# THE CURIOUS HISTORY
## OF THE
# CROSSWORD

BEN TAUSIG

Race Point
PUBLISHING

Quarto is the authority on a wide range of topics.

Quarto educates, entertains and enriches the lives of
our readers—enthusiasts and lovers of hands-on living.

www.quartoknows.com

A division of the Quarto Publishing Group USA Inc.
142 West 36th Street, 4th Floor
New York, New York 10018
quartoknows.com

Visit our blogs at quartoknows.com

RACE POINT PUBLISHING and the distinctive Race Point
Publishing logo are trademarks of the Quarto Publishing Group USA Inc.

Cover, title page, and chapter opener artwork illustrate
a reproduction of history's first crossword puzzle edited
by Arthur Wynne and featured in *New York World* on
December 21, 1913.

Copyright and source information for the individual puzzles in this
book can be found on individual puzzle pages.

Editorial Director:  Jeannine Dillon
Project Editor: Jackie Bondanza
Designer: Rosamund Saunders

ISBN: 978-1-937994-45-7

Printed in China
8 10 9 7

www.racepointpub.com

# TABLE OF CONTENTS

# FUN'S Word-Cross Puzzle.

**F**ILL in the small squares with words which agree with the following definitions:

2-3 What bargain hunters enjoy.

4-5 A written acknowledgement.

6-7 Such and nothing more.

10-11 A bird.

14-15 Opposed to less.

18-19 What the puzzle is.

22-23 An animal of prey.

26-27 The close of a day.

28-29 To elude.

30-31 The plural of is.

8-9 To cultivate.

12-13 A bar of wood or iron.

16-17 What artists learn to do.

20-21 Fastened.

24-25 Found on the seashore.

10-18 The fibre of the gomuti palm.

6-22 What we all should be.

4-26 A day dream.

2-11 A talon.

19-28 A pigeon.

F-7 Part of your head.

23-30 A river in Russia.

1-32 To govern.

33-34 An aromatic plant.

N-8 A fist.

21-34 To agree with.

3-12 Part of a ship.

20-29 One.

5-27 Exchanging.

9-25 Sunk in mud.

13-21 A boy.

# INTRODUCTION

Curiosity is the innate drive to know, and specifically, to know more. It's what compels us to explore what a noisy commotion is about, what moves toddlers to persistently ask "why?" and perhaps what drives our scientific inquiries. Humans aren't the only beings who are curious. But we are undoubtedly a species hungry for knowledge.

Crossword puzzles are for curious people. They begin with an elegantly simple premise and they beg to be unlocked. Empty white squares are arranged in a larger box, each word interlocking in a graceful, symmetrical pattern. When a crossword is blank, nothing is known. By the time the solver fills in the last letter, however, every question has been answered, all of the mysteries and oddities of this particular universe have been illuminated, and it all fits together to tell a story. Longtime solvers know the feeling well. Each day, their curiosity is satisfied. Order returns to the world.

"There's the scarlet thread of murder running through the colorless skein of life," says Sherlock Holmes in the story *A Study in Scarlet*, "and our duty is to unravel it, and isolate it, and expose every inch of it." Crosswords appeal to the detective in all of us, when we feel a need to find solutions. Life so often hands us problems without easy answers, but there's always a solution to the crossword. And if you're curious enough, you can probably find it.

*The Curious History of the Crossword* isn't just a history. As the game turns 100 years old in 2013, there's just so much to know. Not only the facts, like when the first crossword book was published or who is responsible for the rules around its design, but contentious subjects, like who is the greatest constructor of all time, how puzzle makers get paid, and whether using technology counts as cheating. For the truly curious puzzle fan, this book offers the inside scoop on personalities, humor, and the camps of puzzlers who have squared off (no pun intended) to have their style of crosswords accepted in the mainstream. This book is about lively debates—debates the casual solver may not even be aware of—that have been ongoing for years or even decades. Each chapter is an essay on a topic that reveals something surprising or unique about the history of the crossword. Each one takes on a subject that has either never been written about at length, or at least hasn't been tackled for so long that it's worth revisiting.

There are a handful of amazing crossword history books out there—though some are out of date—as well as some interesting and quirky memoirs. What you'll find here is a little history, a little memoir, and *more*. I began my own puzzle odyssey in 2004, after solving for a few years and deciding I wanted to try my hand at making them. I wondered how grids were made, and inquired of some people with experience. Before I knew it, I was freelancing for the *New York Times*, *Los Angeles Times*, and *New York Sun*, and publishing my own syndicated feature in publications nationwide. Within a couple of years, I was the editor for the puzzle in *The Onion* newspaper (which later became the American Values Club), and in the mid-2000s joined the ranks of young constructors then defining a new generation. I've since written thousands of puzzles, and edited hundreds more. But this book isn't really my story. It is the history of puzzles told from the perspective of a relative insider. I know most of the major figures involved in modern construction personally, to varying degrees, and I know *about* all of them. The community is colorful and very supportive. But there's also gossip and disagreement about what constitutes a quality puzzle. I know about that side, too.

For those whom this book leaves out, or whose accomplishments are not recognized sufficiently, I apologize in advance. There are simply more worthy puzzle people than can be mentioned within a limited space. The only conscious editorial decision in this vein has been to "decenter" the role of the *New York Times*. The paper's puzzle is a significant player in crossword history, and many of the best constructions ever have been published there. However, there are already a number of books and other writings that identify the *Times* puzzles as the Cadillac of crosswords, while understating the importance of other puzzle outlets. The average solver may not realize how many fantastic, genre-defying puzzles have been printed in other newspapers, in magazines, newsletters, and online, since the very dawn of the crossword's invention. I hope this book presents an alternative history of puzzles that gives space on the marquee to those bit players who really aren't bit players at all. The *Times* plays a big part here, even takes center stage in some chapters. But it doesn't steal the show.

Finally, this book attempts to stay narrowly focused on

the version of the crossword puzzle that you likely know best: the square, interlocking with across and down clues, printed in good old black and white. Constructors have experimented with lots of variants, from asymmetrical blocks to diagramless grids to offbeat shapes. Cryptic crosswords—which are the British style (explained in Chapter Four)—have a history in American outlets, too. None of these can be written out of a history of the crossword, even a narrow one. Credit is given where credit is due, and I acknowledge that experimentation has been an important factor in the continued viability of the crossword over ten decades. But to some extent it's the very conservatism of the standard American crossword that facilitates so much creativity. It practically demands to be extended, distorted, rearranged, and reshaped. The fact that its Platonic structure hasn't receded largely accounts for the creative ideas that exist in puzzles today. Every puzzle is essentially made in reference to the conventional crossword as a touchstone, and constructors are attracted to the challenge of figuring out new ways to bend the rules.

In many ways, crossword puzzles today are at their most exciting point in history. The quality of themes and grids and the standards of editors are at an all-time high. Crosswords now are made mostly with the enjoyment of the solver in mind. This may seem obvious, but it hasn't always been the case. And while it may sometimes feel like the world is on the brink of running out of puzzle themes, contemporary constructors keep finding ways to expand the game, inventing clever new tricks and approaches. We've undoubtedly come a long way since the early days of puzzledom, when simply arranging some real words (and even some questionable ones) was considered an accomplishment in itself.

But the journey from Arthur Wynne's first crossword—published in the *New York World* in 1913 in the "Fun" section of the newspaper—to today's puzzles (Hey! Look! It's been one hundred years!), has taken many twists and turns. There was a national puzzle craze in the 1920s, the arrival of universal construction standards in the 1940s, a fallow period in the 1960s, and a triumphant resurgence in the 1980s and 1990s. The years since have witnessed a creative gold rush and a diversification of huge proportions. Puzzles today flourish in niches that new technology has made possible, and many more constructors have many more opportunities to share their work. The fact that puzzle construction is an art has never before been so clear.

How did such a simple game come so far? What's so deeply satisfying about crosswords that keep millions of people addicted to them? Who and what is responsible for the success of the crossword, as well as for its evolution and mass popularity? If you're curious, read on.

*It should be noted that the puzzles in this book are reproduced as authentically as possible to preserve their integrity. In an effort to maintain their authenticity, the puzzles are not consistent for style or formatting. Solutions may be found on page 165, please disregard solution pages in the puzzles themselves as these refer to the original publications.*

# CHAPTER ONE

# Crossword Knowledge, Then and Now

Crosswords are, at their core, games of knowledge. They are not games of wisdom or cleverness or logic—though each plays a role—but of being schooled in a certain set of facts and ideas. It naturally follows that crosswords have never been for everyone. In fact, the knowledge they favor tells us a lot about what we, as a society, consider important. It's worth taking a look at how the focus of puzzles has changed over the decades. What kind of things has a crossword solver needed to know, both then and now?

Every era of the crossword puzzle tells us something about the value of knowledge in the world at that time. From the 1940s to the early 1990s (the period at the *New York Times* that has been termed the "pre-Shortzian era") solvers had to be up on their geography, botany, poetry, Latin, and Shakespeare to successfully solve a puzzle, while a solver today might be better off studying IMDb, the Internet Meme Database, and Pitchfork. It's not that older puzzles never made reference to pop culture, or that modern puzzles never have clues about minor poets or biological genera. But more often than not, older puzzles assumed that educated people had a shared awareness of Victorian novels, classical languages, and systems of natural classification, to name a few subjects. Today, this body of knowledge strikes many of us as stuffy and esoteric. But meanwhile, old assumptions have given way to new ones. When and why did this happen?

The story begins in the early 1940s. Though crosswords had existed and been popular since 1913, the *New York Times* made the trend an acceptable pastime for the intellectual in 1942, when it began publishing its own puzzle in-house (the feature went daily in 1950). Not only that, but the editor the paper hired, Margaret Farrar, turned out to be an excellent choice for the advancement of the crossword puzzle. Farrar was by all accounts a talented, supportive editor, and many of the ground rules she created for crosswords persist to this day.

Farrar's appointment in early 1942 came closely on the heels of the United States' entry into World War II. It has been said that war is "geography's best friend[1]," and indeed with global conflict came increased awareness about international places. So maybe it's no surprise that world capitals and foreign currencies populated so many crossword clues in the middle of the 20th century. Both WWII and the Cold War placed heavy emphasis on foreign affairs in the newspaper, in a way that for many Americans felt both personal and urgent. Being an in-the-know "citizen of the world" meant understanding more than a little about the places where U.S. strategic interests were being advanced.

The emphasis on geography in crosswords was in part a way to practice and affirm such knowledge. Thus, in just one week in early March of 1984, solvers were treated to clues about geographic obscurities like:

"Kirghizian range or valley"

"Former name of Kalinin, U.S.S.R."

"Baltic Sea feeder"

"Rhone feeder"

"Belgian Congo today"

… and so on. A solver today might yawn at these arcane references, but just imagine how often the names of Soviet and European cities were in the newspaper in the decades after World War II. Knowing geography was not just about intelligence, it was a civic duty.

Of course, it isn't only geopolitics that explains clues like these. Education played a big role, too. Geography was an informal 19th-century addition to the Quadrivium, an educational system comprised of arithmetic, music, geometry, and astronomy. From the Renaissance onward, the Quadrivium was the key to understanding more or less everything. Long before social studies and economics, a smart student was one who was familiar with Pyxis and Perseus, about the parallel postulate and Thales' theorem. But during the eras of exploration and colonialism, geography was gradually added to the mix. The National Geographic Society (the same group that created the magazine) was founded in 1888, with a focus on spreading knowledge about geography and encouraging resource conservation. It is certainly no coincidence that the society sprang up just a few years after the Berlin Conference, at which the territories of Africa were carved up by the European colonial powers. Learned people like Alexander Graham Bell, who served as the second president of the NGS, understood the growing value of geographic awareness, and promoted it. Geography grew as an educational trend as a result of such efforts, and became a field that every educated person was expected to know.

Other popular crossword subjects have similar stories—from biological taxonomy to history. Looking at the Sunday puzzle from September 14, 1986—written by the famously stodgy editor Eugene Maleska himself—we can break down some of the key knowledge areas of the pre-Shortzian era. This puzzle, called "Book Country Revisited," is an unelaborated list of bestselling books from the previous year that ran at the same time as the now-defunct New York Is Book Country festival in Manhattan. There is almost no wordplay, and nearly every clue asks for either a fact or a synonym. Out of 140 total words, the puzzle includes:

- No less than 40 references to literary titles and quotations.
- Four references to Shakespeare alone.
- Potentially colorful answers like OPERATES, TROTS, CARVE, and COAL clued with bone-dry, one-word synonyms like "Runs," "Jogs," "Sculpt," and "Cannel," (whatever cannel is).
- Six know-it-or-you-don't geographic facts.
- No fewer than six foreign words, and uncommon ones at that ("Sprees, in Scotland" clues GELLS, for example).
- Individual clues about the national French opera, Greek mythology, and the infraorder of shrimp.
- Only one punny clue, a play on words about an obscure Civil War legend.

The ideal of the well-rounded member of the intelligentsia appears here in vivid gray. Editor Maleska, in effect, quizzed solvers on their awareness of the current bestseller list, of the world atlas, and of the general knowledge range of the erudite person. Imagine a solver checking the solution grid for a missed answer—he or she wouldn't groan at the clever puns they failed to catch, but might well feel inferior about their own education and reading habits. In this way, crosswords of the middle 20th century could be pointedly classist, rewarding the best-educated members of the urban bourgeoisie while freezing out those of more ordinary taste. The scent of competition and hierarchy was in the air. Stan Newman may have put it best when he wrote that Maleska "took a pedant's pleasure in flummoxing other people with obscure facts."

Maleska, in fact, represented the apex of elitism at the *Times* crossword. Farrar, as well as Will Weng (who served as editor from 1969 to 1977), each had a flair for wordplay, and both of their puzzles were more fun than Maleska's. But Will Shortz, who took over for Maleska in 1993, changed the flavor of crosswords dramatically. A representative of the "New Wave" of puzzle makers who congealed at *GAMES* magazine in the 1980s (the New Wave was led in part by Stan Newman), Shortz was hired over old-guard candidates such as John Samson. Shortz introduced a degree of wordplay and popular culture previously unknown to the puzzle. The very first puzzle of the Shortz era, appropriately, and I'll bet deliberately, had a rainbow rebus theme created by Peter Gordon. It was, in every way, colorful, being both lively and literally full of color. Sure, there was still geography (with answers like YELLOWSEA, ANKARA, CASBAH), but most of the place names were broadly familiar. Moreover, some of the entries crossing in the other direction were made simpler to help ease the way in difficult spots. Multiword answers that people use every day, like GREENBEANS, EKESOUT, and EVENUP, proliferated instead of

WILL SHORTZ

This year marks the 25th anniversary of the "Stepquote," a crossword featuring a quotation running in stairstep-fashion down the grid. The invention of Eugene T. Maleska (above), now the crossword editor for the *New York Times*, the puzzle made its controversial debut in the *Times* back in July 1964. Many solvers at that time couldn't make heads or tails of the puzzle gimmick, and the paper was deluged with complaints. Today, however, the Stepquote is one of crossword puzzling's standards. The new puzzle on this page is based on a favorite quotation of Maleska's, which he has been saving a long time for a special occasion. Happy 25th birthday to the Stepquote!

## ACROSS

1 Stepquote
5 I.R.A., for one
9 Author of the Stepquote
14 Wing-shaped
15 Whom Moslems praise
16 Sight at New Orleans
17 "Vive ___ ! " (old French cry)
18 Tropical climber
19 Coeur d'___, Idaho
20 The sun
22 Persephone's mother
24 Bedouin
26 "Runaway" singer Shannon
27 Cobbler's equipment
30 TV character from Melmac
33 Studio time
35 Embezzler's target
37 Below, in poesy
39 *Amadeus* setting
40 *Brigadoon* costume designer's choice
42 Spent
44 Pickpocket
45 Still kicking
46 Shepherd's home
48 The Holy Grail, e.g.
49 Digression
51 Robot's creator
55 Fabric first made in 1941
57 Like a tumbler
58 Battle of Britain VIPs
61 Near-sighted cartoon character
64 Pony Express method
65 Minos's mother
67 Two-dimensional
69 Old-fashioned teaching method
70 Pays a short visit
72 Hall-of-Famer Williams
73 Word above WALK
74 Tortoise's snapper
76 Get the wash ready
77 Necessities for hay fever season
80 Mary Hart of *Entertainment Tonight*, e.g.
84 Jim Croce's "I Got ___"
86 Miss USA prop
88 First all-electronic computer
90 Source of the Stepquote, March 15, 1963
91 Plume source
92 Scout leader?
93 Express checkout units
94 Aptly named English poet

## DOWN

1 Sidekick
2 Butter substitute
3 Viscount's superior
4 Walked on
5 Noted retiree of 1979
6 Habilimented
7 Thrashed
8 Henley Regatta site
9 Motorist's headache
10 Flack's issuance
11 Break a watch, perhaps
12 Hundredth of a Brunei dollar
13 Pipe joint
15 Pacified
21 Algerian port
23 Soccer squad
25 Ham's father?
28 Anderson of *WKRP* fame
29 Quick pic
30 How some stocks are sold
31 Charles de Gaulle's birthplace
32 Show one's inability to swim
34 Liqueur-brandy cocktail
36 Boiling over
38 Left in a hurry
41 Leaves in a hurry
43 Miami-to-NYC heading
47 Tavern order
49 Pitcher's "soupbone"
50 All, for one
52 Series starter, often
53 Delight
54 Entered, as computer data
56 Metropolitan business weekly
58 Funnyman Foxx
59 Gold: Prefix
60 Land abutting the street
62 Klutzes
63 Sandlot game
66 Best
68 River that gave Iberia its name
71 Like German words after "das"
75 Stocking shade
78 Pictures
79 Pulitzer poet Teasdale
81 ___ about (roughly)
82 ___-Soviet relations
83 Words from an Exeter exiter
84 Bird: Prefix
85 "The Road ___ Taken," (poem by 9-Across)
87 Cherry, e.g.
89 Barracks feature

deeply buried dictionary terms. "Al Green," "Certs breath mints," "Ren and Stimpy," and "60 Minutes" each made their way into the clues in that first puzzle, heralding the arrival of popular music, television, and consumer products in the crossword. Peter Gordon himself went on to edit the *New York Sun* crossword, which eclipsed even Shortz's puzzles for contemporary flair. November 21, 1993, the day Shortz began, marked a moment of reform, if not flat-out revolution, for the crossword.

The changes that have occurred since then have mostly been a matter of degree rather than type. The *Times* puzzle has grown more modern, nowadays nearly dividing its themes between those that the old guard would appreciate and those that flatter the tastes of pop culture connoisseurs. (A recent themeless puzzle by David Kwong worked answers including TWITTERFOLLOWERS, ARIANNA Huffington, and WISHFULDRINKING into the grid.) In the wake of this transformation, and largely as a result of new media, independent outlets have also sprung up to push the envelope even further. Blog crosswords are inherently flexible enough to jump on up-to-the-minute news stories as theme content.

To many a modern solver, a puzzle with laugh-out-loud jokes about current subjects promises more entertainment value than a humorless quiz about last year's bestselling books. However, it's worth noting that modern crosswords, just like those of last century's, are still games of knowledge. So what kind of knowledge is favored now?

Modern crosswords are often praised for being democratic, in much the same way as the Internet and new

media are. Without question, more puzzle-solving neophytes without an Ivy League education could today pick up the *New York Times* crossword and make more significant inroads than ever before. By reading the news semi-regularly, encountering a handful of movies and pop songs each year, and having a college education, one is likely

## A CURIOUS THING

Crosswords, as we all know, usually run in the back of the paper. There are many reasons for this, including the editorial idea that the fun, whimsical stuff is like dessert after a main course of serious news. But it also usually means that the puzzle is the sweet treat that convinces us to consume a few bites of what keeps the paper healthy—advertisements. It's no secret that crosswords hold one of the longest engagement times of any part of the newspaper. An elite solver can finish an easy puzzle in a few minutes, but the average person will take no less than twenty minutes, and probably more like an hour. All the while, their eyes are wandering toward the ads that pay the bills. In alternative newspapers, these ads can get pretty raunchy—ads for sex shops and escort agencies are just a couple of examples. In classier publications, the surrounding ads may be literary, peddling volumes of classic books. In the *New York World*, where the crossword was born in the 1910s, the ads near the puzzle were for miscellany, much of it medical and all of it spurious-seeming. Spots promised to "develop your bust," to teach you to "throw your voice" and elsewhere how to "be a detective." Cures for asthma, eczema, and tobacco addiction shared one page. The Write Irradiant Co. of Brooklyn even promised, for free, something called "the key to success." No further explanation was given.

*Left: Eugene Maleska, "Stepquote," GAMES, November/ December 1989. Reprinted with permission of Kappa Publishing.*

to be able to tackle the *Times* puzzle at least through the middle-difficulty days of the week (Tuesday, Wednesday, and Thursday). For those who want an even heavier dose of clues about sports, music, books, or movies, the independent puzzles provide a range of options to suit each taste. In brief, crosswords are no longer the exclusive province of the stuffy gatekeepers of classical knowledge. There are puzzles out there for just about anyone, which is why they are considered democratic.

However, by becoming more and more contemporary, puzzles have also become more disposable. Crosswords have been affected by the inclusion of ephemera, in which stories and products from last month are already embarrassingly obsolete. If crossword puzzles were once meant to be timeless, solvable for many years after their publication, it is difficult to imagine a grid filled with references to neologisms and gimmicky web sites having much currency even in two years' time. This state of affairs is, it's worth noting, precisely what the pre-New Wave crossword regime was concerned about. An article from 1988 about the struggle between the New Wave and the old guard noted that "by far the greatest difference is over the use of brand names. [Old-guard constructor and editor William] Lutwiniak said that while he has no objection to brand names that can be found in dictionaries, like 'Xerox,' in recent months he has received puzzles containing the names 'Acura' and 'BOAC.' 'I'm afraid that once you open the door to this kind of thing, you can't stop it,' [said Lutwiniak]."[2]

Modern crosswords ask that solvers be aware of a multitude of material goods, something that a number of editors in the past had expressly forbidden. The mattress company SERTA first appeared in the *New York Times* crossword in 1994; ALL changed from a totality to a detergent in 1997; the Jaguar XJS pulled up in 2004; AXE was first clued as a body spray in 2010. If it's in the grocery store or the mall from coast-to-coast today, it's arguably fair game for the crossword. Bluntly put, solvers now need to know the landscape of consumer products, much as they once needed to know the political divisions of the earth's landscape. And just as a Maleska puzzle patted you on the back for knowing that the PENNINES are a range of English hills, modern puzzles help us practice and affirm our awareness of the stuff we buy.

Crosswords have become, in part, a game of knowledge about the contemporary world, and often the more contemporary the better. A crossword written for *The Week* includes themes about that week's news, a remarkably quick turnaround. Constructor Brendan Emmett Quigley is famous in part for getting entries like the sleep aid ZZZQUIL or Manti TEO into puzzle grids within weeks or days of their appearance on shelves or newsstands. People love seeing fresh words and names in their puzzle grids immediately, but those same puzzles become dated quickly. The rapidity of digital technology raises the value of knowing what's happening right now, a consumerist idea if ever there was one.

That said, crosswords have not *entirely* become an outpost of *The Price Is Right*. General knowledge of history, geography, literature, and so on are still very necessary for solving. And that isn't even to mention the greater role of wordplay today compared to older puzzles; the fun quotient now is unquestionably higher. But the emphasis has shifted toward being in touch with current affairs, perhaps for both better and worse. For worse, there's the disposability. But for better, consider the following anecdote.

On September 1, 2004, around the time I was just getting my feet wet in puzzle construction, I sent an email to cruciverb-l, the listserv where puzzle makers talk shop. I was wondering whether the initialism LGBT—which stands for "Lesbian, Gay, Bisexual, Transgender" and is a very recognizable phrase in the gay rights movement—could pass muster in a newspaper crossword. Of course, even common initialisms like LCD aren't considered great crossword fill because they're boring, barely evocative, and hard to clue in an original way. But considering that obscure or outdated entries like SBC (an old telecom) and OSS (the CIA's predecessor) still show up pretty often, I wondered if LGBT crossed the threshold of usability. I wrote to the list: "I have the common acronym LGBT (half a million Google hits, campus staple, 10% of us) in an in-progress grid. Never seen it in a puzzle, nor is it in the cruciverb.com database. Hopefully this isn't an issue of editor discomfort … Is it?" Nine people responded privately to vote on the acceptability of LGBT, with four recognizing it but expressing serious reservations, and five giving a flat-out "no." All nine respondents voted it down. Eight years later, in 2012, a different list member asked essentially the same question about the entry LGBT. Some of the public responses included "Yes. Enthusiastically so," "I suspect any editor of a major paper would keep it in," and "On what possible basis is LBGT not OK? I'm confused/concerned as to why this is a question." The person who posed the question reported that the response was an overwhelming "yes."

The change that took place between 2004 and 2012 was surely part of a political shift, but it also points to one of the advantages of a more responsive and up-to-date regime of knowledge in crosswords. Editors no longer have a mandate to preserve creaky definitions of what counts as valid information and terminology. The collective pressure to recognize changes in the world as they happen helps keep crosswords relevant and even progressive.

✦⟹ ⟸✦

## Daily Cross-Word Puzzle

### Ruth von Phul
Cross-Word Puzzle Champion, solved this Puzzle in a "bogey" time of
**Eight Minutes**

### By Paul S. Smith
Something new in the puzzle world is offered for your amusement in the Sunday Magazine of the Herald Tribune to-morrow—a puzzle with definitions in rhyme, by W. P. Wooten.

### ACROSS

1 Beast of burden.
4 Possessive pronoun.
7 Mineral spring.
13 Face value.
14 To place.
14 Anger.
15 A metal.
16 Regret.
17 Chosen by ballot.
19 Disrobe.
21 Beverage.
22 Rodent.
24 Perform.
25 Move swiftly.
26 Nuisances.
28 Rind.
30 Unit.
31 A poplar tree.
32 Before (prefix).
33 Granaries.
36 Turned on an axis.
39 A worthless leaving.
40 King (French).

41 A western state.
45 Curving.
49 One (Scotch).
50 Go in.
52 No (Scotch).
53 A separate article.
55 Tumults.
56 Apportion.
57 American humorist.
58 Cat cry.
59 Skill.
60 Italian colony in Abyssinia.
63 Springy.
67 Swimming organ of a fish.
68 Shoemaker's tool.
69 Even.
70 Sick.
71 To dress.
72 Affirmative.
73 Snare.
74 Expression of assent.

26 An associate.
27 Noisy sleepers.
29 Guided.
34 Negative.
35 Period of time.
37 A weight.
38 Help.
41 May (French).
42 A Canadian province.
43 Wanting.
44 Beasts.
45 In intervening position.

46 Sluggishness.
47 Tidily.
48 To turn to the right.
51 A digit.
54 Encountered.
55 Masculine plant or animal.
60 A lizard.
61 Beam of light.
62 Female sheep.
64 Sheltered side.
65 An insect.
66 A diminutive (suffix).

### DOWN

1 Imitate.
2 A sultan's wife.
8 One who steers.
4 To strike.
5 Before.
6 Make reparation.
7 Stammer.
8 Fasten.
9 Conjunction.

10 A rule of conduct.
11 Severe in aspect.
12 Things, in law.
18 Domestic animal.
20 Sharp blow.
23 Serpent.
25 Another domestic animal.

### Solution of Yesterday's Puzzle

VISION FESTAL
ANI WORSTED ONE
SCAN REHAN OLGA
SAMOS FOR SIDED
AS MATUTINAL RI
L MERIT FETED N
SPINDLE ABIDING
IR IL UR GO
INTONES ELICITS
S HAIRY FACET H
OR SASSAFRAS NO
LATIN TIE LABOR
AVES MELTS RENT
TEA DAMSELS ACE
E MITY YEOMEN

---

## Daily Cross-Word Puzzle

### Ruth von Phul
Cross Word Puzzle Champion, solved this Puzzle in a "bogey" time of
**Fourteen and One-half Minutes**

### By Bernard Josephson
Happy New Year! May all your troubles for the next twelve months worry you no longer than fourteen and one-half minutes.

### ACROSS

1 Apparition.
6 Joyous.
11 Bird of tropical America.
12 Defeated.
16 A person spoken of indefinitely.
17 To recite metrically.
19 Famous American actress.
20 Girl's name.
21 Island in the Aegean Sea.
23 In behalf of.
24 Agreed with.
25 Like.
26 Early.
29 Japanese measure.
30 Worthiness.
31 Feasted.
33 A yarn measure.
35 Awaiting.
37 Legendary Irish hero.

38 Prefix: Not
39 City of Chaldea.
40 To move.
41 Utters with a musi, l note.
44 Brings to light.
47 Hirsute.
48 Small surface.
49 Conjunction.
51 Tree of the laurel family.
53 Word of refusal.
54 Dead language.
56 A bond.
57 Toil.
59 Welcoming hailings.
60 Dissolves.
62 Fissure.
63 Social party.
64 Your unmarried women.
66 Hair's breadth.
67 Hostility.
68 English freeholders.

28 Misty.
30 Merriment.
32 One of the first nine figures.
34 Target used in bowling.
36 Expressing negation.
41 To place by itself.
42 Source of joy in monotony.
43 Regular order.
44 Worn out.

45 Emperor.
46 To reduce in amount or size.
50 Intensely black.
52 Is indisposed.
53 The present.
55 A pair of animals.
58 Light ray.
60 To be allowed to.
61 Cunning.
64 Delirium tremens (abb.).
65 Prefix: apart.

### DOWN

1 Servants.
2 Ancient South American chieftains.
3 Asiatic kingdom.
4 Cry of pain.
5 Neither.
6 Marsh.
7 Editor (abbr.).
8 Took effect.
9 Wrath.

10 In front.
13 To disprove.
14 Fired a gun.
15 Spanish seaport.
18 A simple name.
20 Anointed.
22 Native of a Mediterranean island.
24 Ironical.
27 Parts of rudders.

### Solution of Yesterday's Puzzle

HERALD TRIBUNE
AXIS WHOA ARID
BID TAUT OKAPI
IT HURT DUEL T
T PUFF JOSS LO
SPURT PACT SIR
ILL LACK CUE
ALL MILK SLING
ME BANE BOOT
B VANE QUAY WE
IVORY PURR THE
EELS YEAR BAIL
NET BEAK MOIRE
TRADES EQUALLY

**By E. A. R. and F. L. R.**

The worst comes first in No. 1 across. After the solver has nailed down those six letters he will find the rest as comforting as having an extra day off or a refund in his income tax.

**By CHARLES P. HOLTYSON**

"Regardless of size, this is the most difficult construction I have *ever* attempted," says Mr. Holtyson. Regardless of size, the puzzle editor will *enter the* ring with anybody who says Mr. Holtyson has not done a great piece of *work*.

### (First puzzle — E. A. R. and F. L. R.)

**ACROSS**

1 One of the pair of opposite points of an orbit where the moving body is in conjunction with or opposition to the sun.
6 Pure.
12 Chillier.
13 Size of type.
14 Cultivate.
15 Spawn of fishes.
16 Always.
17 Domest c fowl.
18 A fresh set.
20 The largest volcano in the world.
21 Opus (Abbr.).
22 Begun again.
24 Else.
25 Goddess of vengeance.
27 Purpose.
29 Friend of Pythias.
30 Equipped.
33 Nothing.
34 Made strong.
36 Like.
38 Holdings.
40 Mister (Abbr.).
41 Mineral spring.
44 Meadow.
45 Beget.
47 Crazy.
48 Persian fairy.
49 Plaintive.
51 Start.
52 Represented.
53 Festivals.

**DOWN**

1 Bent tube used for drawing liquids.
2 Humorously named.
3 Hill in Jerusalem.
4 Tree, genus Taxus.
5 Grain (Abbr.).
6 Choicest.
7 Personal pronoun.
8 Hail.
9 Hindu deity.
10 Yellow dye from the flowers of the palas tree.
11 Mistakes.
13 Large pill.
18 Plant exudation.
18 Provided with a new sole.
19 Longed.
22 To abate.
23 Small coins.
26 Human race.
28 Coffine.
30 Ventilated.
31 To deserve censure.
32 Defiles.
34 Shrub, genus Rhus.
35 Draws off.
37 Overturned.
39 Rover.
42 Space.
44 Supports.
46 Urge.
48 Vegetable.
50 That is (Abbr.).
51 Happen.

### (Second puzzle — Charles P. Holtyson)

**ACROSS**

1 To bar from a congregation.
13 Pierced.
14 Solitary.
15 Scoffs.
16 Lissome of figure.
17 Parts of ships.
18 Motor maniac.
19 Initials of famous author.
20 1,002.
21 A stitch in knitting.
23 Girl's name.
25 Kind of pastry.
26 And (Latin).
28 Man's name.
29 Manuscript (abbr.).
30 One-masted vessel.
32 Vegetables.
33 To arette or reckon.
35 Beast of burden.
36 Shut up.
39 Safe keeping of goods in a warehouse.
41 Bar for moving weights.
43 Merciful.
44 Roof of the mouth.
45 Build.
46 Animal.
47 Romantically.

**DOWN**

1 A reading or writing table.
2 Internal.
3 Iron refined and combined with carbon.
4 Touches.
5 Makes a mistake.
6 French article.
7 Low Dutch (abbr.).
8 Brandish.
9 Rest.
10 An assault with intent to rob.
11 Time intervening.
12 Without equal.
16 Harp-like instruments.
18 Inhabitants of an Asiatic country.
20 Allowance for expenses a *wit*.
23 A debutante.
24 Land *measure*.
27 Excruciating pain.
31 Petty naval *officers*.
34 Region of *the definite extent*.
36 Greek letter.
37 Use.
38 An insoluble body.
40 One who is against.
41 Bindmost.
42 Depend.
44 Inclosure.
46 To exist.

**By K. C. FAILE**

Puzzledom seems to be unable to evolve a much more satisfactory design than the plain square with a Greek *cross* in the center. Most constructors find it their most useful vehicle for expression without unkeyed letters or abbreviation.

**ACROSS**

1 Prevents.
7 Changes.
13 Velvet or a fabric resembling it.
14 A circus requisite.
15 Related on the mother's side.
16 Equivocate.
17 Pinches.
18 Female sheep.
20 Animate existence.
21 A lighting element.
22 The turmeric.
23 A hint.
24 Cardinal number.
27 Dissolve again.
30 Preposition.
31 Negative.
32 Ultimate atoms.
36 Desire eagerly.
40 Before.
41 Tree.
43 Nothing.
44 Row.
46 Seven.
47 Furnished with a foot covering.
48 Compound of iodine.
50 Expunge.
52 Resin obtained from elemis.
53 Gazer.
54 Parts of a fort.
55 Small candles.

**DOWN**

1 Require.
2 Pardonable.
3 Slip away.
4 Grooves.
5 Prefix: three.
6 Distinguish.
7 Become visible.
8 Pasture.
9 High.
10 Tempt.
11 Doleful.
12 Thoroughfare.
17 Pronoun.
19 By way of.
20 Finish.
28 Being, in philosophy.
29 Implement for washing.
32 Profession.
33 Bird.
35 Required.
36 Numbers.
36 Among.
37 To be a fixed attribute.
38 Roisterer.
39 Seniors.
42 Chinese measure.
45 Philippine bread fruit.
47 Blow.
49 Uproar.
51 Greek letter.

### Last Sunday's Solutions

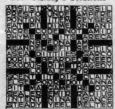

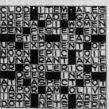

**NUMBER CRYPTOGRAMS**
Introduces. Phylogenic

---

# Meeting Place of the Puzzle Makers

### By DR. ARTHUR ROSENZWEIG

No, No. 104 down is not the kind of a pulse the doctor finds when he grasps your wrist and tells you you'll have to give up eating starchy foods or smoking. Nor is Dr. Rosenzweig the kind of a doctor that grasps wrists. He belongs to the set that tells you the gold crown you had put in a few moons ago won't be in style this season.

### By W. P. WOOTEN

It remains for Mr. Wooten, of Washington D. C., to provide the "Barrack Room Ballads' of the world. He appears to be the pioneer in setting "Acorss" and "Down" to rhyme.

## ACROSS

1 To show absistence.
7 Cud.
11 Relic of prehistoric times.
17 Suddenly.
18 Wavy, in heraldry.
19 Unit of electricity.
20 Portable float used in building bridges.
21 Make note of.
22 Boiling, gushing spring.
23 Gnaw.
24 Mixed type.
25 U. S. silver coin.
26 In continuance.
27 Tropical American blackbird.
28 Measure of area.
30 Body of law.
32 Negative.
34 Among.
35 Composition in verse.
37 Suffix signifying an alcohol.
38 Possessive pronoun.
39 Betel nut palm.
40 Take notice! (abbr.)
42 Girl's name.
44 Part of "to be."
45 Tortuous movement.
50 Newt.
51 Having power to promote putrefaction.
56 On the ocean.
57 Songs.
60 Combining form: flesh.
61 Type of Greek architecture.
63 Having a beard.
65 Indigence.
66 Large migration.
68 Margin.
69 Fatal event.
71 Behold!
72 Liquors.
74 Twelve months (abbr.)
75 Smell.
79 Neuter pronoun.
80 Delve.
82 Demand as due.
87 Besides.
88 Unfortunate.
90 Speck.
92 East Indian money.
93 Trap.
94 Parent.
95 Contest.
97 Pronoun.
99 Cdyle forces.
100 Veasel engaged in seal hunting.
102 Arabian military officer.
103 Movable limb of a sextant.
105 Aim.
106 One of Columbus's fleet.
107 Interest paid for money.
108 Firm.
109 Formerly, an eel.
110 Liquefied.

## DOWN

1 Become visible.
2 To open for the first time.
3 Guard.
4 Suffix of agency.
5 Check.
6 Strengthener.
7 Trifler.
8 Let loose.
9 The same.
10 Deprived of reason.
11 Bundle of twigs.
12 Augur.
13 Discover by close search.
14 Herb.
15 Pacific.
16 Province of N. E. Spain.
29 Square of type.
31 Hawaiian bird.
33 Bone.
34 Measure of area.
36 Destroy.
38 Enfeebled.
39 City of Iowa.
41 River bottom.
43 Particular.
44 Like.
45 Artificially produced.
46 Fresh water fish.
47 Combining form: air.
48 Fresh water chætopod.
49 Longitudinal ridge in a plant.
52 Throe.
53 Woody plant.
54 Frosted.
55 "Buffalo Bill."
58 Formation of monstrosities, in medicine.
59 Fixed.
62 Homage.
64 Arid.
67 In a high degree.
70 Portion of curve.
73 Astral.
75 Blood poisoning.
76 Dependent.
77 Social rank.
78 Compass point.
79 Exclamation of triumph.
81 Move.
83 Musical note.
84 Rub with unctuous substance.
85 Bring on.
86 Assembled.
88 Social gathering.
93 China grass.
91 Fringe or tassel.
94 Alter for better.
96 Dig for ore.
98 Mitigate.
101 Meadow.
104 Split pulse.

### NUMBER CRYPTOGRAMS
### By B. P. Gill

The following long divisions, when solved by translating the letters into the numbers 1, 2, 3, 4, 5, 6, 7, 8, 9, 0, will reveal two ten-letter words as their keys:

```
TRU)NDENCO(UUD
     NRNE
     ────
     NDTC
     NRNE
     ────
     NSEO
     NSCN
     ────
       IT

YL)NLEO(HLI
    GN
    ──
    PGE
    PYG
    ───
     YPO
     YCG
     ───
       I
```

## ACROSS

1 Inert lump of earth.
5 Particular thing.
9 Of these brews there is dearth.
13 This continues to spring.
14 A term used in craps.
15 Presented; fulfilled.
16 A place to pull scraps.
18 Type that is spilled.
19 They're uncertain and coy.
20 You may use this to write.
21 To bother; annoy.
24 It is finished now, quite.
25 Fore part of a boat.
27 To precede or to tower.
29 You and me and the goat.
31 An index of power.
34 Shows owner or source.
36 When the sun's overhead.
38 A heroic discourse.
39 To work till you're dead.
41 A fish (not an eel).
42 Spout wildly, abuse.
43 Fills the hole in the wheel,
44 Implies that you choose.
45 Irascible quite.
48 What "you" was, long ago.
49 It is quick to take fright.
50 Fluids darker than snow.
52 Consumed or devoured.
54 Appearance or seeming.
57 Must often be scoured.
60 The product of steaming.
62 Used with "I," not with "they."
63 Fruit, color or lassie.
65 Metal, hard, strong and gray.
66 A melody classy.
68 Plane space, round or square.
69 Love fondly, adore.
70 Used for tennis or hair.
71 A seed or a spore.

## DOWN

1 To roughen the skin.
2 Erudition complete.
3 Lays bare what's within
4 A place of retreat.
5 Now suppose for awhile
6 Lets a blow lightly tap
7 To collate or compile.
8 Myself, that is all.
9 In the time that has died
10 With legs full of woe.
11 What two can divide.
12 To cause one to go.
17 Where the peak culminates
19 A bird small in form
22 Most high potentate.
23 Describes each thunderstorm.
26 Never lead from this hand
28 Go forward, hell-bent.
29 "To," the archaic brand.
30 Turn sharp or ferment.
32 Who owns this is ill-fated
33 A number that's square.
34 With grease saturated.
35 To beat it from there.
37 Supported or held by
40 He's a most useful beast.
46 What you do to a cry
47 Implies entrance at least.
49 Place wherein to store.
51 The temple's high head.
52 Always wanting some more.
53 A root used for food.
55 To cut off the skin.
56 Outward to send.
58 Neither under nor in.
59 Group seeking one end.
61 Joined together, united.
64 To be unduly slow.
66 A "one" somewhat slighted.
67 When, like or so.

*Dr. Arthur Rosenzweig and W.P. Wooten, New York Herald Tribune, January 10, 1926.*

# Here Are Puzzles to Sharpen Your Wits

"The objective point in the evolution of this puzzle (given below) was the elimination of all prefixes, suffixes, abbreviations and contractions; in fact, all foreign matter has been omitted, but its kick still remains." The foregoing statement accompanied Mr. Latto's contribution, and we must concede that he has attained his goal.

## CROSS WORD PUZZLE

### By Charles E. Latto.

### HORIZONTAL.

2 The 120 part of a plaster.
7 Anguish.
9 Fondle.
11 Allocate.
15 Matter.
18 Size of type.
21 Indivisible particle.
23 Habituate.
25 Liquor.
27 Anxiety.
30 The young of herring.
33 Untanned calfskin.
36 A chime of bells.
39 Prevailing fashion.
41 Dress fabric.
44 Burlesques.

### VERTICAL.

1 Scarf.
3 Suspend.
4 Penetrates.
6 Marshland.
8 Luxurious.
9 Subsequent in time.
12 Regret.
14 Racy.
17 Friendship.
19 Invite.
21 Priestly vestments.
29 Nothing.
33 Recoil.
34 Intrigue.
36 Demure.
38 By birth.

## ANAGRAM

### By Mrs. Ruth Casserly..

**BELLOW, ARTHUR**

**From the letters in the above cartoon** form a sentence that will apply to the picture.

## SHAKESPERIAN ENIGMA

### By A. I. Dotey.

I am a quotation of Shakespeare containing sixty-six letters. Guess the words defined below and distribute them in accordance with the numbers given:

My 12, 29 and 38 is a short, coarse hemp.
My 37, 20, 50 and 3 is a hawklike bird.
My 1, 10, 59 and 63 was a Jap. Admiral in the Rus.-Jap. war.
My 4, 32 and 5 is something Y-shaped.
My 17, 47, 26 and 21 is an astringent mineral salt.
My 9, 22, 31, 34, 43 and 56 is a lodge used by the Indians.
My 30, 49, 16 and 27 is to stud.
My 2, 40, 13 and 53 is a sunk fence.
My 19, 8, 24, 42 and 64 is muscular power; strength.
My 39, 35, 11 and 28 is a strain.
My 51, 45, 6, 7, 52, 41 and 66 is influential.
My 23, 60, 14 and 25 is a caprice.
My 44, 36, 55 and 48 is a light yellowish brown color.
My 15, 54, 65, 61, 59 and 33 is the state or condition of a person.
My 18, 57, 62 and 46 is to lavish extreme fondness.

## AUTHORS' CHARADE

### By Miss Alexandra Dalziel.

My first is just a common boy's name.
An animal, my second, of biblical fame.
My third is opposed to soft, you bet.
My last is a letter of the alphabet.

## WORD SQUARES

### By Mrs. Rose N. Bildhauser.

(1)

A bar, usually of wood or iron.
Given name of a famous danseuse.
A girl's name.
Indolent.

(2)

A boy's plaything.
A common metal.
A tailless, jumping amphibian.
Terminations.

## LAST SUNDAY'S (OCT. 28) SOLUTIONS.

### CROSS WORD PUZZLE

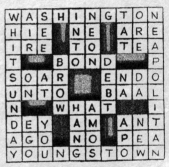

| W | A | S | H | I | N | G | T | O | N |
|---|---|---|---|---|---|---|---|---|---|
| H | I | E |   | N | E |   | A | R | E |
| I | R | E |   | T | O |   | T | E | A |
| T |   | B | O | N | D |   |   |   | P |
| S | O | A | R |   | E | N | D | O |   |
| U | N | T | O |   |   | B | A | A | L |
| N |   | W | H | A | T |   |   |   | I |
| D | E | Y |   | A | M |   | A | N | T |
| A | G | O |   | N | O |   | P | E | A |
| Y | O | U | N | G | S | T | O | W | N |

### ENIGMA

**Read The New York Herald.**

### AUTHORS' CHARADE

**Hawthorne.**

### SHAKESPERIAN ENIGMA

So true a fool is love that in your will,
Though you do anything, he thinks no ill.

### ENIGMATIC PROVERB

Hope deferred maketh the heart sick,
But when the desire cometh, it is a tree of life.

---

Charles E. Latto, New York Herald, November 4, 1923. With its many unchecked squares, this grid resembles a modern British cryptic more than an American-style crossword. We also include some of the other variety puzzles for you to see and even solve.

# Here Are Puzzles to Sharpen Your Wits

ONE of our contributors wishes to know why his cross word construction, which he had sent in ten days before, had not been printed in last Sunday's New York Herald. For his benefit and for the benefit of those who have been wondering, just wondering, as to the fate of their brain children, the following is expounded.

All of the puzzles received that are worthy of the name, subject to revision, of course, will be printed, but none can possibly be published in less than three weeks from the day received. With the cross word puzzles the time limit is apt to be extended as owing to their popularity with the New York Herald readers we receive more of them than the rest of the puzzles combined. Therefore, when submitting puzzles be patient and remember the admonition "Everything comes to him who waits."

---

### CROSS WORD PUZZLE
#### By "Uno"

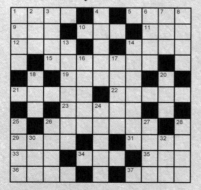

### DEFINITIONS.
### HORIZONTAL.

1. Flesh.
5. Unharmed.
9. Sick.
10. A couch.
11. A pass between two peaks in a mountain range.
12. The scoria of a volcano.
14. A region.
15. A suite.
19. Abate.
21. Med. Ailment.
22. A strip of leather.
23. The Bermuda arrowroot.
26. Solutions.
29. A part.
31. Lateral.
33. Wrath.
34. Local U.S.A. wanigan.
35. A sheltered place.
36. A size of paper.
37. To make monkish.

### VERTICAL.

1. A young girl.
2. Anything shaped like the letter L.
3. Bot. Axillary.
4. A colored twilled cotton goods.
6. 43,650 square feet.
7. An enemy.
8. Ardor.
13. Pertinent.
14. Originators.
16. Figuratively, sorrow.
17. To treat with nitric acid.
18. Before.
20. Hostelry.
24. Cognizant.
25. Dry.
26. The imperial standard of the Turkish Empire.
27. A closed pit in which fodder is stored.
28. Rind.
30. Metal.
32. Refresh.

---

"Uno," New York Herald, *November 18, 1923.*
*The editor explains submission volume above this pseudonymous puzzle. One of the most interesting aspects of the* Herald *puzzles was having a word from the editor each week to demystify crosswords.*

# Here Are Puzzles to Sharpen Your Wits

THIS Sunday's dictionary booster comes to us from up the Sound. New Rochelle, to be exact. We mention the precise location from which it came for a reason. New Rochelle or any other city, town or village on the map should be proud to be the originating place of a perfect cross word construction. Do I hear laughter? If the scoffers think that it is so easy let them try it once. I have no doubt but that they will think twice before sneering the next time.

---

## CROSS WORD PUZZLE
### By Mrs. Rose N. Bildhauser

## DEFINITIONS.
### HORIZONTAL.

1. Luminous heavenly bodies.
5. Mere noise.
9. A people united politically.
11. Print half the width of an em.
13. Mother of pearl.
14. A chinese measure of length.
15. A snakelike fish.
17. A word of command to animals.
18. The lair of a wild beast.
19. A minion.
21. The sister of one's father or mother.
22. Buildings where dyeing is done.
23. A secluded and narrow valley.
24. A long cut.
26. Ever.
27. A venomous snake.
29. To scatter abroad.
30. Similar to.
32. A large body of water.
34. Not any.
35. A fruit tree.
37. A shell.
38. A good fellow.

### VERTICAL.

1. A bendy curve.
2. One or any.
3. A bank of string or twine.
4. An adult male deer.
5. Sensitive.
6. A numeral.
7. Objective case of we.
8. Dishearten.
10. Buildings for storing ice.
12. Small instruments for sewing.
14. Extreme strain.
16. One thickness placed over an other.
18. Combats between two persons.
20. X in Roman numerals.
21. A dull, stupid fellow.
23. Cogwheels.
25. A gambling game.
27. Tart.
28. Elapsed.
32. Of or pertaining to us.
33. A negative connection.
35. Egypt relig. The soul.
36. Egypt. Chaos.

---

*Mrs. Rose N. Bildhauser, New York Herald, November 25, 1923. The editor's introduction is a tad defensive.*

# CHAPTER TWO

# Transcendent Puzzle Themes, Then and Now

This chapter is, on its face, a little unfair. Crossword themes weren't firmly established until the late-20th century, so the earliest puzzles can't really compete with contemporary ones. But the history of the crossword has nevertheless seen its share of great themes. These include ideas that break the mold in surprising ways, but that make perfect sense to the solver right away. They also include never-before-seen twists on existing approaches, or just plain virtuosic work. Bad themes come in different shapes and sizes as well. We'll spill a little less ink on them here than on the good ones, but they include sets of entries that the solver has no chance of understanding, florid obscurities, and bizarre indulgences. Finally, some puzzles are simply offbeat. The pursuit of novelty can take constructors in some pretty unexpected directions.

Even though themes weren't yet in fashion, in certain respects, the puzzles of the 1910s and 1920s were superior to those that came a couple of decades later. The earlier puzzles featured smaller, more irregular grids, and the fill words were nearly always common English. Even today, there's very little from an old *New York Herald Tribune* puzzle that an average adult wouldn't know. Common nouns like MILK, IVORY, and TOT, along with verbs like PULL and HURL, are the same sort of fill that modern constructors prize for the corners of their grids, albeit with a wider and more creative range of clues nowadays.

Moreover, grid design was guided by a sense of playfulness (rather than firm rules) that would not return again with the same energy until the golden era of *GAMES* magazine in the 1980s. Each puzzle in the *New York World* had a unique shape, often a diamond or even an array of four diamonds. Some puzzles were irregularly sized, making a large F shape (for "Fun") or sporting a large empty space in the center. This made them visually appealing in a new and surprising way each week. The puzzle editor also introduced each week's puzzle with a few words, often about the constructor. "Cross-word puzzles for FUN continue to arrive in all shapes and sizes," wrote Arthur Wynne below one puzzle in 1914. "Here is a carefully constructed example, a contribution from Herman S. Gumanow of Sackman Street, Brooklyn. 'I have tried my best,' he writes, 'and am confident that my fellow readers of your worthy little FUN will find it interesting.' " The focus on the personality of the constructor and their process was not thematic in itself, but like a theme it gave the puzzle a special identity each week.

But all told, the 1920s were certainly a simpler time for puzzle themes. The name of the section in the *New York World* in which Arthur Wynne's original puzzle appeared

was, as mentioned previously, FUN—an apt summary of the aim of the game in those days. Erudition, mental workouts, and artfulness came much later. Periodically, Wynne even felt the need to apologize for the difficulty of recent puzzles, and to reassure the solver that this week's offering would be much easier.

When themes began to emerge in the 1940s and 1950s, they could be rough around the edges. One puzzle from 1957 in the *New York Times* called "Getting Your Number" included names such as CHARLESVI, PIPPINIV, and EDWARDII as answers. Not such a blast. Of the thousands of European rulers with numbers following their names, the constructor chose a few with no particular relationship to each other, and which formed no pattern. Some, like Pippin and Richard II, have a relationship to literature or drama. But others don't, which created a confusing mishmash of historical figures only connected by the fact that their male forebears had the same name as them. The placement of the names in the grid is not symmetrical, either (a nearly unbreakable rule for themes today), and there are several non-thematic answers of equal length to the theme entries, a taboo today. There's no wordplay, no twist, and no unifying rationale. The theme offers the solver little in the way of pleasure, while its inconsistency could easily lead to a couple of hours of head-scratching.

Weak puzzle themes are less excusable today, but that doesn't mean they've gone away. In fact, Americans may solve more lousy puzzles than any other kind. Some of these are the product of indifferent local papers that run computer-generated content on the cheap, or in-flight magazines that hire puzzle makers with no experience. Some others are specially commissioned for *People* or other magazines that really only care about keeping things simple. But perhaps no outlet is guiltier than *USA Today*. Jon Stewart jokes in the crossword documentary *Wordplay* that "I'll solve, in a

# FUN'S JANUARY PUZZLE.

## JANUARY

| SUN. | MON. | TUES. | WEDS. | THURS. | FRI. | SAT. |
|------|------|-------|-------|--------|------|------|
| 3 | 4 | 5 | 6 | 7 | 1 / 8 | 2 / 9 |
| 10 | 11 | 12 | 13 | 14 | 15 | 16 |
| 17 | 18 | 19 | 20 | 21 | 22 | 23 |
| 24 / 31 | 25 | 26 | 27 | 28 | 29 | 30 |

Place thirty-one small counters, numbered from 1 to 31, in the spaces indicated in the above Calendar for January. The puzzle is to rearrange the counters so that when each vertical and horizontal lines of figures is added up the totals will be as shown on the right. This can be done, but can you do it?

| S | M | T | W | T | F | S | |
|---|---|---|---|---|---|---|---|
| 3 | 4 | 5 | 6 | 7 | 1/8 | 2/9 | =45 |
| 10 | 11 | 12 | 13 | 14 | 15 | 16 | =91 |
| 17 | 18 | 19 | 20 | 21 | 22 | 23 | =140 |
| 24/31 | 25 | 26 | 27 | 28 | 29 | 30 | =220 |

| S | M | T | W | T | F | S | |
|---|---|---|---|---|---|---|---|
| ? | ? | ? | ? | ? | ?/? | ?/? | =124 |
| ? | ? | ? | ? | ? | ? | ? | =124 |
| ? | ? | ? | ? | ? | ? | ? | =124 |
| ?/? | ? | ? | ? | ? | ? | ? | =124 |

## FROM THIS — TO THIS

Rearrange the numbers on the calendar so that when added up they will give totals as shown above.

---

*FUN's January Puzzle, January 3, 1915. Offbeat puzzles like this "calendar puzzle" were common in the FUN section of the World. In fact, these variety puzzles preceded the crossword, which was created as just another type of game to fill up space on the page. Such puzzles continued to coexist with the crossword for many years.*

# FUN'S CROSS-WORD PUZZLES—NO. 39

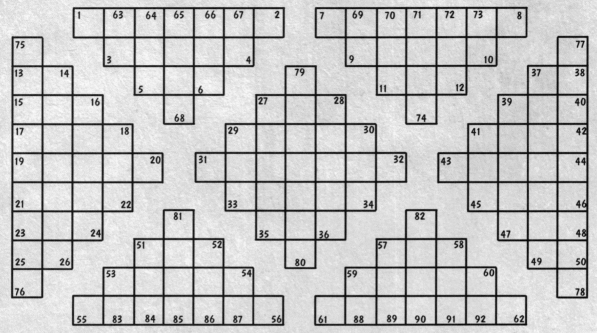

Cross-word puzzles for FUN continue to arrive in all shapes and sizes. Here is a carefully constructed example, a contribution from Herman S. Gumanow of Sackman Street, Brooklyn.

"I have tried my best." he writes, "and am confident that my fellow readers of your worthy little FUN will find it interesting."

See if you can solve it. Fill in the blank squares with works corresponding to the list of clues and definitions given below. The answer to this crossword puzzle will appear in next week's FUN.

| | |
|---|---|
| 1-2 | One who visits. |
| 3-4 | A fog horn. |
| 5-6 | An affirmative motion of the head. |
| 7-8 | A curved sword. |
| 9-10 | Corn storehouses. |
| 11-12 | A cave. |
| 13-14 | A preposition. |
| 15-16 | Fish trap. |
| 17-18 | To ensnare. |
| 19-20 | The path of a planet. |
| 21-22 | The stronger sex. |
| 23-24 | Frozen water. |
| 25-26 | I. |
| 27-28 | Margin. |
| 33-34 | A small piece. |
| 31-32 | Causing motion. |
| 33-34 | A small place. |
| 35-36 | A serpent-like fish. |
| 37-38 | To have existence. |
| 39-40 | A domestic fowl. |
| 41-42 | A running contest. |

| | |
|---|---|
| 43-44 | One who serves on a jury. |
| 45-46 | A girl's name. |
| 47-48 | Placid. |
| 49-50 | In this manner. |
| 51-52 | Covers the head. |
| 53-54 | A titled nobleman. |
| 55-56 | Garland of flowers. |
| 57-58 | Through. |
| 59-60 | Mohammedan female apartment. |
| 61-62 | Loosened. |
| 14-26 | A raised flat area. |
| 16-24 | Piece of furniture. |
| 18-22 | A child's delight. |
| 29-33 | Short for sister. |
| 27-35 | Therefore. |
| 28-36 | A mineral product. |
| 30-34 | To tear. |
| 37-49 | Happens. |
| 39-47 | Injures. |
| 41-45 | To repent of. |
| 51-84 | A possessive verb. |

| | |
|---|---|
| 52-86 | An adverb of degree. |
| 53-83 | To exist. |
| 54-87 | Negative. |
| 57-89 | A partner. |
| 58-91 | Meaning king. |
| 59-88 | A personal pronoun. |
| 60-92 | I, objective. |
| 63-3 | Exists. |
| 64-5 | A base act. |
| 65-68 | A metal. |
| 66-6 | Abbreviation for Theodore. |
| 67-4 | Not off. |
| 69-9 | Third person singular of to be. |
| 70-11 | Middle. |
| 71-74 | An evergreen tree. |
| 72-12 | 3,000 pounds. |
| 73-10 | Likeness. |
| 75-76 | A dumb show. |
| 77-78 | A producer. |
| 79-80 | Venerated. |
| 81-85 | Not the whole. |
| 82-90 | A girl's name. |

New York World, *August 28, 1914.* *The different sections of the grid are not connected—a practice that would eventually disappear—now, all answers must interlock with the rest of the puzzle.*

# FUN'S CROSS WORD PUZZLE

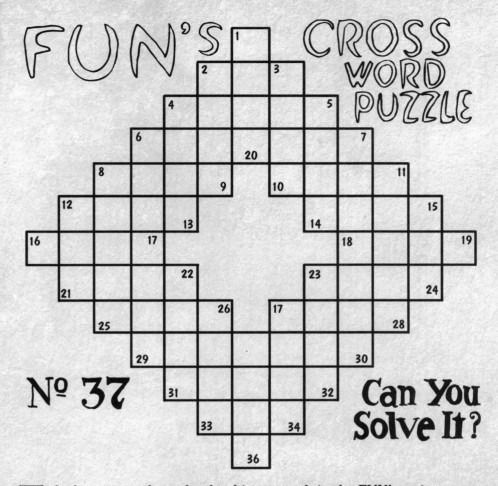

## № 37

## Can You Solve It?

2-3   What boys become.
4-5   What the reckless motorist was, when caught.
6-7   To speak about.
8-9   Of the masculine gender.
10-11   To fall flatly and loosely.
12-13   To separate into grades.
14-15   A famous English school.
16-17   One who entertains guests.
18-19   Hastened away.
21-22   A hollow metallic instrument for giving forth sound.
23-24   A liquid measure.
25-26   Planted in the ground.
17-28   Used in dressing wounds.
29-30   Tantalizing.
31-32   A sharp instrument.
33-34   The best thing to do when hungry.
1-20   Comes high, but we must pay it.
2-9   That which belongs to me.
3-10   A fist, or hand.
4-13   Touched.
5-14   To distribute in portions.

**T**oday's cross-word puzzle, the thirty-seventh in the FUN's series, was sent in by Ernest B. Rust, of Yonkers, N.Y. In a letter accompanying his puzzle he writes.

Just to show you our appreciation of the cross-word puzzles in FUN, the solving of which has give us many hours of pleasure, I have endeavored to make up one. I trust your readers will not require as many hours to solve it as it has taken me to produce it."

Mr. Rust's puzzle was excellent in its original form. If the puzzle editor of FUN were to publish it exactly as it was sent in, Mr. Rust would not have any cross-word puzzle to solve this week. So the puzzle editor has taken the great liberty of changing one or two words in Mr. Rust's puzzle in order that he, too, can have an interesting hour or so solving his own puzzle.

Fill in the small squares with words corresponding to the list of clues and definitions given below. The solution to this puzzle will appear in next week's FUN.

New York World, *August 14, 1914. This puzzle, like others in the* New York World, *was sent in not by a seasoned constructor but just an average reader who wanted to try their hand at crosswords.*

hotel, a *USA Today*, but won't feel good about myself." Just how bad is the puzzle in the nation's most widely circulating paper? The July 9, 2009, puzzle called "Fit as a Fiddle" had phrases with synonyms for fitness at the end: ULTRA**SOUND**, WISHING**WELL**, PARKING-**FINE**. These three are strong entries. They are consistent by all being noun phrases and all having the "fit" synonym at the end. Such consistency is what makes themes fun and clear for solvers. But the fourth entry is simply the word PERFECTION. PERFECT isn't a synonym for fit, and even if it were, it's the only one-word phrase of the set. And the quasi-synonym comes at the beginning, not the end. It's as if the editor never played "One of These Things (Is Not Like the Others)" on *Sesame Street*.

Bad puzzles pretty clearly span eras, but in order to locate *great* work from different periods, we have to be a bit generous. We have to recognize that older themes can't be judged by modern standards. Today, especially with the benefit of construction software, solvers have little tolerance for entries like HALSE ("to embrace about the neck"), which are more than enough to invalidate a great theme if they cross the letters in some of its entries. But in the past this was not so. With a tip of the hat to David Steinberg, creator of the Pre-Shortzian Puzzle Project (an effort to digitize old crosswords), the September 28, 1969, *Times* puzzle by Edward J. O'Brien is worth a look. O'Brien's puzzle has a remarkable 16 thematic entries, where seven or eight would likely be adequate. It's playful, if a bit goofy, featuring rhyming wordplay reminiscent of Dr. Seuss: WHITECOLLARDOLLARHOLLER, OMAHAHAHA, and ALONGSIDETOGUIDE-THERIDE, for example. The answers also interlock at numerous points, meaning the grid was difficult to construct. Even with the obscurities, there's a lot to like about this construction. Most importantly, the spirit of the theme is ambitious and clever, two qualities that solvers of every era appreciate.

But perhaps we should reserve the word "transcendent" for a puzzle published a few years earlier by the legendary Bernice Gordon. On May 30, 1965, Gordon's "Words and Words" ran in the *Times*, and the theme required solvers to place an ampersand in a single square within phrases such as EAST&WEST, SUGAR&SPICE, and FREE&EASY. The concept of the rebus—or use of pictures or symbols to represent sounds—is ancient. An example is a picture of a honeybee + the letter R, to represent "BEER." Until then, a rebus had never before been used in a crossword.

In an interview with David Steinberg, Gordon said of "Words and Words" that "[Editor] Margaret [Farrar] said she had never seen anything like it in her puzzles, and she was not sure readers would accept a rebus. She held it for about six months, and when she published it on a Sunday, the response was overwhelming. She mailed me manila envelopes full of praise for its originality, and just as many who said it was tricky and underhanded and a poor excuse for a puzzle. But it really started a new trend in constructing." If anything, Gordon understated the influence the theme had. Today, rebus constructions are so common that editors warn constructors not to send them in because they already have large backlogs. Most of the obvious ideas for rebuses have been done at least a few times, and original takes are at a premium. In other words, the rebus has become a common element of the crossword landscape. By introducing it, Gordon brought an entirely new dimension to themes, one that had not been thought of previously..

The mixed response to "Words and Words"—which was both delight and anger—is not at all unusual with maverick themes. Another sensational *Times* puzzle that ushered in a new type of theme arrived on Election Day in 1996, and was similarly both loved and hated. The clue for the key thematic entry in this puzzle was "Lead story in tomorrow's newspaper (!)," and the answer could be either BOBDOLEELECTED or CLINTONELECTED. All of the crossing words through BOBDOLE and CLINTON had two possible answers. For example, ?AT was clued as "Black Halloween animal," and the answer could be either BAT or CAT. Will Shortz reported a surge in mail, which included not a few confused souls who thought the crossword editor had somehow rigged the election. But most people figured out the trick, and praised it as one of the cleverest puzzles they'd ever seen. This type of puzzle is now referred to as a Schrödinger theme, after the physicist whose thought experiment posited that a cat in a closed box is simultaneously alive and dead. Schrödinger themes now show up a few times a year in all kinds of puzzle venues,

though the great difficulty in their execution has kept them from becoming overused.

Some constructors have become nearly synonymous with themes they've either invented or done better than anyone else. Trip Payne, who constructs not only standard puzzles but many other variations as well, specializes in one of the stranger twists on the conventional form in the "Something Different" crossword ("*Cuckoo Crossword 2*," *page 35*), said to have been invented by Henry Hook and Merl Reagle. As Payne himself explains on his web site, "Something Different crosswords allow made-up entries that can be clued in any way. For example, the clue 'Flowery poem about one 1980s fad' might lead to ODE ON A RUBIK'S CUBE; the clue 'Like margarine' might lead to OLEOESQUE." Once you get into the mindset of solving silly, invented phrases, a Something Different is just as accessible as a regular crossword, and often much more fun.

Frank Longo has published an entire book of vowelless crosswords, puzzles where all vowels are omitted in the answers. For instance, PDTRCN, or "pediatrician," would be the answer for the clue "Spock was one." Though others have dabbled in this type, it is unquestionably Longo's forte.

In recent years, the meta crossword has seen a surge in popularity, largely thanks to a series of weekly crossword contests run by Matt Gaffney. For a meta puzzle, the solver must not only complete the grid, but also figure out the answer to an additional riddle. Typically, this riddle is posed separately from the puzzle proper, asking something along the lines of "Which fast-food chain is suggested by this puzzle's theme answers?" If the answers are DANQUAYLE,

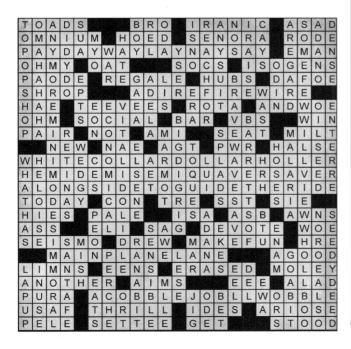

Edward J. O'Brien, "Rhymes from Way Out," New York Times, September 28, 1969.

# FUN'S CROSS-WORD PUZZLES

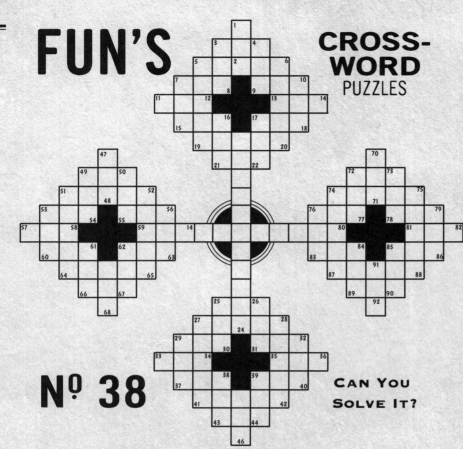

## Nº 38

### CAN YOU SOLVE IT?

1-2 Wrath.
3-4 A unit of superficial measure.
5-6 A view.
7-8 Past tense of eat.
9-10 Not wet.
11-12 A space of time.
13-14 A staff.
15-16 A small violin.
17-18 Never feminine.
19-20 A fast traveller.
21-22 A quarrel.
23-24 An assemblage.
25-26 A small, venomous snake.
27-28 An angler's basket.
29-30 A male sheep.
31-32 Used for fishing.
33-34 Warm in winter.
35-36 A tub.
37-38 Also.
39-40 A tumor.
41-42 Greek word meaning mother.
43-44 A support.
45-46 A shiny metal.
47-48 It stings when molested.
49-50 Used by golfer.
51-52 Large in number.
53-54 Twisted.
55-56 A sharp blow.
57-58 Shelter from the wind.
60-61 A beverage.
62-63 A biting remark.
64-65 A conference.
66-67 Covering for the head.
68-69 We do it when hungry.
70-71 Neckpieces for women.
72-73 Five on each foot.
74-75 Keen.
76-77 Fear.
78-79 A short sleep.
81-82 A tenon.
83-84 An organ for hearing.
85-86 Perceive.
87-88 Swift.
89-90 Fish with long, narrow jaw.
91-92 A cushion.
3-8 A unit.
4-9 Conclusion.
5-19 Series of steps.
6-20 A mistake.
7-15 A place of refuge.
10-18 Beyond.
16-21 A sailor.
17-22 What mother does with a torn garment.
25-30 A limb.
26-31 Used for writing.
27-41 Rebound.
28-42 A bar.
29-37 A furrow.
32-40 Yellowish brown.
38-43 Used for rowing.
39-44 A texture.
49-54 Attempt.
50-55 Corn grows on it.
51-64 Encounter.
52-65 Noiseless.
53-60 Not dry.
56-63 A sharp, quick report.
59-80 One who convokes.
61-66 A curved line.
62-67 Wooly surface of felt.
72-77 An article, denoting special object.
73-78 An eagle.
74-87 Take oath.
75-88 Measured by stepping.
76-83 We did it at dinner time.
79-86 An American poet.
84-89 A tattered cloth.
85-90 A title of respect.

**H**ERE are four cross-word puzzles, all in one, a contribution to FUN'S series from Albert R. Clapsaddle of Gates Avenue, Brooklyn. This puzzle may seem very difficult at first sight, but once you get started  you may find it very easy sailing. It is only fair to state that one of the words used from 59-80 is obsolete although you will find it in the standard dictionaries.

Fill in the blank squares with words corresponding to the list of clues and definitions given below. The solution to this puzzle will be given in next week's FUN.

---

New York World, *August 21, 1914. Puzzles of this era were mostly dictionary exercises. Wordplay, for example, was rare. Solvers mostly had to know definitions.*

Here is a cross-word puzzle which ought to be easier to solve than some of the previous ones. One word, "FUN" is given as a starter. See if you can complete the puzzle by filling in the blank squares with words to the list of clues and definitions given below. The answer to this puzzle will be found in next week's FUN.

| | |
|---|---|
| 1-2 Famous for a confusion of tongues. | 31-32 The third power of a quantity. |
| 3-4 Used by photographers. | 33-34 A Mohammedan prayer leader. |
| 5-6 To construct. | F-6 Worth striving for. |
| 7-8 By word of mouth. | 1-10 To cook by dry and continued heat. |
| 9-10 Ribbon-like. | 3-25 To catch. |
| 11-12 What artists do. | 5-21 A large bird of the parrot family. |
| 13-14 An agreement. | 9-17 An identification label. |
| 15-16 To let fail. | N-7 An Emperor of ancient Rome. |
| 17-18 A native of ancient Gallia. | 2-11 The semi-solid oil of hogs' fat. |
| 19-20 Similar to. | 4-26 A small fish. |
| 21-22 To surround and cover by folding and winding. | 8-24 Birds. |
| 23-24 Never Daughters. | 12-20 Heavy affliction. |
| 25-26 To cast into shadow. | 18-27 To be without. |
| 27-28 A long, loose skirt with sleeves. | 22-29 To interweave. |
| 29-30 Acquired during the summer vacation. | 19-28 Privation. |

New York World, October 4, 1914. Notice that puzzle clues of this era used a period after every clue. This practice was later dropped by the New York Times. Fair warning that some clues are missing from the puzzle.

MRS. MAY HURST of Third Avenue, New York City, who sent in the original of to-day's cross-word puzzle, my not readily recognize it as her own. It has been enlarged. Fill in the small squares with words corresponding to the list of clues and definitions given herewith. The solution will appear in next week's FUN.

## Can You Solve This One?

| | |
|---|---|
| 3-4 Atmosphere. | 39-40 Peeled. |
| 5-6 To concur. | 41-42 One month. |
| 7-8 Ease of speech. | 1-2 A conflagration. |
| 9-10 A holiday. | 3-10 A chill. |
| 11-12 Not this. | 5-14 Between tenor and treble. |
| 13-14 An extinct bird. | 7-18 A baseball league. |
| 15-16 Minerals. | 9-33 Shaping. |
| 17-18 Now fashionable. | 13-29 Indian millet. |
| 19-20 An action. | 17-25 Not thin. |
| 21-22 Injury. | 26-37 A great bustard. |
| 23-24 A young woman. | 30-39 An open-handed blow. |
| 25-26 Three together. | 34-41 The first man. |
| 27-28 To bind. | 43-44 The kingdom of Persia. |
| 29-30 Insects. | 4-11 A tear. |
| 31-32 Used in the kitchen. | 6-15 A reflected sound. |
| 33-34 A monster. | 8-19 It has three feet. |
| 35-36 A conceited person. | 12-36 Overflowing. |
| 37-38 A hollow flatiron. | 16-32 Cauterizes. |

New York World, January 1, 1915. The dimensions of early 20th century crosswords varied dramatically. This week was 15 x 15. The previous week was 38x38 (the square count or dimension of the puzzle).

# FUN'S CROSS WORD PUZZLE

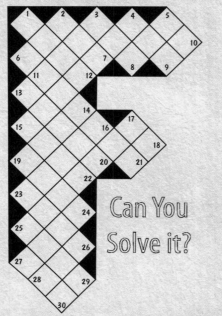

Can You
Solve it?

THERE are going to be three chapters to this cross-word puzzle. The first chapter deals with the letter F. Next week we will consider the letter U, and the week following the letter N. And that spells FUN for every one of FUN's puzzle solvers.

The idea for this puzzle was sent in by George E. Price, of Catherine Street, Hornell, N. Y. Fill in the blank squares with words corresponding to the list of clues and definitions given below. Chapter XI. and the solutions to Chapter I. will appear in next week's FUN.

| | |
|---|---|
| 1-12 To shove. | 9-10 Denial. |
| 2-7 A boy's name. | 13-3 Ornaments. |
| 3-8 To plant seed. | 15-4 It precedes manhood. |
| 4-9 A wild animal's home. | 8-5 Married. |
| 5-10 A verb. | 19-14 A companion. |
| 6-21 A county in Pennsylvania. | 23-16 A country in Asia. |
| 17-13 An adverb. | 25-17 Affirms. |
| 13-20 One who votes. | 27-34 An apartment. |
| 15-22 A young child. | 28-26 Part of your head. |
| 19-24 Fog. | 6-2 It often follows faith. |
| 23-26 A ruler of a kingdom. | 27-30 Charge for professional |
| 25-29 An exclamation of regret. | services. |
| 11-12 An exclamation of surprise. | |

## A CURIOUS THING

Not every crossword has a theme. But themed puzzles have become so standard nowadays that themeless puzzles have to be marked as such. Moreover, themeless puzzles need something to distinguish themselves, since there is no common thread otherwise. For this reason, they tend to have a lower word count than themed puzzles, meaning fewer black squares and longer words overall. Themeless constructors try to include colorful, in-the-language entries spanning nine or more letters, often in stacks of three or four. Naturally, the density of letters makes it difficult to get clean crossings. But that, too, is a prerequisite. A themeless grid should not only be clean but sparkle with fresh, original words. Moreover, the cluing for a themeless puzzle is usually highly challenging. The rise of crossword software has produced something of an arms race among themeless constructors, with regulars like Joe Krozel and Frank Longo taking turns as the record-holders for the puzzle with the lowest word count. While these puzzles are technically impressive, entries like HASANINTERESTIN, TOLERANCELEVELS, RETAP, and ASBIG aren't exactly what we on the inside would call sexy. A debate rages among constructors and hardcore solvers over the value of setting records at the potential expense of user-friendliness.

New York World, *January 24, 1915. A lovely grid shape. This was followed by weeks in which the grid was shaped like a "U" and an "N," to spell "FUN."*

DENNISQUAID, DELAWAREQUARTER, and so on, the solution to the meta would be Dairy Queen, suggested by the initials D.Q. This is just one of Matt's easier recent metas. A meta gimmick ties a puzzle together in an especially cool way that's a little more involved than a typical theme, and Matt provides further incentive by giving prizes to a random selection of people who find the meta solution each week.

Matt's metas, however, never rest on their laurels. The themes range from quirky to breathtaking. For example, one 2012 puzzle titled "At the Present Time" asked the solver to "write a clue for 60-across that completes the theme." The grid featured one hint answer across the center, EVERY5YEARS, meant to tip us off to the fact that every fifth clue (5-Across, 10-Across, 15-Across, and so on) had the traditional anniversary gift material associated with that year's anniversary in the clue. So 5-Across, SWUNG, was clued as "Used a **wood**, say," and 10-Across, TOTO, was "He barked at the **Tin** Man." Without the bolded letters, of course. The answer for 60-Across, NEIL, could thus be clued as "Singer **Diamond**." Matt's metas routinely break the mold in this fashion, and while they have been widely emulated, his are the most elegant and witty.

Of course, a puzzle doesn't have to be impossibly difficult to be great. Actually, producing a refreshing and original easy puzzle is one of the biggest challenges a constructor can face. Elite solver Stella Zawistowski and her constructing partner Bruce Venzke have made an art of the collaborative easy puzzle, publishing many in the *Los Angeles Times*, *New York Times*, CrosSynergy syndicate and elsewhere. The bulk of Nancy Salomon's impressive body of work has appeared on Mondays and Tuesdays—the easiest days—in the *Times*. One young constructor who excels at this type of puzzle is Aimee Lucido, a recent Brown University graduate who writes for the *Times* and the American Values Club, among others. One of her recent A.V. Club puzzles included the revealer CUTTHECHEESE, and within each theme answer a different kind of cheese was "cut up" within the phrase. BRIE, for example, appears in alternating letters within **BURNINEFFEGY**, and EDAM within the slangy **NERDGASMS**. Great easy themes require an intuitive sense of how to make a straightforward idea sparkle.

Constructor Merl Reagle, who syndicates a 21 x 21-sized crossword each Sunday, has contributed his share of incredible themes in a decades-long career in puzzling. Reagle is less an artisan of the high-minded gimmick than the immensely pleasurable and playful one. Possessed of a sense of humor and adventure not unlike Trip Payne's (indeed, Reagle is likely one of his influences), Reagle takes delight in an idiosyncratic approach to themes. He is most famous for his puns, but is hardly one-dimensional in creating them. His 2008 puzzle for the American Crossword Puzzle Tournament, titled "If I Wrote the Dictionary," gave offbeat definitions for real words. LACERATION was clued as "n. the act of tying shoestrings," and so forth. Because the definitions were made up, Reagle had license to include words that might normally be too unpleasant for a crossword, such as SCATOLOGICAL. "If I Wrote the Dictionary" extends the possibility of what a theme can be, strongly injects the personality of the constructor, and cleverly plays with taboo language without cashing in on cheap toilet humor. That puzzle, like many of Merl's, is thematically masterful.

There are, ultimately, far too many great puzzle themes to list, and the worthy candidates only grow by the week. In 100 years, the instinct to extend the boundaries of the crossword has proven powerful. Some of the puzzles in this chapter come from *GAMES* magazine, considered a pioneer in making the theme a key part of the crossword during the 1980s.

# FUN's CROSS-WORD PUZZLE

## № 55

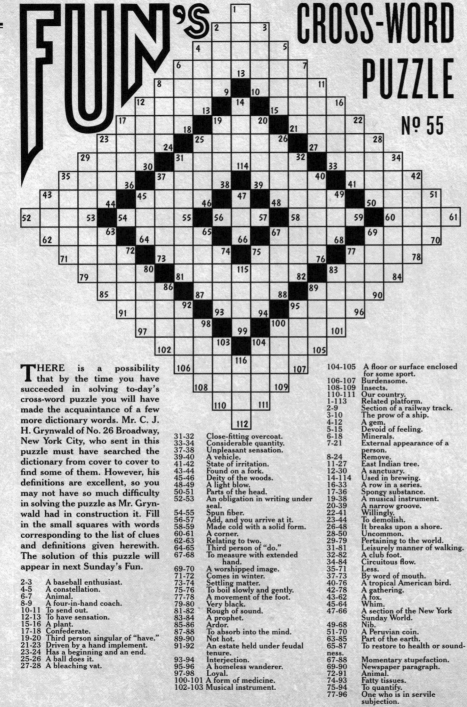

### Can You Solve It?

| | |
|---|---|
| 80-97 | On fingers. |
| 83-101 | Without wind it would be useless. |
| 84-102 | To be in want of. |
| 89-105 | To advance by alternate steps. |
| 92-106 | A game of cards. |
| 93-107 | Victories. |
| 98-108 | Organ of the body. |
| 100-109 | At one time Bishop of Rome. |
| 103-110 | Read in restaurants. |
| 104-111 | A Medieval musical instrument. |
| 115-99 | Woman's hair-net. |
| 116-112 | To efface. |

THERE is a possibility that by the time you have succeeded in solving to-day's cross-word puzzle you will have made the acquaintance of a few more dictionary words. Mr. C. J. H. Grynwald of No. 26 Broadway, New York City, who sent in this puzzle must have searched the dictionary from cover to cover to find some of them. However, his definitions are excellent, so you may not have so much difficulty in solving the puzzle as Mr. Grynwald had in construction it. Fill in the small squares with words corresponding to the list of clues and definitions given herewith. The solution of this puzzle will appear in next Sunday's Fun.

| | |
|---|---|
| 2-3 | A baseball enthusiast. |
| 4-5 | A constellation. |
| 6-7 | Animal. |
| 8-9 | A four-in-hand coach. |
| 10-11 | To send out. |
| 12-13 | To have sensation. |
| 15-16 | A plant. |
| 17-18 | Confederate. |
| 19-20 | Third person singular of "have." |
| 21-23 | Driven by a hand implement. |
| 23-24 | Has a beginning and an end. |
| 25-26 | A ball does it. |
| 27-28 | A bleaching vat. |

| | |
|---|---|
| 31-32 | Close-fitting overcoat. |
| 33-34 | Considerable quantity. |
| 37-38 | Unpleasant sensation. |
| 39-40 | A vehicle. |
| 41-42 | State of irritation. |
| 43-44 | Found on a fork. |
| 45-46 | Deity of the woods. |
| 48-49 | A light blow. |
| 50-51 | Parts of the head. |
| 52-53 | An obligation in writing under seal. |
| 54-55 | Spun fiber. |
| 56-57 | Add, and you arrive at it. |
| 58-59 | Made cold with a solid form. |
| 60-61 | A corner. |
| 62-63 | Relating to two. |
| 64-65 | Third person of "do." |
| 67-68 | To measure with extended hand. |
| 69-70 | A worshipped image. |
| 71-72 | Comes in winter. |
| 73-74 | Settling matter. |
| 75-76 | To boil slowly and gently. |
| 77-78 | A movement of the foot. |
| 79-80 | Very black. |
| 81-82 | Rough of sound. |
| 83-84 | A prophet. |
| 85-86 | Ardor. |
| 87-88 | To absorb into the mind. |
| 89-90 | Not hot. |
| 91-92 | An estate held under feudal tenure. |
| 93-94 | Interjection. |
| 95-96 | A homeless wanderer. |
| 97-98 | Loyal. |
| 100-101 | A form of medicine. |
| 102-103 | Musical instrument. |

| | |
|---|---|
| 104-105 | A floor or surface enclosed for some sport. |
| 106-107 | Burdensome. |
| 108-109 | Insects. |
| 110-111 | Our country. |
| 1-113 | Related platform. |
| 2-9 | Section of a railway track. |
| 3-10 | The prow of a ship. |
| 4-12 | A gem. |
| 5-15 | Devoid of feeling. |
| 6-18 | Minerals. |
| 7-21 | External appearance of a person. |
| 8-24 | Remove. |
| 11-27 | East Indian tree. |
| 12-30 | A sanctuary. |
| 14-114 | Used in brewing. |
| 16-33 | A row in a series. |
| 17-36 | Spongy substance. |
| 19-38 | A musical instrument. |
| 20-39 | A narrow groove. |
| 22-41 | Willingly. |
| 23-44 | To demolish. |
| 26-48 | It breaks upon a shore. |
| 28-50 | Uncommon. |
| 29-79 | Pertaining to the world. |
| 31-81 | Leisurely manner of walking. |
| 32-82 | A club foot. |
| 34-84 | Circuitous flow. |
| 35-71 | Less. |
| 37-73 | By word of mouth. |
| 40-76 | A tropical American bird. |
| 42-78 | A gathering. |
| 43-62 | A fox. |
| 45-64 | Whim. |
| 47-66 | A section of the New York Sunday World. |
| 49-68 | Nib. |
| 51-70 | A Peruvian coin. |
| 63-85 | Part of the earth. |
| 65-87 | To restore to health or soundness. |
| 67-88 | Momentary stupefaction. |
| 69-90 | Newspaper paragraph. |
| 72-91 | Animal. |
| 74-93 | Fatty tissues. |
| 75-94 | To quantify. |
| 77-96 | One who is in servile subjection. |

New York World, *January 17, 1915.*
*A word of warning when solving this one: If you're having trouble with 31-Across, you may not have yourself to blame. The editor seems to have made an error. Mistakes like this were unfortunately common in the early years of crossword puzzles.*

# CUCKOO CROSSWORD 2

BY TRIP PAYNE

In this puzzle, most of the answers are made-up words and phrases. For example, the clue "Stupid plane" would lead to the answer DUMBJET, and "Similar to cartoon character Fudd" to ELMERIC. Normal answers are clued in the regular way.

## ACROSS

1 Blue and richly flavored, as cheese
16 Price-lowering that really should have happened a while back
17 Why the magician's audience was bored
18 Professor's melodramatic assessment of the worst of the term papers
19 XXXIII × XXXV
20 Person who does impressions
21 Mooching dinner, e.g.
29 Zaragoza resident lives it up
30 Raptor that's mostly family-friendly
31 Multitalented musician from South Florida
39 Room arrangement based around salvers from Mumbai
40 CIA head Panetta
41 Poky
42 Wiped a Canadian province off the map
50 Piece that might express disagreement with the actions of an Egyptian goddess
51 Thoroughfare that anyone can change
52 "No pets"

## DOWN

1 "Return whence you came!" and "Get out of my house!"
2 The maximum number of cookers allowed
3 Concerning an American airline
4 Feelin' bad about a loss
5 Vegas numbers
6 Women in black, often
7 Epsilon follower
8 Jazz singer Anita
9 Make messes of S's
10 Literary bitch
11 Basic-level course in which a student might read "Foucault's Pendulum"
12 It's sometimes followed by "Jr."
13 More like a breakfast cereal of the 1960s and '70s
14 Get back into a single dollop, as finger paint
15 In the manner of an old anesthetic
22 Barely beat the Hawkeye St.
23 Have a hard time swallowing
24 "These clues just ___ normal!"
25 U.S. official who evaluates edibles
26 Role lead-in
27 Murder via the Internet
28 Make corrections to
31 Fungicides can get rid of them
32 "You must give that to me!"
33 Hubbubbish
34 "If the canary dies, don't go in," e.g.
35 Category at the Emotional Acting Awards
36 Ninth-inning pitcher for Oakland
37 What the actor who was shunned by The Village Voice received
38 Person to call when you have an ailing sewer
43 "___ the mornin' to ya!"
44 M's place, poetically
45 She played Frenchy in "Grease"
46 Primary
47 Chemical formerly sprayed in orchards
48 Snoot
49 Where some producers and screenwriters work

# VWLLSS CRSSWRD

BY FRNK LNG

This crossword has all of its vowels removed. Enter the consonants into the grid. The letter Y is not a part of any answer. Answer enumerations are on the bottom of page 63.

## ACROSS

1 Dish Network and such
11 Brand-new on the shelves
15 Myopic person's problem
16 In better spirits
17 Stake having a potential monetary gain
18 One of millions in the Oxford English Dictionary
19 Person who establishes and oversees a company
20 Like the hold'em played in the main event of the World Series of Poker
21 Purchases before seeing movies or plays
22 Teeth next to premolars
23 One who gives a player a hand
24 Millimeter vis-à-vis a meter
26 Vigilant
30 Program that blocks some intrusive Internet ads
31 Remove the pigment from
32 Smooth jazz staples
33 Assured
34 Gardeners and masons often push them around
36 "Carnival of the Animals" composer Camille
37 Like writing that doesn't involve the telling of a story
38 Time for many lunch breaks
39 Craps or Yahtzee, e.g.
40 First expedient opportunity
46 Distinctive properties
47 Atypical
48 Not sufficient
49 Discussion for professional advice via a call
50 Walk with faltering steps
51 Make a room dark, say
52 Headless, limbless sculptures
53 Plans on getting even

## DOWN

1 Smelled like a dog
2 Period of three years
3 Unfinished business needing to be tied up
4 Experts in sound reasoning
5 2005 sequel starring Antonio Banderas
6 Carry oneself confidently
7 Isotope used in biochemical tracking, as carbon-14 or iodine-123
8 Bakery item pulled out while wearing a mitt
9 Passé alternatives to compact discs
10 Counterpart of brotherhood
11 Minute Maid product to which water gets added
12 Small, hardy horses with rough coats
13 Choice for therapy
14 Really ripped up
25 Student's document for keeping track of homework tasks
26 Certain chamber ensemble
27 Worker who polishes the text of user guides or system manuals, say
28 Throwing in the towel
29 Officials who supervise seaport operations
30 Strong, hard adhesives
32 Sit-and-spin furniture pieces
35 Address to which bounced e-mail is delivered
36 Installation in Florida named after Kennedy
38 Roosevelt Island's continent
41 Climbs, as a tree
42 What the farmer in "American Gothic" is wearing
43 Provoke
44 Between awful and so-so
45 Frying base that's high in saturated fat

# Can You Dig It?

**HARD INSTRUCTIONS:** This week's crossword grid is missing one letter of the alphabet. Which one is it?

**Across**

**1.** Brush aside

**7.** Having taken MDMA

**10.** Prior to

**13.** English word borrowed from Zulu

**14.** And also not

**15.** Product, often

**16.** Late San Francisco poet Jack

**17.** 1996 movie about four bank robbers

**19.** Occult activity

**20.** Skeleton parts

**21.** Soaring

**22.** Crack ___

**23.** Totals

**26.** Mountain creature, maybe

**27.** Conks

**28.** Untrustworthy individual

**29.** "Who ___?"

**31.** Site of a noted mass suicide

**32.** It revolutionized 20th-century global transportation

**33.** ___+ (French TV channel)

**34.** With "the," system of justice

**36.** Literally, "it is lacking"

**37.** John beat him in the 1979 U.S. Open finals

**38.** ___ fixe

**39.** Yuk

**43.** Western name for a Soviet missile

**44.** Negative particle

**45.** Peninsular nation

**46.** Galileo, Fibonacci, et al.

**48.** Em preceder

**49.** Stops for now

**51.** Learn how to act

**52.** Coax

**53.** One way to go: abbr.

**54.** Enjoys

**55.** Go back

**56.** Capital of Zimbabwe

**57.** A kind gesture from

**Down**

**1.** Perturbation

**2.** Transfix

**3.** Water source

**4.** Amy Goodman's network

**5.** Put in, as Putin

**6.** Afterthought

**7.** Outdoes

**8.** "Find another sucker"

**9.** County of New York and Ohio

**10.** Perfect self-image

**11.** Flag carrier, for short

**12.** Dungeons & Dragons character

**17.** Transmits, as to the other side of a body of water

**18.** Like some flights

**22.** Nash rambler?

**24.** Palindromic family member

**25.** ___-punk (musical genre)

**27.** Clothing discussed in some Judy Blume books

**28.** Together

**30.** Fire ___

**31.** Richard with three #1 hits in 1988-89

**32.** Scam

**33.** Jealous brother

**34.** Rhode Island-based chain

**35.** "Now it's clear to me," in Web shorthand

**36.** Backstab

**38.** Emulated Shakespeare, perhaps

**40.** Harmonize

**41.** Treating impartially

**42.** Lacking

**44.** French department Seine-et-___

**45.** Sort of

**47.** African port

**48.** 2006 role for Whitaker

**49.** Marvel

**50.** ID info

*Matt Gaffney, "Can You Dig It?" Matt Gaffney's Weekly Crossword Contest, July 11, 2008. This and the following two puzzles show the range of difficulty in Matt Gaffney's "meta" puzzles, which require the solver to discern both the solution and an additional unifying answer. This one is hard, "Achy Breaky Heart" is medium, and "Quite Quaint Quintet" is easy." Reprinted with permission of Matt Gaffney.*

# Quite Quaint Quintet

## Across

**1.** "Find someone else to do it!"
**6.** Easily fooled people
**11.** Talking-___ (tongue lashings)
**14.** Truly despise
**15.** Monitor reading?
**16.** NYC subway of yore
**17.** Sleepy fictitious Scotsman
**20.** Pt. of a word
**21.** Letter after "bee"
**22.** Fine with
**23.** Endlessly
**29.** "___ silly question..."
**31.** Creature in sci-fi movies
**32.** Guide to the Himalayas
**35.** Sketch out a course of action
**36.** Nittany Lions' sch.
**39.** Altered a situation's power dynamics
**42.** Put-___ (pranks)
**43.** Word to a gnat
**44.** Latin poet who coined the phrase "carpe diem"
**45.** Noted Irish band, with "The"
**47.** Sign it's time to clean the kitchen
**48.** Cook-off food
**54.** Like many breakfast cereals
**55.** Eugene's state: abbr.
**56.** ___ Flight 800 (still unexplained 1996 explosion off Long Island)
**59.** Vice President from Minnesota
**65.** Airport arrival approximation, abbreviated
**66.** "24" agent Jack ___
**67.** French river known for its valley
**68.** 1998 Irish comedy "Waking ___ Devine"
**69.** Spits out
**70.** "Omigosh!"

## Down

**1.** Dialectical turndowns
**2.** Do what you're told
**3.** Staples Center basketball team
**4.** Lower the lawn
**5.** Hill or Jong
**6.** 1997 title role for Jennifer Lopez
**7.** There, to 44-across
**8.** Bart often crank calls him
**9.** Punching sound
**10.** Schuss
**11.** Chicken ___ masala
**12.** African antelope
**13.** Gadfly journalist Mark ___
**18.** Waikiki wear
**19.** Egg ___
**24.** Astronaut and former Senator Jake
**25.** Innsbruck instrument
**26.** Word in an Agatha Christie title
**27.** Another word from the same Agatha Christie title
**28.** Famous Freud subject, known by her (pseudonymous) first name and last initial
**29.** About
**30.** Avoid socially
**33.** "Goodfellas" actor
**34.** ___ committee
**36.** Voyage among the clouds
**37.** Religious group
**38.** Takes drugs, in slang
**40.** John Deere rival
**41.** Cracklin' Oat ___ (Kellogg's cereal)
**46.** Searches thoroughly
**48.** Ben & Jerry's co-founder Ben
**49.** Terre ___, Ind.
**50.** Have ___ (suffer)
**51.** More common name for caustic soda
**52.** Quarterback's pride
**53.** E-mail program button
**57.** "Where ___ you?"
**58.** Pro team?
**60.** John Riggins and LaDainian Tomlinson: abbr.
**61.** Faucet
**62.** Homophone for 63-down
**63.** Homophone for 62-down
**64.** ___ polloi (general population)

**EASY INSTRUCTIONS:** It may look like this crossword has only five theme entries, but there's a sixth one hidden somewhere in the grid. This sixth theme entry is this week's contest answer.

Matt Gaffney, "Quite Quaint Quintet," Matt Gaffney's Weekly Crossword Contest, May 1, 2009. Reprinted with permission of Matt Gaffney.

# Achy Breaky Heart

**Across**

**1.** Appear alright at first glance

**7.** Small amount of gold or silver

**11.** "Another thing I forgot to mention is..."

**14.** Fighting Midwesterners

**15.** "Don't take that ___ with me!"

**16.** Boxing biopic

**17.** Old issues of Playboy you can bid on?

**19.** Just chill

**20.** Bad: Sp.

**21.** Give pitcher Ryan a makeover?

**23.** Face problems

**25.** Sub ___ (secretly)

**26.** Laundry list

**29.** Death Valley is below it

**33.** Japan's ___ Castle

**34.** Poet killed in the Spanish Civil War

**35.** Cheech & Chong movies, for example?

**41.** KFC rival

**42.** No warmongers

**43.** Sky scare

**47.** John Bobbitt's ex-wife

**48.** ___ the Goalie (hockey nickname)

**49.** Skye of "Zodiac"

**50.** Illegal squirrel-smuggling operation?

**55.** Kind of

**59.** Intent

**60.** Where some amphibians live?

**62.** Encoded material

**63.** Baum barker

**64.** Willie or Craig T.

**65.** Obama, once: abbr.

**66.** Shouts at the successful

**67.** Author of the first

MEDIUM INSTRUCTIONS: This week's contest answer is a five-letter word that ties the theme together.

prominent crossword-based mystery story, 1925

**Down**

**1.** ___ Reap (historic Cambodian city)

**2.** Exile isle

**3.** Transportation to Tel Aviv

**4.** "Princess Mononoke" director Hayao ___

**5.** Unified

**6.** MacColl of '80s-'90s pop

**7.** Court figure: abbr.

**8.** Work very hard

**9.** Not repeatedly

**10.** Average

**11.** Stimulating scientist

**12.** Make happy

**13.** Indicate

**18.** Extra pds.

**22.** Calif. neighbor

**24.** Stuck

**26.** Herbert of the Pink Panther movies

**27.** "This ___ joke, right?"

**28.** Smear

**29.** Some HDTVs

**30.** Jacksonian and Clinton

**31.** UVA, FSU, et al.

**32.** Applied, as flattery

**34.** Popular dogs, for short

**36.** Gullible-getter Geller

**37.** "I'm completely serious!"

**38.** St. Mark's ___ (Apr. 24)

**39.** Uncles, usually

**40.** "___ Man Thinketh"

**43.** Many Tibetans

**44.** Former Labor Secretary Chao

**45.** He gets high at work

**46.** "Perfect Circle" band

**47.** Computer entries

**49.** Stock: abbr.

**51.** Palindromic "Simpsons" character

**52.** Person often taken advantage of

**53.** Use a scale from 1 to 10

**54.** Wedding day exchange

**56.** First, second or third, but not fourth

**57.** Borodin opera "Prince ___"

**58.** Hamiltons

**61.** Actress Thompson

*Matt Gaffney, "Achy Breaky Heart,"* Matt Gaffney's Weekly Crossword Contest, *June 12, 2009. Reprinted with permission of Matt Gaffney.*

# Onion A.V. Club
## November 23, 2011

**Across**

1. Earring or skirt shape
5. Developer's map
9. Like some kids on "Oprah"
15. Command often entered in a state of panic
16. Lira replacement
17. Where much shopping is done
18. "Lord, give her majesty a Brazilian!"?
21. Acronym for an asshole
22. German "rocks"
23. Like a buttinsky
24. Attempt to promote cream cheese?
30. Also
31. Fidel's brother
32. World Series-winning cap letters
33. Stately trees
35. "The doctor ___ "
37. Gwen Stefani purses
42. Still Charlie after all these years?
46. Boy band that had a member go on to play Sean Parker
47. Squished circle
48. ___ Tea
49. It may be bruised if you fall down the stairs
52. See 60-Down
54. Blue Book listing
55. Straitjacket fit for a bookcase?
59. Continent prone to typhoons
61. Subreddit abbr. for outrageous questions and answers
62. Carefully monitored area, for short
63. Cheesy gimmick?
70. Slob's napkin
71. For fear that
72. Instrument often described as "mournful"
73. Scads
74. Uses up minutes
75. Adjective for the man who shirtlessly plays "Careless Whisper" on his saxophone in malls and grocery stores

**Down**

1. Friendly greeting
2. Lennon's second mate
3. Quirky
4. Insane Clown ___
5. Idiot
6. <3
7. Michelle Branch's "___ You Happy Now?"
8. Cobb's spinning top, e.g., in "Inception"
9. Attacks
10. One may be judicial: Abbr.
11. Thrown
12. Attach, like a bow
13. Hydrocarbon endings
14. Say no to
19. Frost
20. Shakira's don't lie
24. Unlikely to crack a smile
25. Book featuring Stanley and Armpit
26. Tommy Pickles' wail
27. Swear
28. Justice Samuel
29. Problems
34. Word in Western city names
36. Exploding stars
38. The first Norwegian band with a number 1 song in the US
39. Word of thanks
40. Started
41. Enjoy, as coke?
43. Drink thrown in the face of 65-Down
44. Sex On The Beach locales
45. Some hipsters
50. Looks intensely
51. "Piece ___ " (Britney Spears song)
53. Architectural piece that becomes weaker when supported
55. Measured
56. Eye color
57. Gather, as the troops
58. What some dealers peddle
59. Response to "Are not!" that's unlikely to resolve the matter
60. 52-Across, for example
64. It runs north-south in NY
65. Michele of "Glee"
66. Nile reptile
67. "May ___ of service?"
68. Sarcastic doctor on "Scrubs"
69. Skeleton ___

Aimee Lucido, Onion A.V. Club, November 23, 2011. Reprinted with permission of Aimee Lucido and Ben Tausig.

# HELL'S KITCHEN
## Eight less-than-scrumptious items from Beelzebub's bakery.

### Across

**1.** Three-liter liquid
**5.** Jordanian neighbor
**10.** Some radios
**13.** Disgusting discovery?
**15.** Dish's co-elopee
**17.** Terrible-tasting tortes?
**18.** Austrian actress Palmer
**19.** Wear
**20.** Japanese theater
**21.** Children's doctor Smith
**22.** Brunch time, perhaps
**25.** ___ and ahed
**28.** Raid victim
**29.** Reason for earthy taste?
**34.** Dishwasher's eclair contribution?
**37.** Thinker's word form
**38.** Del Shannon's "___ Pieces"
**39.** Donut stuff
**43.** A long time
**44.** Wayne and Worth, for two: Abbr.
**45.** Billboard business
**47.** Marked, as a ballot
**48.** Donut stuff
**50.** Mag that "showed off" Burt
**53.** Powerless, in a way
**54.** High-energy sweet stuff?
**58.** Runny puff ingredient?
**61.** The essence of rock
**62.** ___ cropper
**63.** Stay-awake aid
**67.** Key of Beethoven's Second Symphony
**69.** All-purpose truck
**72.** Stovepipe sporter
**73.** "___ Went to Haiti" (Cole Porter tune)
**74.** Unsnappable snap?
**79.** Doc on "Gunsmoke"
**80.** Overly-buttery brioches?
**81.** Airhead
**82.** "___ good money for these tickets!"
**83.** Steamer crew

### Down

**1.** One of the "Three Amigos"
**2.** Like a bucket of song
**3.** Credibility cracker
**4.** "___ longa ..."
**5.** Lowdown, skinny, etc.
**6.** Impulsive
**7.** Blood group
**8.** Sine ___ non
**9.** Computer feed: Abbr.
**10.** See 60-Down
**11.** River in a Smetana work
**12.** "Ta-ta!"
**14.** Electrovalence possessor
**15.** Huskies
**16.** Beethoven's last symphony
**17.** Director's cry
**21.** Actor Cobb
**23.** Officer Obie's most famous arrestee
**24.** Prelude to juin
**25.** "Put a lid ___!"
**26.** Inventor Lilienthal
**27.** Letters on a '68 campaign button
**30.** Heal, as bones
**31.** Caviar, basically
**32.** ___ Jima
**33.** Beanpole Olive
**34.** Feudal estate
**35.** Object of adoration
**36.** Jocular Jay
**40.** Eddie, in "Beverly Hills Cop"
**41.** Relish
**42.** Country crooner Arnold
**44.** Paintings on plaster
**45.** Soviet-Chinese border river
**46.** Feature of St. Peter's
**49.** Wire serv.
**50.** Megaphone's shape
**51.** One of Chekhov's "Three Sisters"
**52.** Boesky's busters: Abbr.
**53.** Showroom model
**55.** Day eponym
**56.** Basketball basket part
**57.** Smuts from South Africa
**58.** Screwdriver part
**59.** Warship group
**60.** Totally tidy, with 10-Down
**64.** African capital
**65.** Last words
**66.** "X, Y and ___" (Liz Taylor film)
**68.** Beam and Bowie
**69.** Tangelo
**70.** What "kilo-" means: Abbr.
**71.** "The Name of the Rose" author
**74.** Tetra less one
**75.** V.T. Hamlin's Alley
**76.** Ending for form or spat
**77.** 'Twixt ne'er and e'er
**78.** Two ___ kind

*Merl Reagle, "Hell's Kitchen,"* Baltimore Open, *April 1987. Reprinted with permission of Stanley Newman.* Crossword tournament puzzles frequently include titles as well as subtitles; the latter provides a clever additional hint to figuring out the theme.

# CATCHING THE 6:15
## A wide-open challenger for the championship. May the best puzzler win.

**Across**

**1.** Scott McGregor or Mike Boddicker

**16.** Gallup finding

**17.** Biased subjects?

**18.** Audacity

**19.** A verse to emotion

**20.** Vision-defying works

**21.** Holiday visitors, often

**22.** Greek goddess of youth

**24.** Eleven makeup

**25.** Chest material

**27.** Snaky horror film of '73

**30.** Ticks by

**33.** Raid the fridge

**34.** Navel display

**37.** Double this after "Da Doo"

**38.** Bud-exciting

**40.** Mobile home: Abbr.

**41.** Covered seats on elephants' backs

**43.** Where a beanery may be scenery

**46.** Earthquake

**49.** Radar O'Reilly's favorite drink

**50.** They really click onstage

**52.** "Bali ___"

**54.** Must

**56.** Gerard, TV's Buck Rogers

**57.** Swamp dweller

**59.** Coexistence thorn

**62.** The zone or the 4-3, e.g.

**63.** Late-arrival query

**Down**

**1.** See 33-Across

**2.** Bully?

**3.** Get used (to)

**4.** Ocho ___, Jamaica

**5.** "Watermelon Wine" singer

**6.** Diminutive suffix

**7.** Mr. Moneybags

**8.** Move effortlessly

**9.** Ghostly

**10.** Common contraction

**11.** Wyoming-Idaho range

**12.** "Geez!"

**13.** Badgers

**14.** "The Hungarian Rome"

**15.** Motion cessation

**23.** Tide competitor

**24.** Erstwhile psywar org.

**26.** Actress Wallace of "E.T."

**27.** Thrill

**28.** Went unused

**29.** Eye sore or eyesore

**31.** Ice skate piece

**32.** Word with two farm-related meanings

**34.** Part of Pres. Monroe's signature

**35.** Benevolent, protective fellow

**36.** Woodwork paneling

**38.** Sleight-of-hand maneuver

**39.** Start of a Faulkner work

**41.** ___ polloi

**42.** Indiana Jones irritant

**44.** "House of Wax" director Andre

**45.** Equilateral parallelograms

**47.** Type of wrap

**48.** Tung preceders

**50.** It always makes the front page

**51.** Ms. Valli of "The Third Man"

**53.** How change may come to the Japanese

**54.** Sound investment?

**55.** Years, in Barcelona

**56.** Half of all square dancers?

**58.** Where Zeno taught

**60.** Jed Clampett, Lucas McCain, etc.

**61.** Vegas venture

Merl Reagle, *"Catching the 6:15,"* Baltimore Open, *April 1986. Reprinted with permission of Stanley Newman. The Open tournaments that took place at various locations on the East Coast from the mid-1980s through the early 1990s were an important factor in the development of a close-knit crossword community, which exists to this day.*

*Answer Drawer, page 78*

## ACROSS

1 Make a two-piece chess move
7 Artist's colors
14 Robe accessories
20 Shaw and others
21 Breakout artist
22 Elvis's birthplace
23 Armstrong's song to NASA?
25 Turkish peak
26 Lamprey catcher
27 1982 Disney movie
28 Compass pt.
29 Merit
30 Buntline and Beatty
31 Indian icon
33 Presidential nickname
35 Wm. Casey's org.
38 Gen.'s underling
39 Movie shown on *Nova*?
44 Examiners
49 Try a new hair color
51 Quietly furious
52 One-time Tarzan
53 Author Fleming
54 Catch
56 Actress Sommer et al.
57 Straws in the wind
58 Rich ruler of a small planet?
61 ____ amis
62 1982 Broadway hit
63 *The Firebird*, e.g.
64 Roman robe
66 Prefix for cycle or centennial
69 Yoko
70 Took first
71 Greek's P
73 Used to be
74 Part of HRH
75 Strongman Ferrigno
76 Devil's home
79 Going out
82 Deal out
83 Greek's X
85 Video game for shuttle pilots?
87 Street's boss
88 "____ in a name?"
90 Soak up
91 Timetable abbr.
92 Part of LEM
93 Small flowers
95 Be economical, in a way
97 Relies
98 Verne tale with a tail?
100 El ____
101 Ariz. neighbor
102 "Bei ____ Bist du Schön"
103 Tie type
106 Menlo Park name
110 Cheese choice
113 Perform
116 "____ does it!"
117 Yorkshire city
119 Party nibble
121 Newspaper akin to *The Martian Chronicles*?
124 Dodger
125 Fit for consumption
126 Used car dealer's deal
127 Soothers
128 *Faerie Queene* writer
129 Shoelace hole

## DOWN

1 Alfresco eatery
2 *Wizard of Oz* composer Harold
3 Panache
4 Read the minutes?
5 Ogles
6 Extremist's suffix
7 Lorry fuel
8 Take ____ (try)
9 Venue
10 Cap type
11 Body of poetry
12 Some July birthdays
13 Nero's tutor
14 Blue zircon
15 Glow
16 Tiff
17 Aurora's theme song?
18 Guido's highest note
19 Souse
24 Some German kings
32 Off one's rocker
34 ____ nova (14th century music style)
36 Angers
37 Also
38 Shout
40 Sound-picture agreement
41 Carousing sprees
42 Diamond and others
43 Prepare a strudel
44 Rock group ____ Harum
45 *One Day at a Time* family
46 Kurt Weill musical for interplanetary performers?
47 Kingsley and Vereen
48 High trains
49 Julia, of *Nine*
50 Go into
53 Bedridden
55 Dracula, at times
58 Hsing-Hsing, for one
59 Multiple choice listing
60 Atlas dots
63 Feathery wrap
65 Fall behind
67 Like folk tales
68 Actresses Dunne and Cara
70 Bleach or blanch
72 Orchestra members
77 Road curve
78 Squall
80 Quick snack
81 Actress Lupino
82 Produced
84 Heavenly headgear
86 Rapier
87 Swabber's need
88 Bride, after the ceremony
89 Falters
92 Size after sm.
93 Erich ____ Stroheim
94 Bio or chem.
96 Actress Hagen
97 Cheerful song
99 Speechifies
100 Mine worker
104 Rough tries
105 Tierra del Fuego's land
106 "Gasoline ____"
107 Co-op contract
108 Mercenary
109 Fred's dancing sister
111 Miami's county
112 Mimic
114 Fellow
115 *Chapeau* site
118 Proofreader's mark
119 Bee follower
120 In the manner of
122 Aykroyd, of *Trading Places*
123 Post's opposite

Philip Greco, "The Sky's the Limit," GAMES, 1983. Reprinted with permission of Kappa Publishing.

# COLORIZING ★★★

### ACROSS

1 Hood's weapon
4 Souchong samples
8 Saw
13 Streetcar
17 Rajah's wife
18 Go ____ (proceed)
19 Woodworker's tool
20 Picture on a $10,000 bill
21 Mammoth
22 Halo
23 Auguries
24 Slow, on staff?
25 Dieter's temptation
27 Breathing
29 What Gelett Burgess never did
31 Wizard's way?
34 Welles and Bean
35 ____ Haute, Indiana
36 ____ van der Rohe
37 Scarfs, e.g.
40 Pressed
42 Rail riders
43 Ambition
46 Topics for Dr. Ruth
48 A Little Rascal
49 Devil, in slang
50 Pretentious talk
51 Sweetie
52 Wheel of Fortune category
54 Tennis or bridge term
55 Belt constellation
56 Eskimo's wrap
58 With it
59 The Snowman in The Falcon and the Snowman
60 Valley guy
63 Civil rights figure Parks
67 Leading Soviet auto
68 Hersey title start
69 Cupolae
70 Architect from Canton, China
73 End of some bus. names
75 "A mouse!"
76 Drape holder
78 Ten times CCCLI
80 Longshoremen, e.g.
82 Harass
83 Landlord's man
84 Loving not wisely, but too well
85 Wally's brother
86 Most distant

88 Ages
89 Subway entrance
93 "True Colors" singer
95 Series losers in '46, '67, '75 and '86
98 Frank
101 Yentl's instructor
102 Don of Hazel
103 Hallowed
104 Prop for Sweeney Todd
106 Slime
108 Superior: Ger.
109 German article
110 Adm. Byrd's story
111 ". . . with sugar ____"
112 Carry on
113 ____ good example
114 Knight's horse
115 Concordes
116 A.M.A. folk

### DOWN

1 Maladroit
2 Fisherman
3 Start of a 1973 #1 song title
4 Belle, Bart, or Brenda
5 Debtor's letters
6 They're done by Hook or by crook
7 Pursued furtively
8 From the top: Lat.
9 Bearing
10 Blvd. crosser
11 4★ leaders: Abbr.
12 Born Free lioness
13 Location for Zane Grey's Riders
14 Full of enmity
15 ____ Martin, James Bond's car

16 Cat calls
17 Butler of fiction
20 Irish county
26 Spaniard, e.g.
28 Part of the Treasury Dept.
30 Excites
32 1975 hit "____ in Love"
33 Shortcoming
38 Like a dunce cap
39 Mr. Mom star
41 "____ bodkins!"
42 Legendary Detroit ballplayer
44 Sleeve item?
45 Authorize
46 It's traditional
47 Poker declaration
48 "Hot enough ____?"
49 ____ Rio, Texas
50 1940s jazz

51 2001 computer
53 Drawing
56 Soothe
57 Playwright James and kin
60 Funnyman Murray
61 Stock buy, maybe
62 Kind
63 Gatsby portrayer
64 Arabian gulf
65 Religious body
66 Query
67 Easygoing
69 Estate
70 Brit. leaders
71 Zoo bird
72 Lacking discretion
74 Keats or Shelley, e.g.
76 Mini-oven setting
77 Columnist Kupcinet

79 Neptune's domain
81 Bestow power upon
82 Stresses
84 Boat with oars
85 Goofs
87 Sports events
88 Cabaret lyricist Fred
90 Weather-map line
91 Sophia and others
92 Put forth
93 Some leaf parts
94 Half of an '80s TV team
96 Able to listen
97 Golden Boy playwright
99 History chapters
100 Sailor
105 Actress Caldwell
107 Prom night woe

ANSWER, PAGE 60

Charles Deber, "Colorizing," GAMES, 1988. Reprinted with permission of Kappa Publishing.

# FOOD STOP!

## *By Stanley Newman*

★★

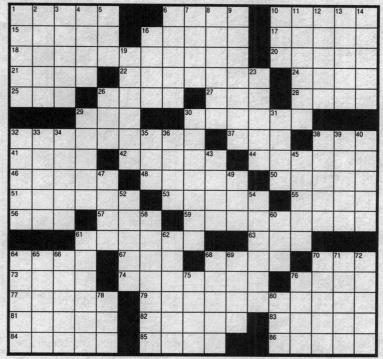

### ACROSS

1 Swell time
6 Their "wait" is taken in pounds
10 Supply
15 Main artery
16 Dudley or Dinty
17 Pointy cap wearer
18 Stuff it!: 2 wds.
20 Miss Thompson of *Rain*
21 Forbidding
22 By ___ (alone)
24 Hang on to
25 Japanese moolah
26 Name of 12 popes
27 KGB's counterpart
28 Goofs
29 Plea at sea
30 Drinking spree
32 Put a lid on it!: 2 wds.
37 Word with willikers
38 Diamond or ruby
41 Retired tennist Arthur
42 "No ___!"
44 Place to hide an ace?
46 Out-and-out
48 Banquet
50 Winter fall
51 Word in a tissue ad
53 Confused: 2 wds.
55 ___ uncertain terms: 2 wds.
56 Spielberg's aliens, for short
57 Astronaut's "all right"
59 Drop it!: 2 wds.
61 Like foam rubber
63 Have debts
64 Channel selector
67 In favor of
68 Bear's order on Wall Street
70 ___ Haw
73 "Ma, He's Making Eyes ___": 2 wds.
74 Unmoved by grief
76 Tailless cat
77 Morocco's capital
79 Can it!: 2 wds.
81 'enry's student in *My Fair Lady*
82 Linda of *Dynasty*
83 Late-blooming flower
84 Cared for excessively
85 Car scar
86 Cause of a blown fuse?

### DOWN

1 Big and loose, as pants
2 Mr. Moto of films
3 "The results ___" (election night announcement): 2 wds.
4 Wine glass part
5 Brown from the sun
6 Dumbbells
7 Klutz's remark
8 Athens' country
9 *Twilight Zone* creator Rod
10 Mister and Asner
11 Name with Oats and Motor Oil
12 Less than
13 More skid-prone, as winter roads
14 Spies on, like Tom?
16 Restaurant or computer list
19 Balances
23 Loses brightness
26 Campaign manager, for short
29 Clay pigeon
30 Like Lauren Bacall's voice
31 Fishes for a sushi bar
32 Outmoded
33 "___ an arrow . . .": 2 wds.
34 Julia Child and colleagues
35 Skippy competitor
36 Neighborhood
38 Actress Davis of *The Fly*
39 Happening
40 Tag-along's cry: 2 wds.
43 Exxon's ex-name
45 Type style
47 Gather grain
49 Vietnamese New Year
52 Housetops
54 Moon-landing program
58 Tied up
60 Wise bird
61 Tawdriness
62 LP track
64 Took chances
65 From Rome or Naples: Prefix
66 Boundary
68 Inadequate
69 Has lunch
70 Must: 2 wds.
71 Opposite of exit
72 Put forth effort
75 "___ Old Cowhand": 2 wds.
76 '70s Alda series
78 Little bit
80 Faux ___ (gaffe)

Stanley Newman, "Food Stop," GAMES, 1988. Reprinted with permission of Kappa Publishing.

# EASY AS ABC

## By Trip Payne
★

### ACROSS

1 Where doors get stuck?
6 Red-breasted bird
11 Umpires, for short
15 Thin as ___: 2 wds.
16 Steer clear of, as the draft
17 Banishment
19 Deep-voiced opera singer
20 Prison compartments
21 More evil
22 A: 3 wds.
25 Chef Julia
26 Lancelot's title
27 Adam's mate
28 Kind of machine or cars
31 "Welcome to Hawaii"
34 Having layers, as a wedding cake
36 Sunbather's quest
37 Emergency signal
38 Extremely happy
40 Brainstorms
42 Overused, as a phrase
43 "Would ___ to You?" (1985 Eurythmics hit): 2 wds.
47 B: 5 wds.
51 Marshes
52 "Button your lip!": 2 wds.
53 Tent peg
54 2,000 pounds: 2 wds.
56 Cambridge, Mass., college, for short
58 Christie's ___ Little Indians
59 Fir popular as a Christmas tree
62 Uncle ___ (Br'er Rabbit's storyteller)
64 Degrees after M.A.s or M.S.s
65 Miners dig it
66 Golf peg
68 Bone: Prefix
70 C: 4 wds.
76 Go ___ (begin fighting): 2 wds.
77 Wounds with a tusk
78 Things
80 Plantation worker, once
81 "Once upon ___": 2 wds.
82 "___, won't you blow your horn"
83 Hair colorings
84 Baseball star Pee Wee
85 Twenty, old-style

### DOWN

1 Poke in the ribs
2 Smell ___ (be suspicious): 2 wds.
3 "Monster ___" (novelty hit of 1962)
4 Cut into two equal parts
5 Splash about, as water
6 Remembers
7 Go too far
8 Comedienne Lucille
9 Not busy
10 Birds' homes
11 Daydream
12 Sign by a highway ramp
13 Kind of cigarette
14 "Nothing up my ___" (magician's words)
18 Made a mistake
23 Italian "good-bye"
24 Throw garbage around
28 Rigid
29 Serving spoon
30 ___ a million: 2 wds.
32 Juliet or Joan of Arc
33 "Need ___?" (words to a hitchhiker): 2 wds.
35 King's decree
37 '60s draft organization: Abbr.
39 TV's One Day ___ Time: 2 wds.
41 Lhasa ___ (small dogs)
42 Voice below alto
44 Reluctant
45 Irritated
46 Paradises
48 Some old-time deliverers
49 Not "dis"
50 Superlative ending
55 Dispositions
56 Four-star film, to reviewers
57 Words in an analogy: 2 wds.
59 Winter footwear
60 Muscleman Schwarzenegger
61 Room to maneuver
63 Computers' telephone hook-ups
64 In verse form
67 Ventriloquist Bergen
69 Author Bagnold and others
71 Possess
72 Learning by memorization
73 New York canal
74 Nevada "divorce" town
75 Actor Sharif
79 That lady

Trip Payne, "Easy as ABC," GAMES, 1988. Reprinted with permission of Kappa Publishing.

**ANSWER, PAGE 54**

## ACROSS

1 Harvest
5 HI hi
10 Ont. or N.B.
14 "The wolf ___ the door"
18 "___ want for Christmas . . ."
19 Vitamin C source
20 Quietly, to the orchestra
21 Burrito's kin
22 *Cut wood?*
24 *No more?*
26 Quiz show contestant
27 Body shop fixes
29 Whoopi, in *The Color Purple*
30 Bowlers, e.g.
31 Inclines
32 Muslim judge
33 Lumberjacks
36 Jigsaw minutia
37 Like Charlie McCarthy, e.g.
41 ___ *Irish Rose*
42 *Artless?*
44 ___ *Got a Secret*
45 Dudley Do-Right's girlfriend
46 Over
47 Vikings landed there
48 Re hosp. doings
49 Actress Dolores ___ Rio
50 *No exits?*
54 They're owed on the road
55 Incentive
57 Plant ___ of doubt
58 Cook slowly in liquid
59 Alleviates
60 See 12-Down
61 "___ sec!"
62 Got the gas
64 One who's beside himself?
65 Nursery furnishing
68 Egg silhouettes
69 *No win?*
71 *Ben-___*
72 Acts of the Apostles writer
73 Shopping aid
74 Golden Rule word
75 Figure skater Thomas
76 ___ du Diable
77 *Strike one?*
81 Prove otherwise
82 Lives it up
84 Hot dog garnish
85 Merchant
86 Cockney's quests
87 Flip response?

88 French comic actor Jacques
89 "Ya ___ believe!"
91 Opposite of 20-Across
92 Rotary-wing aircraft
96 *Far out?*
98 *Take off?*
100 Clock numeral
101 Kate's mate
102 Winning side in '65
103 Subdued
104 *Cliff's Notes* info
105 Present time?
106 Polar explorer
107 *National Enquirer* competitor

## DOWN

1 Asian noble
2 Photographic developing powder
3 Hamlet's cry re Yorick
4 Pyrotechnic spinner
5 Puts on the qui vive
6 Yukon river
7 Gen. Bradley
8 Not vert.
9 "The woods are lovely, dark, ___": Frost
10 Actress ZaSu
11 Stadium shouts
12 With 60-Across, singly
13 Pelée and Krakatoa, e.g.
14 *Like this*
15 Ranee's wrap
16 Ranch component
17 Tot's Xmas gift
20 Vaudeville comedian Joe

23 Approaches
25 Track relentlessly
28 @
31 British tar
32 Stallone flick
33 MGM Grand rival
34 Red as ___
35 *Lost shoe?*
36 Toughs
37 "And be ___ for such disguise . . .": *Twelfth Night*
38 *Man overboard?*
39 Sermon subjects
40 Thickheaded
42 *Witch word?*
43 Pageant host
46 Distributed
48 Raccoon's relative
50 Dodges, in a way
51 Koch bestseller

52 "With ___ in My Heart"
53 Taylor or Richards
54 Actress Van Devere
56 Sap source
58 Low figure?
60 Rorschach designs
61 Imperfections
62 Henry of *Webster*
63 Palatal pendant
64 First asteroid
65 *The Hunted,* in a 1987 movie
66 Musicmaker Blake
67 Judge, perhaps
69 *What's this?*
70 Dupes
73 Crusoe or Gilligan
75 Tickles pink

77 Coup group
78 Held wide apart, in ballet
79 ". . . ___ or a miss?"
80 Angry
81 Pick to win
83 Rig
85 Soft and smooth
87 Comedienne Fields
88 Coach
89 Cager Goodrich
90 Lima locale
91 Hew
92 Minor place?
93 "___ your disposal"
94 "___ Lama Ding Dong" ('61 song)
95 Nonpareil
96 Sartorial mishap
97 Actor Gulager
99 Nantes number

*Nancy Ross, "Name-Dropping," GAMES, 1988. Reprinted with permission of Kappa Publishing.*

# SPEECH! SPEECH! ★

BY WILLIAM LUTWINIAK

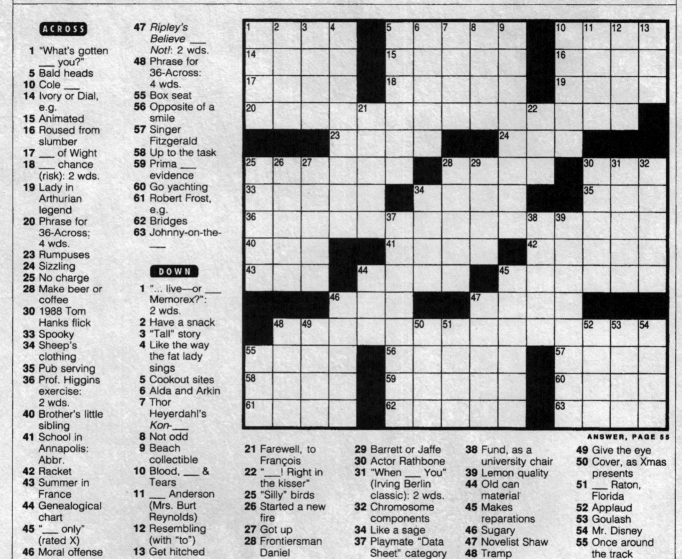

### ACROSS

1 "What's gotten ___ you?"
5 Bald heads
10 Cole ___
14 Ivory or Dial, e.g.
15 Animated
16 Roused from slumber
17 ___ of Wight
18 ___ chance (risk): 2 wds.
19 Lady in Arthurian legend
20 Phrase for 36-Across: 4 wds.
23 Rumpuses
24 Sizzling
25 No charge
28 Make beer or coffee
30 1988 Tom Hanks flick
33 Spooky
34 Sheep's clothing
35 Pub serving
36 Prof. Higgins exercise: 2 wds.
40 Brother's little sibling
41 School in Annapolis: Abbr.
42 Racket
43 Summer in France
44 Genealogical chart
45 "___ only" (rated X)
46 Moral offense

47 Ripley's Believe ___ Not!: 2 wds.
48 Phrase for 36-Across: 4 wds.
55 Box seat
56 Opposite of a smile
57 Singer Fitzgerald
58 Up to the task
59 Prima ___ evidence
60 Go yachting
61 Robert Frost, e.g.
62 Bridges
63 Johnny-on-the-___

### DOWN

1 "... live—or ___ Memorex?": 2 wds.
2 Have a snack
3 "Tall" story
4 Like the way the fat lady sings
5 Cookout sites
6 Alda and Arkin
7 Thor Heyerdahl's Kon-___
8 Not odd
9 Beach collectible
10 Blood, ___ & Tears
11 ___ Anderson (Mrs. Burt Reynolds)
12 Resembling (with "to")
13 Get hitched

21 Farewell, to François
22 "___! Right in the kisser"
25 "Silly" birds
26 Started a new fire
27 Got up
28 Frontiersman Daniel
29 Barrett or Jaffe
30 Actor Rathbone
31 "When ___ You" (Irving Berlin classic): 2 wds.
32 Chromosome components
34 Like a sage
37 Playmate "Data Sheet" category
38 Fund, as a university chair
39 Lemon quality
44 Old can material
45 Makes reparations
46 Sugary
47 Novelist Shaw
48 Tramp
49 Give the eye
50 Cover, as Xmas presents
51 ___ Raton, Florida
52 Applaud
53 Goulash
54 Mr. Disney
55 Once around the track

ANSWER, PAGE 55

William Lutwiniak, "Speech! Speech!" GAMES, 1989. Reprinted with permission of Kappa Publishing.

# HOW SWEET! ★★

BY MARGARET RIGBY

## ACROSS

1 Stop, as a subscription
7 "How ___ the little busy bee..."
11 Cookie container
14 Peter of *Lawrence of Arabia*
15 Ending for "buck"
16 Let sit, as wine
17 The "A" in A-bomb
18 Eatery sign
19 Prefix with fit, fire, or file
20 Win first prize, so to speak: 3 wds.
22 Hit B'way sign
23 Brimmed with activity
24 Triangular street sign
26 Plumb crazy
29 April initials
30 Muir or Calabash
31 Timetable abbr.
32 Dumbo's "wings"
34 In balance
37 Vegas casino ___ Palace
39 Indianan
40 Slip by
41 Pillow filler
42 Mineral source
43 "Merry month"
44 London's "big timer"
45 TV problem up north?
46 Toyota model
48 Woodwind musician
51 Baton Rouge campus
52 Made more palatable
57 Channels 14 and up
58 High school exam, for short
59 Connected by computer: 2 wds.
60 Gridiron official
61 Concerning, legally: 2 wds.
62 Joan of Arc, ___ Orleans: 2 wds.
63 Fourth year students: Abbr.
64 Chows down
65 Mr. Hemingway

## DOWN

1 Parka or slicker
2 "___ boy!"
3 Alcove
4 Regain consciousness: 2 wds.
5 Upper crust
6 *Café con ___* (coffee with milk)
7 The Rockettes, for example
8 Mountain nymphs
9 Conned
10 Lovers' holiday
11 Informal performance: 2 wds.
12 "I want ___ just like...": 2 wds.
13 Put in a new lawn
21 Asian rulers
25 Eye part
26 Queen Anne's, for one
27 Evangelist Roberts
28 Sissies: 2 wds.
32 Simple: 3 wds.
33 '50s series *You ___ There*
34 "___, right in the kisser!"
35 Architect Saarinen
36 Actress Barrymore
38 Practice with Mike Tyson
39 Kind of card or guard
41 Pre-election events
44 *African Queen* skipper
45 Yalta Conference host
46 Speaks drunkenly
47 Theater seater
49 "Ready or not, here ___": 2 wds.
50 Submarine gadget
53 Annapolis inst.
54 Ebb or neap
55 Baseball's Slaughter
56 Adroit

ANSWER, PAGE 55

Margaret Rigby, "How Sweet!" GAMES, 1989.
Reprinted with permission of Kappa Publishing.

# CLEF NOTES ★★

BY RANDOLPH ROSS

## ACROSS

1 Skips over
6 The dole
12 Mosque features
14 "Prettiest town I ever seen," in song
16 "Nobody doesn't like ___": 2 wds.
17 Oil-carrying ships
18 Just skin and bones
19 Bemoan
21 OK, but not great
22 The daily routine
23 Not now
24 Scandinavian goddess of the underworld
25 *National Velvet* author Bagnold
27 Actress Esther of *Good Times*
29 CIA's predecessor
30 Pinnacles
32 Vitality
34 Play based on the Von Trapp family: 4 wds.
40 Boredom
41 Broadway hit
42 It may be sliding or revolving
44 Summer ermine
47 ___ gin fizz
48 Fall mo.
49 Kind of casserole
50 ___ de France
51 Banned pesticide
52 Bank jobs
54 Actress Gardner and others
55 Cousin or aunt
57 Arrive at a ballpark figure
59 Gives, as one's time
60 Symbolizes
61 Abhor
62 Michigan and Ontario, for two

## DOWN

1 Intuitively: 3 wds.
2 Nautical
3 Teheran's country
4 ___ Aviv
5 Starlike
6 Where Wellington defeated Napoleon
7 Israeli statesman Abba
8 Pocket fluff
9 Columbo's portrayer
10 Peanut butter cup brand
11 Signs up for
12 Abuse
13 Former Asian alliance
15 Exxon's old name
20 Sweet-sounding
24 Expressions of boredom
26 Leave in the lurch
28 Dynamo's force: Abbr.
31 Charles, to Elizabeth
33 Evening times, for short
35 Young ___ (kids, in dialect)
36 Most bizarre
37 Anticipate a good meal
38 Puts under quarantine
39 Brie and cheddar
42 Scribbled
43 Musical range
45 Joined the poker game
46 Mortarboard accessory
51 Famous slave Scott
52 Sex researcher Shere
53 December 31 and others
54 Run ___ (riot)
56 Two-year-old
58 Rock's Turner

ANSWER, PAGE 54

*Randolph Ross, "Clef Notes" GAMES, 1989.*
*Reprinted with permission of Kappa Publishing.*

# CHAPTER THREE

# The Puzzling Question of Crosswords and Gender

"Congratulations to the 4 women and 34 men who debuted as constructors [in the *New York Times*] this year," reported xwordinfo.com at the end of 2012, without apparent surprise. The difference in the numbers was mentioned as the most neutral of facts. But many were surprised. Which should not surprise us.

This chapter wades into difficult, controversial waters. But it is worth writing for exactly that reason. For its entire history, women have made enormous contributions to crosswords but, for reasons no one seems to fully understand, have lately been vastly underrepresented in prominent publications, as both editors and constructors.

The question of why this is so vexes the crossword community, where it comes up often, causing tension at times, with many reacting as if they wish the question would go away. I can hardly claim to have a clear answer. Matters like this are always a bit speculative. Moreover, I know most, if not all, major crossword editors to be honest people who would never knowingly discriminate against anyone. There is something more subtle at work than overt bias, it seems.

A solver and constructor named Mark Diehl, who has helped digitize many old *Times* puzzles, noticed that in several randomly selected weeks during 1967 and 1979, there was a nearly equal number of work by male and female constructors. Diehl offered the following chart based on his findings in an email to the cruciverb-l list:

**Female Constructors Per Week**

Eugene Maleska era

        03/26/79 – 04/01/79: 4/7
        04/02/79 – 04/08/79: 3/7
        08/06/79 – 08/12/79: 3/7
        08/13/79 – 08/19/79: 3/7
        08/20/79 – 08/26/79: 3/7

Margaret Farrar era

        04/24/67 – 04/30/67: 4/7
        05/01/67 – 05/07/67: 3/7
        05/08/67 – 05/14/67: 3/7
        05/15/67 – 05/21/67: 4/7

As Diehl notes, the sample is not comprehensive, and a closer analysis of a longer period would be necessary to suggest anything more conclusive. Both those proportions are hard to imagine today, even anecdotally. In the entire month before my writing this, for example, there were only two solo puzzles by women, as well as one male and female collaboration. That's a ratio of more than ten-to-one in favor of men.

Among the most prolific female constructors in the history of the *New York Times*, most who are still living, there has been a decline in contributions in recent years. Liz Gorski, the second-most published constructor of all time, ran her highest rate of puzzles in the late 1990s and early 2000s, slowing to less than ten per year recently. Similarly, Paula Gamache has also slowed her puzzle contributions. Nancy Salomon, Cathy Allis, Sherry O. Blackard, Sarah Keller, Nancy Nicholson Joline, Stephanie Spadaccini, Karen M. Tracey, Dana Motley, and Nancy Kavanaugh, frequent contributors all, have as a group slowed dramatically or stopped contributing altogether. The great Frances Hansen died in 2004. For various reasons, including a lack of mentorship and minimal effort from editors to reach out to them, women have diminished in the bylines of the *Times* and other papers. And while a number of exceptional female constructors have recently come along—including Aimee Lucido, Zoe Wheeler, and Zhouqin (C.C.) Burnikel— joining the already active Stella Zawistkowski, Sarah Keller, Emily Cox, Andrea Carla Michaels, Deb Amlen, and others, the ranks of new women in constructing have thinned overall.

I talk about the number of women constructing for the *Times* here mainly because of the availability of data, but the situation seems to be similar, if not more extreme, at other papers. One prominent weekly crossword hasn't run a puzzle by a woman in over *two years*. Perhaps this would be less unusual if it weren't for two facts. First, that women continue to wield

# HANDYMAN'S SPECIAL by Cathy Millhauser

## ACROSS

1 Big, to Brutus
6 Community event
10 Night times
14 Farmland
15 Milieu
16 Word for the wise
17 Where handymen advertise?
19 Be sure of
20 Where the buoys are
21 Banquet spot
22 Clockmaker Terry
24 Fall guy
26 Prevailing conditions
30 Pen pals, perhaps
31 Venerated
32 Spill the beans
34 Inverted "v"
35 Time delay
36 On the road
37 Doesn't raise
38 Existence: Lat.
39 What boys will be
40 Alley offerings
41 Numbered rds.
42 Saves on postage
44 Falafel bread
46 Gives out
47 Destructive bugs
49 Nanakuli necklace
50 Swit's costar
51 Word of wonder
53 Teller's bailiwick
56 Handyman teams?
59 Candid
60 Does something
61 TV's "Friend" et al.

62 Boxing boundary
63 Some boys of summer
64 "I __ reason why not!"

## DOWN

1 Welcome sights
2 Pains' partners
3 Handymen's favorite tools?
4 Innovative
5 My Life __ ('85 film)
6 Socrate composer
7 Some nest eggs
8 Nemo's harpoonist

9 Graceful Africans
10 Pie man?
11 It may move you
12 Inflation victim
13 Darn
18 Reminds too often
23 Light rhythm
25 Grease-filled
26 Bernstein and Betz
27 Top handyman's contest?
28 Coquette
29 Outer limits
31 Nathan and Alan
32 Buccaneers' home
33 They'll hold water

34 Inclines
37 Fair
38 Dufy contemporary
40 Ballpark section
43 Mum
44 Detachable containers
45 Saddam subjects
47 Sanctify
48 Enclosed car
50 Bit of legalese
52 Sinclair rival
53 Inner ear?
54 Imitator
55 Set
57 Sculptor's medium
58 Ending for press

Cathy Millhauser, "Handyman's Special," Crossworder's OWN Newsletter, October 1991. Reprinted with permission of Stanley Newman.

prominent, powerful roles in the realm of crosswords *outside* of editing and constructing. And second, that many leading lights in the history of the game have been women. We may not find an easy answer as to why the 100th anniversary of the crossword is a time of skewed representation, gender-wise. But we can certainly find reasons why it doesn't have to be this way.

The story of women in crosswords begins with ace solver and constructor Ruth Von Phul of Manhattan. Von Phul was not only the winner of the *New York Herald Tribune*'s National All Comers Cross Word Puzzle Tournament in both 1924 and 1926, but was a noted scholar of the work of James Joyce—a model of erudition in the classic mold, to be sure. She appeared on the cover of *The Cross Word Puzzle Magazine* in March 1925 above a caption that said "The champion trains for her next bout." Von Phul routinely set the bogey time for puzzles, meaning that she had solved it the fastest in competition. Newspapers printed her name and time next to the puzzle so that solvers would have a point of comparison for themselves.

Von Phul was a serious celebrity during the crossword craze of the 1920s, but she disappeared from the public eye for many years when she took to studying and publishing on Joyce. She returned to an audience of puzzle enthusiasts in 1981, when Will Shortz invited her to speak at that year's American Crossword Puzzle Tournament, which he continues to run. Von Phul had been contacted just two years earlier by the *New Yorker*, which profiled her under the headline "Renewed Acquaintance." The magazine had written about her in April 1925, at the height of her puzzle fame, in one of its very first issues.[3] The former champion, though she no longer solved many puzzles, had plenty to say. She had attended but not finished college, worked for the New York Office of Postal Censorship decrypting potentially subversive messages in civilian letters, appeared on the game show *The $64,000 Challenge*, and become an expert analyst of

Joyce's novels. "There is obviously a connection between my interest in crosswords and cryptography and my fascination with Joyce," she told the magazine. "When you're solving puzzles, you let your mind float with respect to words."

The story of Margaret Petherbridge Farrar has been told elsewhere, but no history of crosswords would be complete without her. Farrar was the first-ever editor of the *Times* crossword. She had more than 20 years' experience with the form when she began, having been an editorial assistant to Arthur Wynne (the inventor of the crossword) at the *New York World*, and later having been co-author of the first crossword book in 1924, published by Simon & Schuster (it was published under a different imprint as the company was concerned about associating its name with a fad that might not last). She was the foremost editor of crosswords in the country when the *Times* established its puzzle and an obvious choice for the job.

Her editorship began at a time when puzzles could be pretty riotous in design—a square grid here, a diamond there, letters that only crossed in one direction, repeating words, and so on. Farrar established a set of rules to standardize puzzles, most of which persist to this day. The familiar design of a crossword, with its perfectly square grid, rotational symmetry, and interlocking white squares all over, was the work of Farrar. Moreover, she introduced the idea of themed puzzles and permitted multiword answers. And she was equally concerned with regularity and loveliness. Thanks to her eye, the crossword is not only a game of language with serious rules, but its grid is an iconic image.

During her remarkable 27 year run as the puzzle editor—still the longest tenure in the paper's history—Farrar's reputation was impeccable. She was helpful to aspiring and established constructors alike, and was rigorous in her review of submissions. She also published more than 100 books independent of her newspaper duties. Farrar ultimately achieved no less than laying the groundwork for the *Times* puzzle's current reputation. As Rosen and Kurzban put it: "It is impossible to count the people who owe thanks to Mrs. Farrar."

When I began constructing in the early 2000s, it wasn't a young gun cruciverbalist I admired most, but an 85-year-old woman named Frances Hansen. Hansen, who died just a few months after I discovered her puzzles, had been constructing for the *Times*, *The Washington Post*, and the *Los Angeles Times* for decades. According to her obituary, she "had written every [*New York Times*] Christmas puzzle since 1995 and had become the second most prolific living writer of Sunday puzzles and the fourth most published of all time." Hansen was, in certain ways, resolutely old-fashioned. One of her favorite theme types was a homage to old entertainers like Fred Astaire or Emmett Kelly, with the theme answers being straightforward lists of their films.

But she was also quite idiosyncratic, including her own original poetry in many grids.
H A N G U P Y O U R S T O C K I N G S D O /
B U T P L E A S E D O N O T S U P P O S E /
T H A T S A N T A Y E A R N S T O V I E W
S W E A T S O C K S O R P A N T Y H O S E ,
she penned for the December 22, 2002, Sunday puzzle. The cuteness of the phrase disguises the difficulty of writing poetry under such constrained circumstances. Not only did Hansen satisfy the usual conventions of verse, but she arranged each segment so that it contained exactly 21 letters.

Still, Hansen's chops were only one reason to admire her work. I appreciate in particular that her voice was so unique. One simply doesn't put their own original quotations in crosswords, except that Hansen did. I continue to admire her singularity, and as a beginner took it as inspiration to try to write puzzles that stood out from the crowd.

Von Phul, Farrar, and Hansen are not tokenistic examples of success by women in crosswords. All three are as foundational as it gets. But it doesn't end with editing, solving, and constructing. As writers of history and criticism, women have also been more than well-represented.

Helene Hovanec, who today does much of the behind-the-scenes work for the annual American Crossword Puzzle Tournament, was perhaps the first true historian of crosswords, with her *Puzzler's Paradise* in 1978. Michelle Arnot followed soon after, in 1981, with *What's Gnu? A History of the Crossword Puzzle*. Arnot's book is an exhaustively detailed account of American and British-style puzzles, with rich descriptions of major figures in both countries. Hovanec followed up with *Creative Cruciverbalists* in 1988, and constructor Coral Amende's *The Crossword Obsession: The History and Lore of the World's Most Popular Pastime* came out in 2002. Blogger Amy Reynaldo, who routinely finishes among the top solvers American Crossword Puzzle Tournament, published *How to Conquer the New York Times Crossword Puzzle: Tips, Tricks and Techniques to Master America's Favorite Puzzle* in 2007.

Reynaldo, along with a cohort of helpers, runs crosswordfiend.com, which "review[s] the best crosswords in print and on the web." Crosswordfiend is the thinking solver's site for discussion of a variety of puzzles, from mainstream to niche. Reynaldo, as both a great solver and a professional copy editor, is perhaps the most qualified judge of crosswords in the world. She has significant clout in the community, and editors pay careful attention to her evaluations as well as those of the people who frequent her site.

Constructor and author Deb Amlen, meanwhile, runs the *New York Times* crossword blog called Wordplay. Amlen, who has contributed to outlets both major and indie (including the American Values Club) as a puzzle maker, reviews the puzzle each day for the online edition of the paper. In addition to being an especially inventive cluer in the puzzles she writes, Amlen has one of the best eyes

# PUZZLER AT WORK
## A verse from the Poet Laureate of Puzzledom.

**Across**

**1.** Little archer

**6.** Chewy candy

**13.** Dud

**18.** Sight for sore eyes?

**19.** Promote

**20.** Multi-gun greeting

**21.** START OF A VERSE

**24.** Serenely rustic

**25.** Farmer's field

**26.** Results of film flubs

**27.** After deductions

**28.** Element's elements

**30.** Part of a G.I. address

**31.** Old lady

**35.** The sea

**36.** High tor

**37.** Red's rustic

**41.** Fill up with cargo

**42.** Contribute communally

**43.** Baby bouncer

**44.** "Darling, Je Vous ___ Beaucoup"

**45.** MORE OF VERSE

**51.** Letters next to a phone number

**52.** Frilly collar piece

**53.** Subjective sensation

**54.** Donut-shop staffers

**55.** "Steps in Time" autobiographer

**57.** Analyst Alfred

**58.** "Portrait of ___ " (James novel)

**59.** Raged

**62.** Made possible

**64.** Writer Sinclair

**66.** Emotional intensity

**68.** Young or Swit

**72.** Fleeced

**73.** Rested

**74.** Sun Valley's state

**76.** Sounds of surprise

**77.** MORE OF VERSE

**82.** Second word of a New Year's song

**83.** It's all in the running

**84.** Hercules' captive

**85.** Arizona city

**86.** Quaker pronoun

**87.** One, in Wassy

**88.** Iraq's only port

**90.** MacDonald of soaps

**91.** ___ Gabriel Mountains

**92.** Robust

**93.** New England soda shop

**95.** ___ point (depart from procedure)

**99.** Hill builder

**100.** Ruby anniversary

**105.** END OF VERSE

**109.** Matt Dillon portrayer
**110.** William and Harry's daddy
**111.** Charge
**112.** "Sorry, it's ___ table"
**113.** Least loose
**114.** Stiller's spouse

## Down

**1.** Castro country
**2.** "Exodus" author
**3.** "The Great Commoner"
**4.** Recite musically
**5.** "Nothing runs like a ___" (ad slogan)
**6.** Honeycomb unit
**7.** Former ring champ
**8.** One's good name
**9.** "Venus" singer
**10.** "Go ahead, ___ day"
**11.** Cone-shaped heaters
**12.** MGM mascot
**13.** Attack vigorously
**14.** Exile isle
**15.** Darkness
**16.** Western Indian
**17.** Format of some radio stations
**18.** Traveler's aid
**20.** Did the town, with "out"
**22.** Rebel Turner
**23.** "The Rose of ___"
**28.** Got off the couch
**29.** Pinball problem
**31.** Bow or Barton
**32.** Hotel posting
**33.** Specialty versifier
**34.** Originally called
**35.** The two
**36.** Asian capital
**37.** Waterfall
**38.** Took to
**39.** Federal Express competitor
**40.** London alleys
**42.** Onetime igloo-shaped auto
**43.** Valentine or Carpenter
**46.** Large mollusks
**47.** Cheboygan's waterfront
**48.** Roll of bills
**49.** Swiss mathematician
**50.** Part of an airplane wing
**56.** Back in the saddle again
**57.** ___ Ababa
**58.** Hawaii hi
**60.** Ill will
**61.** Wipe out
**63.** Raucous noise
**64.** "Yeah"
**65.** Grace ___ ("Jane Eyre" character)
**67.** Sean Lennon's mother
**69.** "... woman oweth ___ husband": Shak.
**70.** That and more?
**71.** Swinging in the breeze
**72.** Police team
**74.** African Coast
**75.** Oscar ___ Renta
**78.** School escapees
**79.** "___ and her Sisters" (Woody Allen film)
**80.** Santa's paperwork
**81.** Peruvian chanteuse Sumac
**88.** "Last of the Frontier Demigods"
**89.** John Jacob and Mary
**90.** "Actors are ___": Hitchcock
**91.** Wimp
**92.** Shaping machine
**93.** Sauce source
**94.** King of Troy
**95.** Lake of ballet
**96.** "Comin' ___ the Rye"
**97.** Go crazy
**98.** "Up and ___!"
**100.** All tied up
**101.** ___ de Pascua (Easter Island)
**102.** Once-over giver
**103.** Garb for Scalia
**104.** Shade
**106.** Pretense
**107.** Ending for mod or nod
**108.** His: Fr.

*Frances Hansen, "Puzzler At Work," Baltimore Open, 1987.*

for evaluating crosswords in the business, and brings an acerbic wit to discussing them.

Given the degree to which women—both today and in the past—have been successful and influential in the world of crosswords, what can explain the recent dearth of female bylines? According to some constructors, there is a subtle but pervasive bias against women with children making art, as if to do so were selfish. One beginner constructor told me that: "[Making puzzles is] hard work, focused work, and creatively exhausting. There are many false starts and a lot of bad results, especially in the beginning. Once you know what you're doing, it's still exceedingly difficult to stand out in a competitive, driven, and talented crowd, to say something original, something an editor will want to publish, within an accepted form. It's like any art form in these ways. I've also faced some pressure from my family and from myself to pull back, give it up, let it go. For a period of months, I resorted to doing my constructing and cluing at 5 A.M., while the family slept ... familial and internal discouragements aren't trivial—it can seem not worth the perpetual lack of sleep, the compromise of family time, or the continuous domestic conflict, and I imagine (can't prove) that many more women run up against this particular roadblock to progress ..."

While undoubtedly this kind of biased expectation is a hurdle in some cases, not all women are mothers. I suggest we might also consider the near-monopoly men have on editorships today. The *New York Times, Los Angeles Times, Washington Post, New York Newsday,* and *Wall Street Journal* each have male crossword editors, and the indies generally follow suit. Editors set the tone for a feature's humor and subject matter. They decide what constitutes an outstanding puzzle, and on the other hand, a fatally flawed one. They may not intend to be biased in their selections, but hints of preference seep through nevertheless. Since it's

been quite some time—decades, actually—since any major paper has employed a female puzzle editor (the last prominent female editor anywhere was the great Amy Goldstein at *GAMES* magazine), I suspect that aspiring constructors are hearing the message all too clearly.

This is a shame since, as we've seen, puzzles have historically been a pretty egalitarian pursuit. But today, it's a problem that won't be fixed by editors pointing the finger at the low number of submissions they receive from women, or by claiming to be gender-blind. The puzzle world has to first openly recognize the biased situation in which it finds itself, and then take proactive steps to invite women back into construction and editing. There's no shortage of talent—it's our job to find and encourage it.

### A CURIOUS THING

In 1968, Stephen Sondheim wrote an article in *New York* magazine on the difference between American crosswords and British cryptics. Needless to say, he was not a fan of the American version. "There are crossword puzzles and crossword puzzles," explained the playwright. "The kind familiar to most New Yorkers is a mechanical test of tirelessly esoteric knowledge: 'Brazilian potter's wheel,' 'East Indian betel nut,' and the like are typical definitions, sending you either to *Webster's New International* or to sleep." Sondheim was tweaking the abiding regime of American puzzles at the time, and not unreasonably so. But it was ironic that he penned his words in *New York* magazine, because in 1980 that publication would hire a weekly constructor whose sensibilities helped lead the way to a more humorous and graceful era in U.S. puzzles. Maura B. Jacobson contributed a weekly crossword for more than 30 years, in addition to having a puzzle at the American Crossword Puzzle Tournament in every year since its inception until recently.

# Shakespeare Uses a Computer

*New York Crossword by Maura B. Jacobson*

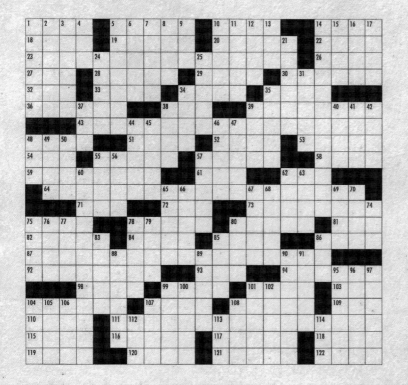

9 Upper House: abbr.
10 Unsophisticated
11 Fudd of cartoons
12 Bellow from Simba
13 Excavated
14 Devices with handles for pushing small loads
15 The scarlet letter
16 Enraged
17 Hamilton bills
21 Rubble
24 Lowest deck
25 Peter O'——
31 Get the suds out
34 Lamp insert
35 Throat-clearing sounds
37 Recipe amt.
38 Overdo on the barbecue
39 Urban haze
40 Shrek, for one
41 Astronaut Armstrong
42 Exxon, formerly
44 Gets by sweat
45 It can be sweet or sour
46 —— law (legal code of the Franks)
47 "First —— see tonight"
48 Pat on
49 What the suspicious smell
50 Ho Chi ——
55 Delhi dress
56 Singleton
57 Swoon
60 Boundary indicators
62 Memorable restaurateur Toots
63 Belonging to a woman
65 State of northeast India
66 Hospitality recipient
67 Mother-of-pearl
68 Unit of heat
69 Sushi-bar offerings
70 Italy's shape
74 G-men's org.
75 Barcelona snack
76 "—— Well That Ends Well"
77 Send packing
78 Flat hat
79 Love god of the Greeks
80 "Today —— man" (bar mitzvah assertion
83 Winter sportsman
85 Stooped
86 Popeye's yes
88 Dowdy ones
89 West Indies land
90 Calendar page
91 Lyons' river
95 Mauler
96 Bullring hero
97 Made smooth, in a way
99 Con game
100 Performed onstage
101 Pays to play, in poker
102 Blarney Castle attraction
104 Wise elder
105 Resign from the job
106 Beehive State
107 The Flintstones' pet
108 Taj Mahal city
112 Crater edge
113 Zero
114 Thurman of "Kill Bill"

## Across

1 In among
5 Prods
10 Schmo
14 Habeas corpus, e.g.
18 Start of a soliloquy
19 Follow as a result
20 Audibly
22 Roll-call reply
23 What a screen saver is: "12th Night": Act II, Scene 4
26 Adam's address
27 Longest Swiss river
28 Actress Mercedes
29 Done with
30 Pumpernickel, rye, etc.
32 106, to Brutus
33 Low-cal
34 Dutch South African
35 Seed covering
36 Buster or Diane
38 ——-de-sac
39 Tibia
43 What e-mail is: "Merchant of Venice": Act I, Scene 1
48 Somewhat wet
51 Bedouin
52 Nuclear particle
53 "To —— human": Pope
54 Jackie's second
55 More miffed
57 Color-guards' totes
58 Move away, in realtor lingo
59 Colorful neckerchief
61 Lungful
62 Premium cable channel
64 Pleased comment when browsing: "Othello": Act III, Scene 4
71 Fallen space station
72 Solar-system hub
73 —— a different color
75 Fictional plantation
78 Harass
80 Cake decorators
81 High tennis shot
82 Then: Fr.
84 Periods in history
85 Roseanne's original surname
86 —— spumante
87 How to access old data: "Macbeth": Act V, Scene 3
92 Fred and Adele of dance
93 Before a B
94 Shortchanges
98 Germanic: abbr.
99 Fish lure
101 In re
103 Constrictor snake
104 Wriggle
107 Tear canal
108 Playwright Chekhov
109 Ceramic of a Keats ode
110 "Wheels"
111 How to make copies: "Henry VI, Part II": Act IV, Scene 7
115 Menotti's first name
116 From the time when
117 "Good Night" girl of song
118 Adjective for a pittance
119 Ordinal-number endings
120 State of mind
121 Surgeon's beam
122 Alex Rodriguez's nickname

## Down

1 Go at
2 California desert
3 Spain-Portugal combine
4 Santa's mo.
5 Not counterfeit
6 First symptoms
7 —— crow flies
8 Double, as citizenship

*Maura B. Jacobson, "Shakespeare Uses a Computer," New York magazine, October 27, 2008. Reprinted with permission of Maura B. Jacobson.*

# I Come From Iowa

New York *Crossword by Maura B. Jacobson*

**ACROSS**

1 Swearing-in recital
5 Trivial commotion
8 Anti-infection liquid
13 Bower
18 Mitch Miller's instrument
19 M.D.'s
20 Capital of Eritrea
21 Ballerina Shearer
22 FIRST LADY
25 Deep dental filling
26 Hymn in the Bible
27 Crooner Crosby
28 Get by sweat
30 Lowest female voice
31 "Rings on —— fingers . . ."
32 PITCHER
36 Super or infer ending
38 Hankering
39 Almost
41 Hear here
42 Armadas
44 Pain reliever
46 POLLSTER
49 Prepared-food mart
50 Tivoli's Villa d'——
52 One's born days
53 Actors' homework
55 Fox comedy series named for a magazine
57 Carries in stock
59 Canonized femme: abbr.
60 Begin's co-Nobelist
61 PRESIDENT
67 Prefix with puncture
68 Sirius of the sky
71 Yahoo! competitor
72 Passed on, as a message
75 Ellis or Staten, briefly
76 ASTROPHYSICIST
81 Masticates
84 Throat-exam sound
85 Mardi Gras king
86 Texas A&M footballer
90 Palindromic belief
91 Downed space station
92 Shade of blue
95 Sea eagle
96 SINGER
101 Break a law
103 Marshy ground
104 Advised medicinal amt.
105 Attached, in a way
106 Kimono cummerbund
108 OPEC abundance
109 PLAYWRIGHT
111 Seminary deg.
114 Future tulip
116 Past due
118 Blanc's opposite
119 Not as high
121 Cove
123 SHOWMAN
127 First month on a calendario
128 Bob who sang with the Dorseys
129 "—— was saying . . ."
130 Item in Claudius's closet
131 Damascene's land
132 "Bad, Bad —— Brown" ('73 hit)
133 Inc., in the U.K.
134 Sappho's poems

**DOWN**

1 Glamour-girl's asset
2 Degrade
3 ACTOR
4 Third Reich greeting
5 After Gator, in a drink
6 Ball-bouncing basketball maneuvers
7 Harden into bone
8 "Silence!"
9 Comedian Philips
10 Less cooked
11 Compound synthesized from ammonia
12 Wedlock
13 Pierre's pal
14 Barrett of gossip fame
15 EVANGELIST
16 Speechify
17 Fabric used for linings
20 Director of "Brokeback Mountain"
23 Surround, as with a body of water
24 180 degrees from W.S.W.
29 PBS science program
33 Caen's river
34 Thai's neighbor
35 Miscalculate
37 Rivulets
40 Piaf and Wharton
42 Beersheba's desert
43 Two-time Oscar-winner Kazan
44 Top U.S.N. officer
45 Teachers' org.
46 Shifter's concern
47 Cat, in Cancún
48 The "P" in R.I.P.
51 Word with Bronx or Hague
54 Kind of poker
56 Fido's doc
58 Hide away secretly
59 Type of eclipse
62 British rule in India
63 Bikini top
64 Lane for cars with more than one occupant: abbr.
65 "The ——-King" (Goethe poem)
66 Kinsman, for short
68 Where to look up a wd.
69 Actor Milo of "Barbarella"
70 BANDLEADER
73 Meadow
74 Designer Giorgio Sant'——
77 Sends by post
78 Rank above viscount
79 Butterfly catchers
80 Lumberjack's tool
82 "—— Our Part," New Deal slogan
83 Foam prefix
87 PAINTER
88 Savings-acct. payback
89 Very wide shoe size
91 Affix the wrong tag
93 Keeper of a bird sanctuary
94 Beloved, in Bonn
97 Siren's sound
98 One of the Gershwins
99 Part of speech ending in -ly: abbr.
100 For the most part
102 "Island of the Blue Dolphins" author
105 Pertaining to Native American groups
106 Kin of the Tonys
107 Rabbit, at Easter
109 Put off temporarily
110 Scooby-——
112 Avoid commitment
113 As —— dust
115 Double this for a vitamin deficiency
117 London subway
120 Numerical prefix
122 "Get thee —— nunnery"
124 To's go-with
125 Khan who wed Rita Hayworth
126 Pot cover

*Maura B. Jacobson, "I Come From Iowa," New York magazine, February 11, 2008. Reprinted with permission of Maura B. Jacobson.*

# It's in the Genes

New York *Crossword by Maura B. Jacobson*

**ACROSS**

1 Killer whales
5 Useful
10 Sultana's residence
15 "Yay, team!"
18 Hockey on horseback
19 Kind of eclipse
20 Minneapolis suburb
21 Opera set in Egypt
22 Very much
23 Offspring of a detective and an arsonist
25 Glitch
26 Breed of chicken
28 Like a conger
29 Mark of disgrace
31 Goes off the tracks
34 Offspring of a minister and a therapist
37 Throw fear into
39 Versifier
41 Snick-a—— (dagger of yore)
42 Hydrocarbon suffix
43 Divinely-sent food
44 Chem. workplace
45 Refrain start
47 Identical
50 Circle segment
51 Offspring of a dentist and a soldier
58 Too-late E.R. report
59 "The Faerie Queene" author
61 Chiang's foe
62 Spuds
64 Super-sandwich
65 Rock-concert need
67 Inebriated
70 Food put through a blender
71 Offspring of an orthopedist and a gunman
75 Berth choice
78 Hi-fi setup
79 Gun-lobby inits.
80 Sides, in cricket
84 Iran, until 1935
86 —— Lingus
87 Paintings and such
89 Third numero
90 Offspring of a shoemaker and a student
96 Lyon king
97 Evict
99 Muff it
100 Web-entry co.
101 "Good Night" girl
103 Pronoun for a ship
105 "Time —— My Side" (Rolling Stones hit)
108 Ranch vacationer
110 Almanac contents
111 Offspring of a genius and a baker
115 Royal accoutrements
117 Inheritance
118 Nanking nursemaid
120 Works to land a fish
123 Memorable Guinness
124 Offspring of a mortician and an architect
129 Start of a birth announcement
130 Half of N.B.
131 Eero Saarinen's father
132 Tenth pope
133 At no time, to Byron
134 Between ready and go
135 One of the Quaids
136 Feel intuitively
137 Zane or Lady Jane

**DOWN**

1 Milky gem
2 Acting assignment
3 Offspring of a plumber and a choreographer
4 Ann who played Maisie
5 The "U" in UV
6 Thick-root vegetable
7 Pig —— poke
8 End of Chou's name
9 Literary Gardner
10 Greece's name, formerly
11 "What is so rare as —— June?"
12 Rice, in Rouen
13 Antipole of W.S.W.
14 Swamp
15 Offspring of a jeweler and a bandmaster
16 What there is "nothin' like"
17 "Horrible" Viking of the comics
21 Mongolians, e.g.
24 Previous to: abbr.
27 Mountain nymphs
30 Afternoon social
32 Recline lazily
33 Christmas paste-on
35 Head: Fr.
36 Wife of Zeus
37 Overhead power play, in tennis
38 —— diem (seize the day)
40 Ted Turner channel
46 Intruder in the grass
48 Oliver Twist's request
49 Relieve tightness
52 Where to move, on a bus
53 "La Douce" and "My Friend"
54 Ham actors
55 Dustin's "Midnight Cowboy" character
56 Roman Empire invader
57 VCR insertion
60 Facial protuberances
63 "Presumed Innocent" writer
66 Cherry discard
67 Make confetti
68 Longest time division
69 Famed Miami golf resort
72 Smallish combo
73 Equipment
74 Fictional plantation
75 —— snuff (satisfactory)
76 Andes land
77 Offspring of a reporter and a spy
81 Offspring of a golfer and a fisherman
82 Opposite of 52-Down
83 Planetarium vistas
85 Tomahawk
88 Something of little importance
91 Word on José's faucet
92 Approximately
93 No gentleman
94 Clock hand
95 Merrie —— England
98 Region of Greece
102 Balustrade
104 And so forth: abbr.
106 Gave the green light
107 With agility
109 Exit
111 Concrete blocks
112 Brawl
113 Computer-network prefix
114 Perrier, par exemple
116 Eagle's dwelling
119 Pair before hooray
121 "That explains it"
122 —— a one (none)
125 Ending for pay or cup
126 Clamor
127 Tell it like it's not
128 Pester for payment

*Maura B. Jacobson, "It's in the Genes,"* New York *magazine, September 18, 2006. Reprinted with permission of Maura B. Jacobson.*

# Rejected Olympics Events

### New York *Crossword by Maura B. Jacobson*

## ACROSS

1 Start of a famous soliloquy
5 Ruined city of Jordan
10 À votre —— (Gallic toast)
15 Examined by touch
19 Israeli statesman Abba
20 Lucy's TV friend
21 Mountain nymph
22 Scent
23 Move on wheels
24 Carpentry-class event?
26 A single time
27 Dispute settler
29 Manicure site
30 Opposite of output
32 '50s V.P. candidate Kefauver
33 Carpenter's joint: var.
35 Signify
36 Redcap
38 No great shakes
39 In midflight
43 Standish's rival
44 Nighttime events?
47 Pigs' digs
48 Crack a book
49 Large: prefix
50 Loads the hook
52 Dumbo's wings
53 Boxing coups, for short
54 Strikebreaker's event?
57 Depart (schedule abbr.)
58 Items no longer provided in New York restaurants
60 Smell to high heaven
61 Out of bed
63 Snake's sound
64 "Saturday Night Live" segments
66 Dick and Jane's dog
67 Blossoming
70 Prescribed capsule
71 Bathed, in a way
75 ——-Magnon
76 Sprint among family members?
80 Ending for spat or form
81 Soviet news agcy.
83 More clearheaded
84 Informal shirts
85 F.B.I. operatives
86 Areas of the eyes
88 Event for tellers?
90 Coffeepots, in brief
91 Part of Iberia
93 Fouls up
94 11th C. Danish king of England
95 Heathen's worship
96 What body-shops fix
98 Poe's one-word bird
99 Texas border city
102 Reach for the floor
103 Like Mom's instincts
106 Advice to the chubby
107 Event for fugitives?
111 Seine tributary
112 Green Gables girl
113 Muse of poetry
114 African language grouping
115 The "U" in B.T.U.
116 Repair
117 Repeat a statement
118 "—— of robins in her hair"
119 Three-chevron GIs

## DOWN

1 Semester
2 Double-reed woodwind
3 Event for those with hair loss?
4 Joined the military
5 Annoy persistently
6 Cultural traits
7 Norse thunder god
8 Dem.'s opponent
9 Everybody
10 Up to now
11 Shaw of swing music
12 Simon who wrote "The Odd Couple"
13 Result of sunning
14 More irritable
15 Bottom-of-the-page comment
16 Dame enacted by Barry Humphries
17 Key's target
18 Arboretum specimen
25 Being pulled along
28 "—— o'clock scholar"
31 Arrests, slangily
33 Julianne or Demi
34 "The quality of mercy —— strained"
35 Peruvian volcano, after "El"
36 Arctic jacket
37 Butter subs
38 Anklets
39 "I Get —— Out of You"
40 Iranian coins
41 Chutzpah
42 Germany's Pittsburgh
44 Big sign on 34th Street
45 As red as ——
46 Highway demarcations
49 Noxious swamp vapors
51 Certain metallic fasteners
54 Previous
55 Ruffled trim, e.g.
56 Gets taller
59 Despite the fact that, short style
62 Inhabitant of: suffix
64 Wailing warning device
65 F.W. de ——, South African Peace Nobelist, 1993
66 Discharge a gun
67 Misbehave
68 "Take a bow!"
69 Defeated one
70 Pertaining to punishment
71 Memorable Beverly
72 Drinkers' marathon?
73 Vote in
74 Parisian prom
77 Clique of political plotters
78 Not together
79 Troupes' trips
82 Filled to the gills
85 Far from stingy
87 Soapy water
89 Sold: Fr.
90 Put down asphalt
92 Peanut, familiarly
94 Cord used for racket strings
96 Airline based in Atlanta
97 Derive pleasure from
98 Delivers a tirade
99 Kin of Gouda
100 Queue
101 Oscar-winner Sean
102 Partiality
103 Buried explosive
104 "—— is in heaven"
105 Tennis do-overs
108 "Right you ——!"
109 Future C.E.O.'s degree
110 Wok

# Wordies

### New York *Crossword by Maura B. Jacobson*

**Across**

1 Not us
5 —— donna
10 Bone: prefix
14 Gradually lose color
18 Permeate
19 Sharpens
20 Junior cities
22 "—— corny as Kansas in August . . ."
23 KCOLC EHT
26 Engrossed
27 Speechifies
28 Meets the bet
29 —— roof (make an uproar)
31 Dickens's Uriah
33 LISTANDSNE
36 Playtime activities
39 Self-banking device: abbr.
42 Calendar pgs.
43 Din
44 In the style of
45 Jai's go-with
46 Used a chair
47 With Magog, a Biblical assailant
48 OR OR O
54 Fake
58 Would-be husband
59 "My Way" songwriter Paul
60 Urgent-care hosp. areas
62 Loyal
63 Transports for E.T.'s
65 OPEC abundance
66 Ham it up
68 Mag. execs
69 YOUJUSTME
74 Chemin de ——
75 Farm storehouses
76 One of the Stooges
77 Ocean motion
78 Give temporarily
80 El ——, national hero of Spain
81 Prefix with dextrous
83 Subtle shade of meaning
87 Unexpected win
89 THE PRIZE GO
93 Nonstick frying spray
95 See 108-Across
96 Bible bk. after Amos
97 Hatchback, e.g.
98 Mattress brand
100 Pointillist's mark
101 Sopping
102 It comes before febrero
104 TIME AND AND
108 Baked-goods company, with 95-Across
110 Envoy
111 Had on
114 Engines
118 Russian fighter planes
119 NO WAYS IT WAYS
123 Peel
124 To have, in Le Havre
125 Hurriedness
126 Pilaf grain
127 Change for a five
128 —— 'acte (intermission)
129 Contort the face disdainfully
130 Topic in the news: abbr.

**Down**

1 Dog that went to Oz
2 Time of day
3 Poet Pound
4 Crème de ——
5 Stage of development
6 Sinbad's bird
7 Signs a document: slang
8 Portion out
9 Cigarette droppings
10 Future lts.' school
11 Fifth note of the scale
12 Sabers, épées, etc.
13 Pizarro's victims
14 Illumination from the hearth
15 Famed Cremona violins
16 Du Maurier who wrote "Rebecca"
17 Lauder of cosmetics
21 Winter sport
24 Honey bunch
25 Superlative suffix
30 Nosy one
32 —— Alto, California
34 Nanking nursemaid
35 Reply to the Little Red Hen
36 Flits about
37 Family name in baseball
38 Second largest Hawaiian island
40 Fictional plantation
41 Small silvery fishes
45 Kind of exercise
46 Impasse, in chess
49 Air-cond. units
50 Warehouse upper levels used as dwellings
51 1930's Dust Bowl refugee
52 Verne's underseas captain
53 Tile fixative
55 Utah city north of Provo
56 Without a stitch
57 Aye
61 Destined for the cleaners
64 Baseball Commissioner Bud
66 *Facial feature*
67 Result finally
69 Rugged Chrysler vehicle
70 Samovars
71 Heading on a list of chores
72 Alaskan gold-rush city
73 Expensive
74 Grippe
79 Disheartens
82 "Wouldn't —— Lovely?"
84 Neighbor of Cannes
85 Royal Russian: alternate spelling
86 Son of Eliel Saarinen
88 Informal good-byes
90 Easy as falling off ——
91 Greek cheese
92 Millinery
94 Tomorrow, to Tomás
98 Apelike
99 Expatriate of a sort
100 Aviation city of Ohio
102 Slangy ending for sock or switch
103 Human or Mother
104 Musical speed
105 Took the wheel
106 Early radical labor union inits.
107 Webster and Wyle
109 Fossil resin
112 Actor O'Neal of 1970's "Love Story"
113 Latin 101 infinitive
115 Pertaining to the ear
116 Puerto ——
117 British carbine
120 Humorist's talent
121 Hockey great Bobby
122 Ingested

*Maura B. Jacobson, "Wordies," New York magazine, March 30, 2009. Reprinted with permission of Maura B. Jacobson.*

# WHAT'S BLACK AND WHITE AND RED ALL OVER?

*By Karen Anderson*

★★★

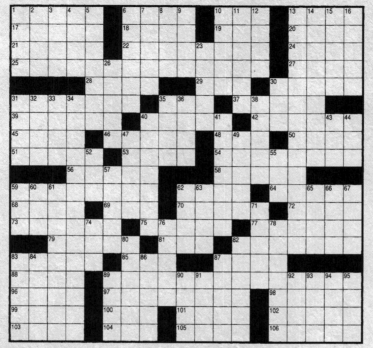

**ACROSS**

1 Swiftly
6 Difficult position
10 Pitcher's pride
13 Paleozoic and Mesozoic
17 Clunker
18 Horn or Fear
19 ___ favor (help)
20 Athletic event
21 They drive kids buggy!
22 Chance for heads, e.g.
24 Crude
25 Answer to the title
27 Oodles
28 Turns informant
29 Dian Fossey subject
30 Falls head over heels
31 Magicians, e.g.
35 Hearing aid?
37 Diary spans
39 Fall away
40 Expressway gas/food stop
42 Symbol type
45 Place for Poe's Ligeia
46 "Back at the ___ ..."
48 Go (for)
50 Spanish ayes
51 Water servers
53 Bath bar
54 13" x 16" paper
56 Sponsorship
58 Indian's A-frame
59 Sends on
62 "___ Not There" (Zombies hit)
64 To the point
68 Russian range
69 " ... say, not ___ do"
70 Play statues
72 Salmon type
73 Made concave
75 Union work sites
77 Prince's stand-in
79 Moving experience?
81 Flock founder
82 Judith Martin subject
83 Mr. Frome
85 Ages and ages
87 Give a bash
88 Stratum
89 Answer to the title
96 The O'Hara homestead
97 Most plastics
98 Electronic keyboard brand
99 Aphrodite's son
100 Mined matter
101 Mob boss
102 Start of a Roman quote
103 Girl Scout's accessory
104 ___ Boot
105 Ere long
106 Wooden rod

**DOWN**

1 Where edelweiss grows
2 Where the Amazon begins
3 "___, a plan, a canal ..."
4 Search meticulously
5 Guaranteed
6 Lemon Fresh and Evergreen
7 Makes lots?
8 Columnists' page
9 Second column
10 Make sense
11 Chevy's *Caddyshack* costar
12 1985 Cher movie
13 Answer to the title
14 Practical
15 Storytelling slave
16 Keeps as is
23 Giraffe's kin
26 Less cooked
30 Make doilies
31 Comic Johnson
32 Catty remark
33 Tiptop
34 Answer to the title
35 Pushpin kin
36 Arthur of the courts
38 Prevent
40 Jackie's O
41 Eases
43 ___ *Today*
44 Drink hot tea
47 Litmus reddeners
49 Bard's output
52 Neptune's domain
55 Shepherd's site
57 Alums
59 Rubik's cube, once
60 "Bravo!"
61 Hacienda dwellers
62 Stash
63 Word before and after "against"
65 It's knot necessary
66 At all
67 Viking landing site
71 Jerk
74 Still, to poets
76 One of the Fords
78 Tums or Rolaids
80 Toledo lady
82 Canadian brewer
83 Belittling suffixes
84 Diana's topper
86 Gawks
87 Silent screen star
89 Snake, e.g.
90 1979 Village People hit
91 *Blind Ambition* author
92 Mexican hero?
93 Words after 102-Across
94 J'___ (I love): Fr.
95 Coward of the theater

Karen Anderson, "What's Black and White and Red All Over?" GAMES, 1989. Reprinted with permission of Kappa Publishing.

# CHAPTER FOUR

## Humor, Then and Now

A great joke is tricky to unpack, at least partly because unpacking a joke usually ruins it. But that's what I'll try to do in this chapter, hopefully without spoiling puzzles for you in the process. What kind of sense of humor does the modern crossword have, and how does it differ from past eras?

Eras, of course, don't have singular senses of humor. Part of the beauty of having open submissions from constructors is that each puzzle has a different voice and point of view. Certainly, though, the preferences of the editor tend to lean toward certain kinds of laugh lines, be they punny, dry, zany, or ironic. And the zeitgeist makes a difference, too. Without making overly broad claims, we can locate some of the trends in humor that have come and gone through the years.

The crossword has attempted to be fun since its inception, but not necessarily to be *funny*. The earliest puzzle clues were just dictionary definitions, and the satisfaction of solving came in testing your vocabulary and general knowledge rather than being bowled over by clever wordplay. Old puzzle clues ended with a period, suggesting that they were each a bounded sentence, a fact that took a direct path toward corresponding with another fact. There was to be no funny business along the way. As Frank Sinatra put it in a 1989 letter to Eugene Maleska in thanks for putting his name in a puzzle: "What a wonderful way to pass the time and also learn new answers every day[4]." Ol' Blue Eyes made no mention of laughing.

Maleska actually dialed back what had been an incipient move toward wordplay by his predecessor. Editor Will Weng, in the late 1960s and early 1970s, ran clues like "Place of no return" for ONEWAYSTREET[5]. According to veteran constructor and puzzle historian Vic Fleming, writing in the *Memphis Daily News*, "Weng brought a sense of humor and playfulness to the *Times* that was said to be lacking in his predecessor. And that his successor surely quashed."

Farrar was generally beloved as an editor, but comedy wasn't her thing, exactly. And Maleska, well … common adjectives used to describe him include "gruff" and "harsh." Uproarious, not so much. Today, even an editor like Rich Norris at the *Los Angeles Times*, who is less apt than some of his colleagues at other papers to publish jokey themes, still runs them at least a couple of times per week. And any given puzzle in the *Los Angeles Times*, no matter the day of the week, will have its share of wordplay intended to make the solver grin. It's simply expected.

Perhaps we can blame it on the Brits. As Stephen Sondheim explains in the "A Curious Thing" sidebar in Chapter Three (*page 58*), the sensibility of a British-style cryptic crossword is devious and playful. Cryptics have a special internal grammar that requires the solver to unravel a mysterious phrase or sentence to deduce the answer. There are no straight definitions at all. In the 1960s, when the American crossword had been around for a few decades without substantial experimentation in cluing conventions, it began to look stale by comparison. Sondheim was among the first to publicly call for a recognition of cryptics on these shores. His call was answered in the 1980s by constructors like David Ellis Dickerson, Henry Rathvon, and Emily Cox. Cox and Rathvon, who construct together as "Hex," are known for their *Boston Globe* crosswords and their specialty puzzles, such as acrostics. But they are loved for their cryptics.

The arrival of this new kind of puzzle—and its very different sense of humor and wordplay—heralded another kind of British invasion, this one more than a decade later than the musical variety. Like soccer, cryptics now have a foothold in the U.S., but there has yet to be a fully fledged craze. They remain a foreign concept in the minds of many solvers. Perhaps it's because at the same time that cryptics arrived in America, lots of other new specialty puzzles did, too. The 1980s were a moment of experimentation with layouts and concepts that sought to turn the crossword on its head. Specialty puzzles and new thematic ideas were busy fixing exactly what Sondheim had diagnosed in the American puzzle scene, introducing a renewed sense of fun and play.

Even in conventional crosswords, the clues were getting funnier. Merl Reagle led the way here with a true comedian's touch. Take, for instance, an entry like ELOPE. In the Maleska or Farrar era, this would have been clued as a definition, but once puniness entered the picture, it became ripe territory for sly jokes. Reagle has clued it with "Double up in Vegas?" "Tie a quick knot?" and "Split to unite?" among others, rarely missing the opportunity to be cute given the wealth of opportunities available. Trip Payne, another fan of the funny clue, went with "Waive one's rites?" in 1994. Bob Klahn nailed it with "Take the honey and run." Frances Hansen, impressively since ELOPE had by the 2000s become a prime target for joke clues and the pickings were growing slim, devised "Skip church, maybe" for a puzzle published in 2004.

Fleming found some other great joke clues for his article, including "Punch with a kick" for SANGRIA (Tony Orbach and Patrick Blindauer) and "Where to see the writing on the wall?" for FACEBOOK PROFILE (Caleb Madison). But there may now be even newer kinds of humor. Part of this is a predictable consequence of the envelope being pushed ever further along. In the indies in particular, answers like ARSE (Seat in the British Parliament?), ENEMA (Process of elimination?), and THA (Hip-hop article?) open up new avenues for the kind of edgy cluing that reads as slightly taboo but not obscene. But even beyond this, an interesting trend has emerged lately. The need to be careful with size in a print newspaper dovetails well with the preference of many crossword editors for economical clues. Historically, a great clue is one that uses the fewest words possible.

But more recently, with many puzzles going digital, brevity has become less urgent. Some constructors have experimented with longer clues for effect. Consider Francis Heaney's "Gp. that keeps planes from hitting each other" for ATC (which stands for Air Traffic Controllers). Whereas ATC is a dry abbreviation, which has been clued into the ground with straight definitions by now, and it's pretty hard to think of a funny way to clue the entry in the first place, Francis magically revives it. His tactic is to be a mite sardonic, like a Borscht Belt comedian, simultaneously giving us a fair clue and tacitly acknowledging that the entry is tedious. Such clues rely on the constructor to assume an authorial voice that was unheard of 20 or 30 years ago. Above all, they require a self-effacing posture and an honest acknowledgement of the less delightful aspects of crossword solving—like Roman numerals, obscurities, stale clues—that can never be avoided entirely.

The use of an informal tone has also become a device in less sardonic clues. Gareth Bain, a top young constructor, wrote the clue "Cool place to live?" for IGLOO in a June 2013 *Los Angeles Times* puzzle. His clue takes advantage of the fact that the word "cool" here reads like it means "excellent." But Bain pulls back from the idiomatic by using "cool" as a straight description of temperature in a phrase that sounds far more casual. This is the kind of humor that plays well in the modern crossword—we've come a long way.

# Commentary

## Across

**1.** Roundball assist

**5.** Trapper's haul

**10.** Ready at a pull

**15.** Spelunker's funhouse

**19.** Sole

**20.** Entertaining Cheri

**21.** "Don't panic"

**22.** A-Rod's A

**23.** Judge

**24.** Crime on the books

**25.** Firm with foil

**26.** Russo in pictures

**27.** "Can anyone unlock this door?"

**30.** "... o'er the ramparts..."

**32.** One of the Twin Cities

**33.** Chinese cooking style

**35.** Height increasers

**36.** Tree-climbing plant

**39.** Fries, slaw, chips, etc.

**41.** Downed the above

**42.** "Hello, is this Glenn?"

**46.** "Gotcha, you rascal!"

**51.** CD follower

**52.** Willful?

**54.** New Mexico arts spot

**55.** What LeBron was, once

**56.** Pretty good

**58.** Great Depression figure

**59.** Some sushi fish

**60.** Freethinking Tom

**62.** High Seas danger

**65.** "First rise, then balance on two feet"

**68.** Primary

**71.** Tolkien's Treebeard, e.g.

**72.** Danny of the Celts

**73.** "Captain Hook's had a bad week"

**78.** Think about

**82.** Sweetie pie

**83.** "Zwei" preceder

**84.** Lady in Arthurian tales

**87.** Singer about Alice

**88.** Post-op spot

**89.** Make ___ dash for

**90.** Frondlike red algae

**93.** "La mer" contents

**94.** "What goes around comes around"

**98.** "I secretly spiked it"

**100.** Plastic ___ Band

**101.** Shrub of the genus "Rhus"

**103.** Lock your eyes

**104.** An elder Alou

**107.** Stalking cats

**109.** Panned item

**113.** "Well, I'm stuffed"

115. "Put your John Hancock right here"

118. Move, to realtors

119. Two-door roller

121. Weepy one of myth

122. Vidal's Breckinridge

123. Past the salad days

124. Common expression

125. Bed definer

126. Power co. output

127. Braxton or Tennille

128. Nest in a high place

129. Positives

130. Adam's number three

**Down**

1. Birds no more

2. All thumbs

3. Go to Nod

4. Service books

5. People as a mass

6. Must-learn French verb

7. Floral neckwear

8. Something pledged

9. The Dog Star

10. Rogers Centre anthem

11. Bruins' org.

12. Second sound

13. Plants yielding balm

14. Put the camp to bed

15. Yule vocalist

16. Not missing a trick

17. Does some selling

18. Splitsville residents?

28. Peace partner

29. Getting cooled

31. "Also starring..."

34. Made as a profit

37. Steve of the Suns

38. Sax sort

40. Reagan Court appointee

42. Photoshop option

43. Trickster from Asgard

44. Epps who acts

45. Where white coats are worn

47. Egypt's Mubarak

48. With wit that bites

49. Fit to stand trial

50. At any time

53. Family emblems

57. Pleasure cruiser

59. Main course

60. Strip set in a swamp

61. Where contenders vie

63. Chuck by another handle

64. The Dark Side?

66. Racket-swinging Ivanovic

67. Econ. indicator

69. Woe to a plant

70. Dominicans, e.g.

73. Of ears

74. Points of convergence

75. Typical par

76. Turns out to be

77. Chip, as flint

79. "Zwei" follower

80. Panache

81. Licentious fellow

85. Broadcasting Don

86. "Hold off!"

89. Baldness

90. One of wisdom

91. Data readers

92. Noncommittal sign

95. Pinocchio's creator

96. Whole thing

97. "I need to hear a joke"

99. Garden goodies

102. Oft-mimicked gangster player

104. Fire, to Latinos

105. Talk-show host

106. Get worn

108. Awfully sarcastic

110. Country's Crystal

111. Wader in white

112. Impart learning

113. Campus house

114. Mrs. who met a ghost

116. Things that we saw

117. Ali simile words

120. Polynesian staple

## A CURIOUS THING

Regular solvers will recognize the phenomenon of a question mark appearing after certain clues, as in "Mountain flower?" The question mark is simply a tip-off to the solver that something unusual and probably punny is going on with the clue. In this case, the answer is LAVA. Because we are used to interpreting the word "flower" as a colorful thing in the garden, we might be caught off-guard when it's being used to mean "a thing that flows." The clue is deliberately misleading in this way, but the question mark serves as a guide, nudging the reader to recognize the fact that the constructor is being devious. If the editor wants to make a clue extra hard, they can withhold question marks where they might be helpful. This is just one way of manipulating the general difficulty of a puzzle, by throwing the solver more or fewer bones.

*Emily Cox and Henry Rathvon, "Commentary," October 23, 2011. Reprinted with permission of Emily Cox and Henry Rathvon.*

# Elevens

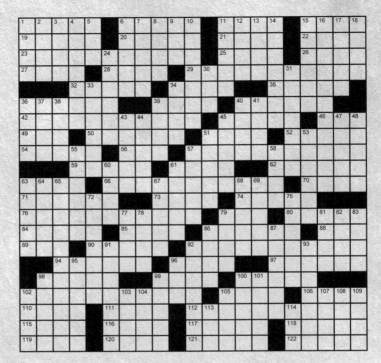

## Across

1. One more than eleven
6. Buck who sang "A-11"
11. Early lesson
15. Big bruisers
19. Denom. of FDR
20. Dehumanized sort
21. Role for Carrie
22. Sir Jagger
23. 11th
25. Neeson of "Rob Roy"
26. Do at Woodstock
27. On the main
28. Like 11-Across
29. 11 am
32. Aussie swimmer Gould
34. Unsafe, for ice
35. Mementos of mending
36. "Cat's Eye" author Margaret
39. GM Epstein
40. Small RV type
42. Apollo 11
45. Hamlet's vision
46. Philanthropist Hogg
49. Psyche, in part
50. Buck feature
51. Verve
52. Code for fonts
54. "J" sound
56. UK lexical tome
57. Side of 11
59. Chaucerian pilgrim
61. Blueprint
62. "Good heavens!"
63. Ex-Yank Martinez
66. 11/11
70. Banned "juice"
71. Jingoistic chant
73. Not in effect
74. Ill-prepared
76. "Ocean's 11"
79. Drink, for short
80. Some SASE inserts
84. "24" agent Jack
85. "That," in Latin
86. Creator of Jo and Beth
88. "Mer" makeup
89. PC text-to-speech aid
90. Worries
92. 11
94. Home to Denali
96. Coveter's sin
97. Penn's partner
98. Height of happiness
99. Move in the breeze
100. Diary note
102. #11 on skates
105. Saab of fashion
106. Celtic retiree of 2011
110. Sunburn application
111. Gas in tubes
112. 11, for 11 theme entries
115. Eat the last of
116. Spun yarn
117. Lavishly laud
118. Solder or steel
119. A mere
120. Be in a funk
121. Campus bigwigs
122. "Mad Libs" choices

## Down

1. ___ vu
2. Artistic work
3. Online mag
4. Ex-Bengal Boomer
5. Cpl. or sgt.
6. Sound at Fenway
7. Not so good
8. PayPal parent
9. Start to doze
10. Crane or King
11. Sort of wrench
12. Flower-power event
13. "Later!"
14. Asian appetizers
15. Some native Nebraskans
16. 11, classically
17. Off-white shades
18. Hershey bar with toffee
24. Add to memory
30. Kia subcompact
31. The Wolfpack's school
33. Tip of the hat
34. Red-bearded god
36. Iowa college town
37. Land next to Benin
38. Collie's comment
39. 11-11, e.g.?
40. Trend-setting
41. "Get a load of this!"
43. Range in the home
44. Pelletized shower
45. Happy faces
47. Dolphin-lovers' locale
48. Had the intent
51. See 100-Down
53. Launches
55. Company on the road
57. Insurance filing
58. Frozen treat maker
60. Flood zone op
61. Working stiff
63. Sort of engine
64. Designer Mizrahi
65. 11, in craps
67. Pandora's box escapees
68. On deck
69. Smithy fixture
72. Wit with a bite
75. Chalkboard accessory
77. Homer-hitter Gibson
78. Type of market
79. Like a Honda Element
81. Wedding wear
82. Apply asphalt to
83. Party in court
86. Historian of Rome
87. Gold Rush name
91. Gives the go-ahead
92. In a tangle
93. Go it alone
95. Odds-on
96. One of the flock
98. Slick band-mate Marty
99. Ancient cord material
100. With 51-Down, NBA forward
101. Physicist Bohr
102. Fast-moving shark
103. Pre-flight assignment
104. Boot base
105. Bluesy James
107. TV video website
108. Erelong
109. Amts.
113. PC program suffix
114. Put up, as preserves

*Emily Cox and Henry Rathvon, "Elevens," December 30, 2012. Reprinted with permission of Emily Cox and Henry Rathvon.*

# Supergroups

**Across**

1. Himalayan capital
6. Barton or Bow
11. Mineral band
15. In the pink
19. Composer Copland
20. UConn athlete
21. 55-Across, in "Casablanca"
22. Van Halen drummer
23. Musical merger called "Venom"?
25. Mordant Mort
26. Egotistic entertainer
27. Not a bit concerned
28. "Jam" band pairing?
31. M. Magritte
32. Far from firm
34. Blue to the max
35. Role in "Amadeus"
38. Shaving tool
39. Canadian rapids
40. Chopper
41. On the bus
43. Bands forming "Charon"?
47. "Of Course" combo?
50. Director von Trier
51. 11-Across makeup
52. Susan of "Baywatch"
53. Things with Xings
54. Gaston of baseball
55. See 21-Across
58. Lake District pools
60. "Caravan" linkup?
62. NH lake or town
65. Cherish
66. As a group
67. "The Loop" supergroup?
69. Swedish sedans
70. Receivers, in part
71. Eight, in Italy
72. Cape once called Tragabigzanda
73. Bottled fuel
77. PC bailout key
78. Seconds
79. "Cork" duo?
81. "Oh, Them" coalition?
85. Candace of the WNBA
86. Anti-Brady bunch
87. Hair reddener
88. Much-feared eel
89. Say yes to
92. Swath of land
95. "Jet" sister mag
96. Truant, as a GI
97. "Food Fight" fusion?
99. Ready to rumble
103. Can't be
104. Not just you or they
105. "Pie" partnership?
108. Box office take
109. Fretted feature
110. Toss out
111. Sonja on skates
112. Pinstriped infielder
113. Pale sort of pinot
114. Pumper's pride
115. Plum in the middle?

**Down**

1. Secure at sea
2. Can't stand
3. Indy racer Luyendyk
4. Locke of Hollywood
5. Reel employer
6. Elected
7. Sox great Tiant
8. Mule's sire
9. "King Kong" studio
10. Objectivist author
11. Fraidy-cat
12. Valley in a 2007 film title
13. Where butts may rest
14. "La Condition Humaine" author
15. Got flustered
16. Bio subtitle, often
17. Popular jeans
18. On the button
24. Quintet
29. Diminutive chord-maker
30. Scopes Trial org.
32. Thick cuts
33. "B.C." cartoonist Johnny
35. Rudolph of "Bridesmaids"
36. Some yokemates
37. Sidecar garnish
38. Falls in buckets
39. "Killer Bs" team
42. Sarawak's island
43. Composer Erik
44. Cornet, tuba, et al.
45. Cat Nation constituents
46. Give a new hue
48. Catch sight of
49. ___ with (equal to)
50. "Mephisto Waltz" composer
54. Tahrir Square site
55. Hebridean isle
56. With no feeling
57. Understands
59. Rules, briefly
60. Speak for the masses
61. Moreau of "Jules et Jim"
62. 24-Down + 3
63. "Put a sock in it!"
64. From then on
65. Ancient city of rock
68. Ruckus
69. Full of twists and turns
72. Showy spread
74. Trait carrier
75. Over-50 org.
76. Blind strip
78. "Jaws" shark, e.g.
79. Place with a loft
80. Attract
82. Piqued or honed
83. Get 15-Across again
84. In progress
85. Long shot
88. Financier's deg.
90. Trumpets for Tritons
91. Red Bordeaux
92. PC of the 1980s
93. "Dog Whisperer" Millan
94. Totaled
95. Sci-fi fuzzballs
96. Olympian Ohno
98. Crucial points
99. Pac-12 team
100. Truckee River town
101. Big pipe
102. Hook henchman
106. Chef's gadget brand
107. Colo. ___, CO

*Emily Cox and Henry Rathvon, "Supergroups," December 12, 2012. Reprinted with permission of Emily Cox and Henry Rathvon.*

# Wacky Readings

**Across**

1. Electronic censor

6. Tennis arena name

10. Old-time sailor

13. Hug givers

17. Tony winner Rivera

18. Feudal figure

20. Bob whom Bill beat

21. "Come again?"

22. Tnempiuqe?

24. Dueling blade

25. Top-notch

26. New bout with old rivals

27. Chickchick?

30. South American monkeys

32. Night out

33. Trying experience

34. Sri Lankan lingo

37. Bruin or Flyer

39. Benefit

41. PROFIT?

43. Pops a question

44. Baroque master

48. Cry of one grabbed

49. Aussie waltzer

51. Computer shortcut

52. "Sting like __"

53. General Bradley

55. Reggae cousin

56. Pierre with a theorem

57. Jarring sight at the shore

60. *Current events?*

62. Wheedle

63. Giant's antithesis

64. Roman called "the Censor"

65. Earth, or hater?

70. Whales and dolphins

75. Verbally abuse

76. Outstanding

77. Filmdom's Lancaster

78. Zoologist's wings

79. Hill of a Hill hearing

80. Changed for the better

82. Leg warmer

85. Diatonic scheme

86. Kiss Kiss Bang Bang author

87. Circl?

89. Amazing deed

90. Matter for Mulder

91. Decline

92. Place to chow down

96. Gallic girlfriend

98. Call across vales

100. AcheS?

103. Fitting one within another

107. Mongolian for "desert"

108. Waikiki's island

109. Ji / ffy?

112. Idi of ignominy

113. Enterprise empath

114. Prefix for thrift

115. Baton event

116. Had resonance

117. Show you're human

118. Tippy-top

119. Union member

**Down**

1. TiVo forerunner

2. Moonstruck actress

3. Place of buzziness

4. Bullet point

5. Opposite of a host

6. Smart guy?

7. Sounding wistful

8. Giggle bit

9. Old "Omigosh!"

10. Allerina?

11. To the sheltered side

12. Shoes for Yao Ming

13. Plaque or trophy

14. Island preceder

15. Crazed excitement

16. Railroading need

19. Naturally wearing down

20. Red state?

23. Hogan's Heroes setting

28. Former Mideast inits.

29. Displeasure squared

31. Tribal magician

34. Billy Blanks workout

35. More fitting

36. Quiet cards

38. Tale-weaver

40. Alias letters

41. With something on

42. In-the-shower item

43. Seltzer starter

44. Owl hangout

45. High point

46. Where things may stick

47. Lover's excitement

50. Castaway's spot

51. Red Bordeaux

54. Mother, pa?

56. Cheese for a salad

58. Amtrak's "bullet train"

59. Solitary

60. Unit on a court

61. Be a teller

63. St. Paul's architect

65. Stoker who wrote of Dracula

66. Twin city of Sparks, NV

67. Roman poet

68. Controlled flier

69. Ayla's inventor

70. Huggable

71. Pioneering

72. Crazy as __

73. Star Wars home of Jar Jar Binks

74. Ooze

77. "Goods," in Italian

80. Penlight battery

81. D, in many sports

83. Size up

84. Liturgical collections

86. Tonic, in music

88. Like the King of Beasts

89. Work wk. end

90. Caligula's dozen

92. On-screen Samantha

93. Trail to a pie?

94. Saw actor Bell

95. NBA great Patrick

97. Island near 108 Across

99. Straighten out

101. Teri in pictures

102. Shelter org.

104. "Rhyme Pays" rapper

105. Vincent Lopez's theme song

106. Midge or punkie

110. Prune

111. Hue changer

*Emily Cox and Henry Rathvon, "Wacky Readings," September 26, 2010. Reprinted with permission of Emily Cox and Henry Rathvon.*

# Twenty Under Thirty
## by Zoe Wheeler

**Across**

**1.** Stiffener for working stiffs

**7.** Perform a smooth operation?

**11.** Uses rolls as a prank

**14.** "Trust me on this"

**15.** Very, in slang

**16.** Works on a wall, say

**17.** Candy advertised by Jordan on a Schwinn?

**19.** "THAT lady?"

**20.** Week ender, briefly

**21.** Clarks alternative

**22.** Traditional Irish language

**23.** Fo' ___

**25.** You may rub one out

**27.** Ice, biblically

**28.** Mockumentary series "___ Life"

**30.** Candy used for a staged "Jersey Shore" scene?

**32.** Capital of Samoa

**33.** "Can ___ honest with you?"

**34.** "Who, me?"

**35.** Candy shaped like a young, foxy Duchess of Cambridge?

**37.** Gum sold with copies of "Ulysses?"

**41.** Collaborator on "Let Me Blow Ya Mind"

**42.** Pro's word

**43.** A fair to remember?

**44.** Candy with a silver-voiced dog mascot?

**48.** Arthur Conan Doyle or Andy Murray

**49.** Episode of "30 Rock," e.g., after its seventh season

**50.** Surrealist Max

**52.** Jumping ability, so to speak

**53.** Not relaxed

**54.** Mani-___

**55.** Things used during crunch time?

**57.** Going grey, say

**58.** Certain candy slogan, and a clue to this puzzle's theme

**62.** Math that may be linear: Abbr.

**63.** Swedish chain

**64.** One who might get sexiled

**65.** Use Clairol, say

**66.** Frond plant

**67.** Noted sportscaster Howard

**Down**

**1.** Family member in a '90s video game

**2.** Exclamation after a graphic description

**3.** Be bad, say

**4.** One filled with regret

**5.** Comedian Ferguson

**6.** ___ Party (Brit's bash for a bachelorette)

**7.** "What I Got" band

**8.** Put up with

**9.** New Pornographers singer Case

**10.** Rapper who does not practice, despite how it sounds

**11.** Arab Spring square name

**12.** "Ta-da!"

**13.** "It's Complicated" actress

**18.** Second-longest European river

**22.** Zynga game "___ & Allies"

**23.** Pierre's place: Abbr.

**24.** Tribe in the Southwest

**26.** Put in a good word, say?

**27.** Pollution portmanteau

**29.** Reach first base

**31.** Eskimo boats

**36.** Company with a familiar ring?

**37.** 2011 Jack Black film

**38.** "The nerve!"

**39.** Each

**40.** Cities, on many maps

**42.** Character out of pornography central casting

**44.** Reckless driver in "The Wind in the Willows"

**45.** Flabbergasted question

**46.** A vindictive person might hold one

**47.** Posh wheels, casually

**51.** Hasbro word guessing game

**54.** Certain fish, road, or weapon

**56.** They come before hos, in a terrible expression

**58.** Image file format

**59.** Ball's trajectory, perhaps

**60.** Not feel so hot

**61.** Kenan's partner on "All That"

*Zoe Wheeler,* Twenty Under Thirty, *2012. Reprinted with permission of Ben Tausig. The* Twenty Under Thirty *collection was the result of a contest in which puzzles by younger constructors were judged anonymously, with the winning entries published together.*

# Twenty Under Thirty
## by Anna Shechtman

**Across**

1. Miffs
5. "Why England ___" (JFK's Harvard thesis)
10. Part of a baseball used to throw a curve
14. Barrett of gossip
15. Holy book with a pointer
16. French cleric
17. Matt Damon role
19. Like some garish clothing
20. Big name in motion
21. Natural heat?
23. South of Houston, roughly speaking
27. Part of IPA
29. Final beach trip occasion, often
30. Mounted
32. Submissive, in bondage
33. Slip
37. Flock, on the ground
39. One of two political houses
40. Sign of resistance?
41. Bad growth
44. Asia's terribly polluted ___ Sea
45. Placed
48. "Very funny" TV station
49. Subject of the 2002 documentary "Devil's Playground"
53. May event for many seniors
54. Place for those about to rock
57. Doofus
58. Like 17-, 23-, and 49-Across, in multiple ways
62. "The Voice" competitor, briefly
63. Further downhill
64. Erato, e.g.
65. Nile vipers
66. Modern readers
67. Former New York Archbishop Edward

**Down**

1. "Persepolis" setting
2. Date offering
3. Epistemologist's concern
4. ___ Domingo
5. Really primitive, as technology
6. Reed who started out writing canned pop songs
7. Blunder
8. ___-Asianism
9. Famous last words?
10. "The one who does not remember history is bound to live through it again" philosopher
11. Siskel's partner, once
12. On the order of
13. High IQ society
18. It's often packed in a dorm room
22. Oil resource
24. Game-winning hit stat
25. Sibling's cry
26. Dada co-founder Hans
27. Ship protected by Hera
28. Topsoil
31. What the cautious walk on
34. E, e.g.
35. Attempt
36. Unagi sources
38. Secular sorts
39. Foot emanations
41. With, on diplomas
42. Caribbean staple food
43. "Rugrats" dad
46. Where Mr. Deeds goes, in a 1936 Frank Capra comedy
47. Calamitous
49. Group providing protection
50. Sugar and Cream holders, say?
51. Brownstone feature
52. Facebook user's request, perhaps
55. Simpson sister
56. Utopia
59. ___ Fighters
60. Do with a pick
61. Sound of disapproval

# CHAPTER FIVE

## The Breakfast Table Rule

Which topics would be so offensive, so upsetting, or so obnoxious that you couldn't finish your eggs and coffee while thinking about them? In journalism, this question is called the Breakfast Table Test (or Breakfast Table Rule). When a newspaper editor is unsure about running an unseemly picture or story, he or she is advised to envision an unsuspecting, robe-clad old lady sipping tea at dawn, as she prepares to sit down and catch up on the day's news. If this imaginary reader might shake her fist toward the sky or punch a wall upon encountering an item in the paper, then that item is said to violate the Breakfast Table Test (BTT), and should be left out.

The term *Breakfast Table Test* has an unrelated history that precedes its use in journalism. Psychologist Francis Galton developed a method of evaluation by this name in the late 19th century, and used it to assess his patients' capacity for mental visualization. The patients were asked to mentally picture their own breakfast table, and to try to describe the things on it. According to journalism historian and former *Washington Post* staff writer Maurine Beasley, the phrase was brought to the news world by Adolph Ochs around the turn of the century. Whether Ochs knew about Galton's test is unclear. But Ochs, like Galton, was concerned with visualization. Among the slogans used by the *Times* when he ran the paper was "It Does Not Soil the Breakfast Cloth," in reference to the paper's commitment to decency during a period of intensely sensational and partisan reporting. His version of the Breakfast Table Test was intended to ensure both editorial balance and a pleasant experience for the reader.

In the ensuing decades, the BTT was applied in newsrooms around the country, and news editors used it as a basic litmus test. (It also had a life in other contexts. The *Miami Daily News* cited the BTT in one outrageously sexist fashion column: "Nothing is more discouraging to the man of the house than to be faced over the breakfast table morning after morning by a shoddily clad woman."[6]) The suitability of images of disease, war, and suffering were judged by this principle. During two world wars, in particular, the test was an especially useful way to think about the proper relationship between newspaper and reader.

Margaret Farrar, inaugural editor of the *Times* crossword, unsurprisingly applied the BTT to her puzzles, according to an interview with Mel Rosen[7]. In fact, she was probably the first editor to do so. Rosen, who published puzzles with Farrar, had grids rejected for seemingly benign entries such as BLOODTESTS, which apparently evoked disease. While crosswords of the 1920s and 1930s in other papers were not exactly bawdy, they were certainly permissive by comparison. The *New York Herald Tribune*, for example, allowed references to putrefaction and liquor (during Prohibition), and the *Daily News-Record* had answers such as NAKED in the grid in 1925. Papers of the period were committed to fun before decency, and their only standard for what was fair game in the puzzle was to look to the pages of the paper itself. In the celebrity-obsessed, headline-grabbing world of 1920s New York City media, crosswords could get away with quite a lot. They were decidedly not BTT-compliant and appropriately so, since the peddlers of yellow journalism in which they appeared were busy showing skin, crime, and scandal. In that sense, the propriety of the *Times* was an outlier as well as a novelty when it first appeared.

## A CURIOUS THING

In the 1920s, especially in 1925, America experienced a crossword craze. There was a book of celebrity crosswords with contributions from Will Rogers and New York Governor Al Smith, among others. There were popular songs, items of jewelry, and magazine covers related to the new pastime. Nearly every paper jumped on board by adding a puzzle feature. Papers in New York, where the phenomenon began, were particularly eager to jump on the bandwagon, with the *New York World*, *New York Herald Tribune*, *New York Graphic*, *New York Journal American*, and many others adding their own unique crosswords as weekly and eventually daily content. Although the crossword is popular from coast to coast and in between, it is in the biggest city where it has thrived most heartily. Perhaps it has something to do with the subway?

In fact, much of the recent evolution of crosswords has involved pushing the limits of the BTT. In the modern puzzle era, this is a much more self-conscious process than it was 80 or 90 years ago. The reputation of crosswords as being dry makes edgy content all the more attractive and exciting, and constructors have tried to plug in blue language in a number of ways, sometimes secretly. Martin Schneider snuck the entry PENIS into a *New York Times* puzzle in 1995 by cluing it as a fill in the blank: "The ___ mightier than the sword." (Leonard Gravis pulled the same trick in *USA Today* in 2009). Because crossword grids don't include spacing between sequences of multiple words, the answer appeared in the solution as a racy double entendre. Bob Klahn, perhaps no fan of Bill Clinton, clued the answer SAX as "Clinton blows it" in the CrosSynergy puzzle mere days after George W. Bush was elected in November 2000. Partisanship is usually forbidden in the puzzle, as it introduces a potentially breakfast-spoiling degree of controversy. But a clever and determined constructor can usually find a workaround.

The *New York Sun* puzzle, edited by Peter Gordon from 2002 until the paper folded in 2008, once clued SEX playfully as "Word with play or act" rather than adopting the conventional tactic of anesthetizing the term by talking about application forms ("Questionnaire question," "Census datum") or science ("Chromosome factor," "Kinsey subject.") The *Sun*, in turn, helped push the *Times* toward a gradually higher level of permissiveness. But the envelope has only been pushed so far to date. The answer HORNY, for example, has been permitted for many years in just about every crossword, though only if the clue is something along the lines of "Like rhinos." Only the alternative crossword market has taken the next step of cluing HORNY according to its more common usage.

The alternative puzzle market, discussed in the next chapter, is an entirely different animal when it comes to the BTT, although that market has limits, too. Words like PEE ("Number one material?") and ASS ("It may be shaken in a club") show up all the time, and clues for SEX can be as playful as one imagines ("It might make you a new person"). In a puzzle by someone like Brendan Emmett Quigley, a solver wouldn't be shocked to solve an entire theme about drunkenness or STDs. However, certain subjects from rape to racial epithets to violence to extreme political partisanship remain tacitly off-limits. It's not that they couldn't be used, strictly speaking, but that they don't afford a lot of great jokes in this medium. And since the highest priority for a crossword is to entertain and amuse, titillation can only happen in tandem with successful humor.

What counts as a violation of the BTT is, of course, in the eye of the solver. One reader of the busy crossword blog Rex Parker Does the *New York Times* Crossword Puzzle was miffed after filling in the entry DREDAY, a hit single by Dr. Dre from 1993. The reader wrote: "I wonder (in a world where many, many solvers are going to Google the clue) how this could possibly have passed the Breakfast Table Test? First off, there appear to be a number of songs which include those lyrics, many of which were released in 1993. Furthermore, all of them contain extremely explicit lyrics which are not welcome at my breakfast table[8]." Others came to the song's defense for being a good piece of music, and no more offensive than many Hollywood movies that frequently populate puzzle grids. Debates have raged among puzzle constructors over whether KAFFIR, clued as a type of lime, might offend some South Africans, whether RUSSKI is offensive, and whether MAILMAN is inappropriate because it isn't gender-neutral. Apparently, there are different kinds of breakfast tables and different rules as well.

Offensive entries have, on occasion, found their way into puzzles due to editorial oversight. Two notable recent examples include Will Shortz running one crossword with SCUMBAG and another with ILLEGAL. Although SCUMBAG had the mundane clue "Scoundrel," and the word seems fit for a G-rated movie, in fact it has a saucier etymology, being a synonym for condom that essentially means "semen bag." ILLEGAL isn't controversial on its own, but clued as "One caught by border patrol," as it was in a 2012 puzzle by Jim Page, it becomes a politically contentious description of an undocumented person. Shortz was widely criticized in both cases. Whether the criticism was warranted is clearly a matter for debate.

The justification for using entries, though, ultimately lies in the content of the paper or other venue where the puzzle runs. Alternative crosswords, which often appear amidst classified advertisements for erotic massage and other services of questionable legality, have every reason to be unrestricted in their material. But even the *Times* has gotten in on the trend lately. *Skinny Bitch*, a best-selling diet book published in 2005 that has spawned a number of successful spinoffs, became a *Times* crossword entry in 2008. Peter Gordon also used the word to comic effect with the clue "Bitch of a dick of fiction" for ASTA in 2012. Although BITCH, on its own, probably wouldn't pass muster even

if clued as "female dog," as part of the name of a bestseller that has appeared many times in the Book Review section, it passes the BTT. Similarly, ETHNICCLEANSING was part of a *Times* themeless grid in 2008. The clue was "Heinous war crime." As tragic and horrific as the phenomenon certainly is, this is a topic that the *Times* would be obligated to cover as a journalistic organ. The crossword simply followed the paper's lead.

Is the Breakfast Table Test still a useful arbiter of what should go in a crossword? It depends. The rule was originally devised at a time when newspapers in general were overrun with scandalous content, and perhaps it helped offer a fresh model for the industry. But transferring the BTT from the front page of the paper to the crossword assumed that solvers wanted the same thing from their puzzle that they wanted from their news. What if the puzzle itself is a kind of escape from dark stories of conflict and crime—not through avoidance, but through commentary? What if it can offer not only a reflection of what's in the paper, but a comic spin on that content? That seems like one way of filling the crossword's entertainment mandate. For many solvers, breakfast goes down better with a side of laughter.

# X-SPELLED

★★

BY JOY M. ANDREWS

**ACROSS**

1 Apr. professional
4 Spa spigots
8 Slotted the mail
14 Rolled bit in a bowl
15 Gillette shaver
16 Like some Basin Street cuisine
17 Espy party-mix cereal?
19 Draw back in horror
20 Med school model
21 Pop in
22 Rapper whose debut album was "Rhyme Pays"
23 PC spinner
25 "Kisses Sweeter ___ Wine"
28 Secretary of State Vance
30 Yolk ___ (egg part)
31 Bowling pin wood
32 Spruce juice
34 Offhand
36 Young den denizen

39 Smoked salmon from New Haven?
41 Put a mark next to
42 Popular puzzle type
44 Mich. neighbor
46 Student of Socrates
47 ___ Diego
49 Igneous rock source
53 Graham of rock music
54 "I bet you can't" sayer
56 ___ airbags (common car safety feature)
57 Monica with a racket

59 Straight path
61 Part of a rack
63 Formalwear for a belly?
64 Experimental Navy underwater habitat
65 Reunion attendee
66 Caroline's stepfather
67 German state whose capital is Dresden
68 Mercury 7 org.
69 Legal thing

**DOWN**

1 Vast
2 Vatican leader's term in office
3 One who makes amends

4 Moolah
5 Personal code
6 Prevailing inclinations
7 Stan Getz's instrument
8 Theater backdrop
9 Miner's quarry
10 Musical performance
11 Dracula movies?
12 Quarterback Manning
13 Oscar winner Benicio ___ Toro
18 New Testament book
21 Apt to speak out
24 It makes pit stops
26 Nautically safe
27 Socially inept sort

29 Authority
31 Alternative to Stuff magazine
33 Trite
35 Solemn promise
36 Crunch's title
37 Golden State sch.
38 Levy on generals?
40 Singers Loeb and Stansfield
43 Desdemona's husband
45 With regret
48 Cloud of interstellar dust
50 Fender product
51 Fertilizer ingredient
52 Supermodel Kim
54 Bowler
55 Uncle of animal tales
58 Slant
60 Samms of "Dynasty"
61 Stubborn person
62 D.C.-based culture sponsor
63 Fan-___ (card game also called parliament)

# HOW'S THAT AGAIN?

★★

BY TRIP PAYNE

## ACROSS

1 Hairball sufferer
4 Suck up soup
9 Apply concealer, for example
12 Some microbrews
14 Says something suddenly, with "up"
15 U2 vocalist
16 Participate in an ovation
17 Architect born in Canton
18 Clued in about
19 #1 hit for the Crystals
21 Runs away
22 Driver's license information
23 First among the children
24 Letter with the largest section in a dictionary
25 ___ section (geometry topic)
27 Liberal foil of Archie
30 It might be put under a pillow overnight
34 Illegal firing
35 Far from the dock
36 Movie beekeeper played by Peter
37 In ___ of (rather than)
38 When Caesar was killed
39 More than just ticked off
40 The cellar, in sports
42 Innie or outie
43 Airline that had a low-cost carrier called Song
44 Lose firmness, in a way
45 Virtuoso Spanish cellist
48 Spoiled rotten
53 Knock the socks off of
54 What a flush pays, in Caribbean stud poker
55 Off-white shade
56 "___ Attraction"
57 "Once ___ a midnight dreary ..."
58 Decorated with a pastry bag
59 It might be read and then deleted
60 Stopwatch count, for short
61 "Conjunction Junction" conjunction
62 Star-___ Sneetch (Seuss character)
63 It can replace a woman's name

## DOWN

1 Hidden hoard
2 Strike zone
3 Josh
4 Carnival barkers' pitches
5 Contest at the bar?
6 OTTAWA
7 Angling need
8 Final one-syllable Greek letter
9 Gift getter
10 Hold'em fees
11 Shoplift, in slang
13 G r o g g y
15 Intrepid
20 1953 A.L. MVP Al
21 Dart here and there
23 She had a 1989 hit with "Orinoco Flow"
26 Unlike gymnasts
27 Rat's hangout?
28 Song that's often in a foreign language
29 Plays for a pawn
30 Having no talent for
31 Name of several Norwegian kings
32 Head of the French Academy?
33 Vulnerable spot for Achilles
38 Travails
39 Unsuited
41 Santos superstar
44 Rank
45 Log home
46 ___ Ultimate (fuel at BP stations)
47 More sensible
49 Prove beneficial
50 They ring rings
51 Ancestor of Noah
52 Jam-packed
54 Category in the game Careers
56 The second mo.

# WEEKEND WARRIOR

★★★★★

## BY KAREN M. TRACEY

**ACROSS**

1 Extended operatic solo
6 Apple ___ (nickname of Tasmania)
10 Radiation units
14 Retort to the indiscreet
16 ___ Sinclair (protagonist of Hesse's "Demian")
17 Plant of the mint family
18 Marjorie Weinman Sharmat's young sleuth
19 Weenie roast desserts
20 Birth
22 Father of Horus
24 Oscar-winning screenwriter Ben
25 Amsterdam soccer team
28 1956 Ingrid Bergman film
30 Very thirsty
32 Innsbruck Olympics surface
33 Group granted U.N. observer status in 1974
35 "Waking Ned Devine" star Ian
36 Minnesota iron range
38 "Wheel of Fortune" purchase
39 Dewar's denial
41 "Tired blood" tonic
42 "Las Meninas" painter
45 Some govs.
46 Like flattened flats
47 Brought to ruin
49 Nets
51 "The Railway Children" author Edith
55 Home to many elephants
56 Central question in the search for extraterrestrial life
58 Ireland's Shannon-___ Waterway
59 Nonconformist
60 Cardiologists' charts, for short
61 She played Maxine on "Judging Amy"
62 Rash

**DOWN**

1 Samples
2 Cut bait
3 Saarinen who designed Yale's Ingalls Rink
4 Aleve, generically
5 "Café Terrace at Night" setting
6 "___ Not About the Bike" (Lance Armstrong book)
7 First name in country
8 Author of the cookbook "Louisiana Real & Rustic"
9 French quarters?
10 Actress O'Connor and others
11 Deliver
12 Hank Azaria role opposite Jack Lemmon's Morrie Schwartz
13 Hard fall?
15 His son was on the cover of the first issue of TV Guide
21 Shot follower
23 Letters after Sen. Javits's name
25 Contemporary of Moshe
26 Portrayer of one of the Ewing wives on "Dallas"
27 John Denver hit that begins "You fill up my senses"
29 Atlantic and Pacific, e.g.
31 "Gracias" reply
34 Many Manets
37 Crosswind landing maneuver
40 Personal attendant in the British royal household
41 Coll. prereq, perhaps
43 Shooting equipment
44 Invisible
46 Pulitzer-winning biography by Douglas S. Freeman
48 Half-moon tides
50 Host
52 Tora ___ (2001 battle site)
53 Monogram ltr.
54 "Alouette" body part
57 Bantam

# COMMON SORT

BY PATRICK BERRY

**ACROSS**

1 Gold rush asset
6 Lumber jacket material
10 Flavorful plant
14 Uninteresting
15 Looking for a catch, say
16 Waikiki wingding
17 Wood used to build the Kon-Tiki raft
18 Like some checks / Removed errors from
20 It's neat to make this
21 Give up
23 Casino fixtures
24 Vacuuming obstacle
26 Bathtub stain, maybe
29 Thus far
30 Prove the truth of
32 River around Notre Dame
34 Bovid in 1996 headlines
35 Intellectually primitive / Lend support to
39 Celebrate Thanksgiving
40 Knockoffs
41 Nick Charles's wife
42 Preface to a hazily remembered anecdote / Brand of acne medication
44 Title girl in a Ritchie Valens hit
45 Allotted, with "out"
46 Started up, as a computer
47 Parliamentary negative
50 Culmination
51 Spray container
52 Avoid committing oneself
54 Imposing tooth
56 Computer that Dell doesn't sell
59 Nonconducting sheath / Musical TV show that first aired in 1971
62 Concord
64 Word used in 7-Eleven drink sizes
65 Work hard
66 Ice cream store freebie
67 A smaller amount
68 Patriarch of a former MTV reality show
69 Contract conditions

**DOWN**

1 Queequeg's captain
2 Niger neighbor
3 Brainless
4 Type of amusement?
5 ___ duck (red-faced New World bird)
6 Edging material
7 How you should enter the letters of each Across answer in this puzzle
8 Provoke sharks, possibly
9 The end of eternity?
10 "Joanie Loves Chachi" costar
11 Beethoven dedicatee
12 1980s Red Sox pitcher Bruce
13 Like poorly tended dirt roads
19 Threw with force
22 Hang out, maybe
25 Bored one's audience
27 Goes on a quest
28 Final number in a team's record
30 Old Icelandic literary work
31 Doodle bug?
33 Some beachwear
35 Fair ball figure?
36 R&D genius, e.g.
37 Inadvisable action
38 Harness race pace
40 Novelist Waugh
43 Sawtooth Range setting
44 It pairs with uracil in RNA
46 Traveler's burden
47 Wise words
48 Actor Sam of "Jurassic Park"
49 Frightened cries
53 Serengeti herd
55 Monkey (with)
57 Suit in a tarot deck
58 Hit 1993 computer game from Brøderbund
60 Subcompact from Kia
61 Artful
63 Thing given to a bébé

# CHAPTER SIX

# Indie Puzzles

For nearly all of its life, the better part of 100 years, the crossword puzzle has been paper-bound, and mostly newspaper-bound. Intimately linked to the printed page, many solvers even in the digital era cannot fathom solving with a keyboard. For them, pen or pencil and paper are the only way to go. But, as with so much content that used to run in the newspaper, puzzles today have moved on to electronic devices of all kinds, for both better and worse.

Chapter Eight *(page 111)* will address changes in puzzle technology, and Chapter Ten *(page 147)* covers some of the history of crossword puzzle economics. But for now, it's time to introduce you to the crossword features that have sprouted like wild strawberries from the ashes of the newspaper industry's scorched forests—independent puzzles.

Independent puzzles as they exist today aren't without some precedent. Stan Newman self-published a short magazine called *Crossworder's OWN Newsletter* (later *Tough Puzzles*) from the early 1980s to the early 1990s. Newman's monthly (sometimes bimonthly) issues were mailed to subscribers and printed without binding. The pages were folded and stapled at the crease, each using just three sheets in total. *Crossworder's OWN* was of a piece with *samizdat* pamphlets and 'zines, in the sense that it partook of the most affordable and direct method of distribution available at the time— black-and-white printing and the trusty old postal service. The initial price, $21 a year, was hardly cut-rate, however. The general air of *Crossworder's OWN* was that of a premium product for serious enthusiasts.

Newman, already a respected figure in puzzles by that time, adopted an authoritative and knowledgeable tone in the introduction to each issue. He commented, sometimes pointedly, on the state of crosswords. "The quality of the *Times* puzzle has declined recently," he wrote in one issue, and in another catalogued some of editor Eugene Maleska's errors, including misspelling the name of New York City mayor Jimmy Walker and cluing the single word FAREWELL as "two words." He also criticized Maleska's esoteric bent, for instance in his cluing LOA in reference to Loa, Utah—a town of no particular distinction that was home to a whopping 364 people.

Unless one went to bed snuggling their world atlas each night, Newman seemed to imply, the *Times* puzzle wasn't really for them. Meanwhile, *Crossworder's OWN* became something of a refuge for those no longer willing or able to follow Maleska down his rabbit hole. One poor solver wrote in to ask how the answer BRDS in one *Times* grid could possibly make sense clued as "B's slide on them." Newman didn't know, either, but he asked Maleska, who explained that "B's" here stood for "bishops," and that BRDS was an abbreviation for "boards," as in chess boards. The explanation was as baffling as it was revealing of how completely the *Times* puzzle had lost touch.

Newman was part of a movement of puzzlers growing increasingly critical of the most famous crossword in the world for its pomposity and lack of color, and *Crossworder's OWN* was in the 1980s the voice of this New Wave movement. In this way, Newman was a leader of the first true community of independent constructors and editors. There had been no equivalent in any prior period, despite the popularity of crosswords. For whatever reason, popularity hadn't translated into a lasting community until around this time.

The story of the independents, however, was to be for a time interrupted. Will Shortz became editor of the *Times* in November 1993, bringing his own pop-culture-positive approach squarely into the mainstream. Newman, meanwhile, lost his day job on Wall Street after the stock market crash of 1987, and began searching for new employment. When the opportunity arose for him to assume editorship of the *New York Newsday* puzzle in 1994, he decided that a regular paycheck was too appealing to turn down. *Crossworder's OWN* would have been impossible to continue along with his new editing duties, and so he folded the publication.

The magazine, however, left an important legacy behind. When it launched, many of the puzzles were well constructed but otherwise ordinary; by the early 1990s, some of the top up-and-coming constructors, including Matt Gaffney, Peter Gordon, and Trip Payne, were contributing

# SATURDAY STUMPER by Matt Gaffney

## ACROSS

1 Phrase on Rhode Island plates
11 Hines specialty
14 Nine-time Wimbledon champ
16 The Buckeyes
17 Citrine coolers
18 Durocher's nickname
19 Bring to naught
20 Magic stick
21 Think-tank output
23 Film holder
24 Robert's daughter on *Father Knows Best*
26 Mr. McGrew
29 Dawson or Deighton
30 Erstwhile auto
33 Printer's proof
35 Long time: Abbr.
36 Jerk's locale
37 Worthless talk
38 Martian feature
40 European car
41 Track alternative
44 Senior member
45 Styling job
46 It's refined
47 Mouse-o-phobe's cry
48 *A Civil Tongue* author
50 "This can't be!"
54 Lamb Chop's handler
56 Wherein you'll see the light
59 Tooth's partner
60 Finless fish
61 Card game
64 Entirely
65 African high spot
66 Get a load of
67 Breathed colleague

## DOWN

1 "Maladies are taxes __ joys": Byron
2 Judy of *Laugh-In*
3 Get around
4 Army leader
5 Harper
6 Internalize anger
7 Mia Farrow's sister
8 *The Heart Is __ Hunter*
9 Rug rat
10 Spacewalk, to NASA
11 Range of variation
12 See 25 Down
13 Little boxers
15 A-apple link
22 Arcade game
25 With 12 Down, Gunther book
27 Uris hero
28 ". . . __ at the inn"
31 Young of *The Boost*
32 Wise, man
33 Hitchcock thriller
34 Ever
37 Short flight
39 Iowa college
42 Vocal filler
43 Bhutto of Pakistan
49 Lighter part
51 Mirthful sounds
52 Soup
53 Game-show announcer Johnny
54 Black and Red, but not Green
55 Beatles #1 tune
57 "For shame!"
58 Thunderous sound
62 Horse and carriage
63 One __ million

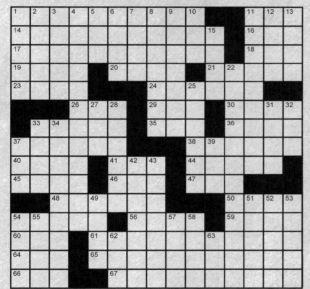

*Matt Gaffney, "Saturday Stumper," Tough Puzzles*, Crossworder's OWN Newsletter, April 1994. Reprinted with permission of Stanley Newman.

# B MOVIES  by Peter Gordon

## ACROSS

1 Embarrass
6 Whale of a movie
10 Nostrils
15 Metal fastener
18 Arnold's wife
19 Hawk
20 Fictional seaman Arden
21 "Scat, cat!"
22 B movie about a big party on a reservation?
26 Mentally bushed
27 Alencon is its capital
28 Schindler's List extras
29 Summer treats
33 B movie about the 1974 Ali-Foreman fight?
36 City on the Po
37 Bar-mitzvahed boy, e.g.
39 Acapulco gold
40 Babbles
41 Incorrect marks
42 Battery, e.g.
44 Page
48 L.A. Law character: Abbr.
49 "While you're___..."
51 Los Angeles event of 1994
52 Sicilian city
53 B movie about fluorescent material?
57 Composer Schitrin et al.
58 Lash of the West
59 Single or double, e.g.
60 French Oscars
61 B movie about a neurologist?
64 State of Hope: Abbr.
65 B movie about a post game winner's interview?
67 Notorious name in old Italy
68 Three-way intersection
69 Slow
70 Roman Empire invaders
71 B movie about a Charles Dickens expert?
77 Textbook chapter, perhaps
78 Stand-up material
80 Pout
81 Sea eagle
82 Stack part
83 Hip to
84 ___ Te Ching
85 Swirls
87 Citrus drink
88 Nome home: Var.
90 Free game of pinball
91 B movie about a know-it-all?
98 With tranquility
100 Cedar Rapids citizen
101 Pennsylvania port
102 Computer software company
103 B movie about what's left after the milk is drunk?
111 Bit of fishing tackle
112 California lake
113 On in years
114 Icicle's spot
115 Printer's measures
116 Organized methods: Abbr.
117 ___-deaf
118 Vane's place

## DOWN

1 Qty.
2 Scrooge's exclamation
3 "These ___ the times…"
4 Only child's lack
5 90 minutes past noon: Brit.
6 Davis of Do the Right Thing
7 Check again
8 Dullard
9 Visitor to the Tanner family
10 Gandhi's father
11 As to
12 One gentleman of Verona
13 Foucault's Pendulum author
14 "Zip your lip!"
15 Muslim soldier
16 Classical order of architecture
17 Nova precede
21 Psychological injury
23 Some New Yorker covers
24 Roger Rabbit's compatriots
25 Dirt
29 March honoree, for short
30 Straight up, in a way
31 Speechify
32 B movie about litter, homelessness, etc.?
33 Borscht ingredient
34 Divide, as a road
35 Johnson of Laugh-In
38 Way to go?
42 Cluster of feathers
43 Ox
44 B movie about a snake?
45 Zhou___
46 Huge, in poetry
47 Like granny dresses
49 Oaxaca water
50 Now's partner
51 Ovaltine rival
54 Sari wearers
55 1963 Shirley MacLaine role
56 Cast
57 Start of a waffle slogan
60 King, for example
61 Kid's weapon
62 Television's Arledge
63 Ars gratia ___
64 Ship responses
65 Sky-colored: Ger.
66 Pink, in a way
68 "Stop pouring"
71 Ring decision, for short
72 Adult insect
73 Animal sci.
74 Fiancée, eventually
75 Actress Barbara or Tricia
76 Hot
78 Karate's cousin
79 Neighbor of "#"
84 Everest locale
85 Beige colors
86 Treats a wound
87 ___ time (never)
89 Grand slam component
91 It's found on the spine
92 Boring
93 Lemonade servers
94 "¿Quién ___?" ("Who knows?": Sp.)
95 Words of assent
96 Believe It ___
97 Bona ___ (credentials)
99 Practice piece
102 Danish toymaker
104 Oz. and lb.
105 Nonprofessional
106 Tricorn, for example
107 Mouth, in slang
108 LIII x II
109 Atmosphere: Prefix
110 Mao___-tung

Peter Gordon, "B Movies," Tough Puzzles, Crossworder's OWN Newsletter, April 1994. Reprinted with permission of Stanley Newman. This puzzle originally appeared at the annual American Crossword Puzzle Tournament in Stamford, Connecticut.

# CIRCULAR REASONING by Charles E. Gersch

## ACROSS

1 "R-A-G-G" follower
5 __cloud (solar-system region)
9 Saratoga stats
13 Learning place
16 Queens, for short
17 I Don't Care et al.
18 "Poetry Man" singer
19 Under, to Umberto
20 U.N. member since 1960
22 *Garfield* guy
23 Bumper-sticker word
25 Fort Courage company
27 Bustles
30 Not up to par
32 Extreme degree
33 With 34 Across, VIP group
34 See 33 Across
35 Chiang Kai-shek in-laws
38 John__Lennon
39 Guadalcanal's archipelago
41 *Barney Miller* actor
42 Start of an Oliver Stone film title
44 Destiny
45 *You Light Up My Life* star
46 Horror-film director Browning
47 Tupolev product
48 Mah-__
49 Associate
51 Autogiro capability: Abbr.
53 School of whales
54 Italian prime minister of the '60s
56 Diamond shape
59 About preceder
61 Dorm area
64 Rank quality
65 Beach Boys tune of '66
66 Outside: Fr.
67 Bats
68 Confused states

## DOWN

1 Autograph purchases: Abbr.
2 *Der Rosen-kavlier* character
3 "Rats!"
4 *Twenty Years After* character
5 Game-show announcer Johnny
6 Leftover morsel
7 Etymology concern
8 Cap
9 Dictionary abbr.
10 *Paradise* star
11 Lose tautness
12 Dispersed
14 Four Holy Roman emperors
15 An NCO
21 "Smoking__?"
24 Architect of German reunification
26 Oklahoma Indian
27 Second-floor apartment
28 Mr. Bill's shriek
29 Like some sales routes
31 Yo-yos
34 Took
35 Lush
36 Tea-ceremony need
37 Number
39 A "city of the Plain"
40 Witty remarks
43 Japanese drama
45 *The __Mone*y
47 Promenade
48 General Pershing
49 Oceanfront flat
50 Mythical birds
52 Sphere starter
53 Big seller in bear markets
55 Herman Melville is its main character
57 Earth layer
58 Bell sound
60 AT&SF et al.
62 Soft shoe, informally
63 Larry King's radio

*Charles Gersch, "Circular Reasoning," Tough Puzzles,* Crossworder's OWN Newsletter, *August 1992. Reprinted with permission of Stanley Newman.*

## COP-OUT by Henry Hook

### ACROSS
1 Ring master?
6 Vertical
11 Love-seat capacity
14 Gladiatorial milieu
15 Ingredient in French toast?
16 Whammy
17 '45 flyer film
19 Aberdonian's uncle
20 Estevez's brother
21 *Juno and the Paycock* playwright
23 Think quietly
26 Jock
27 From square one
28 Barrel downhill
29 __ *Man Answers*
30 Pack to the future?
32 Page of music
35 Cacophonies
37 Pondered
39 Baseball's Saberhagen
40 Hospital liquid
42 Sophia Loren film of '66
44 *L'eau*land?
45 Still packaged
47 Revolutionary's incendiary
49 Rickles' repertoire
51 Private payments of a sort
52 Ex-Secretary Weinberger
53 Nicely-Nicely's creator
54 Where *on parle francais*
55 Pipe smoker's accessories

60 Many, many years
61 "Were __ That Special Face"
62 On __ (busy)
63 Actress Woods
64 Star's statue
65 Berlin products

### DOWN
1 Apprehend
2 Acapulco gold
3 Deleted
4 Strand
5 Least cautious
6 So far
7 Grief
8 Blow up: Abbr.
9 Item in a Biblical quid pro quo
10 Whopper topper
11 Headline event of '25
12 "Haven't __ before?"
13 Daisy variety
18 Ousted Arizona governor
22 Preakness winner in '42
23 Bookies' nightmares
24 Miss Klinker
25 War of 1870-71
26 Did something
28 "Don't look __" ("Smile")
31 Robert wrote them
33 "You can __ man from Harvard . . ."

34 Gossip-column fare
36 Dawn
38 Superenergetic one
41 One of mixed ancestry
43 Blueprints
46 Coors rival
48 Blanketlike cloak
49 More aloof
50 Shell lining
51 NBA member
53 *Two Years Before the Mast* author
56 Pen name
57 Which came first?
58 Which came first?
59 Letters for help

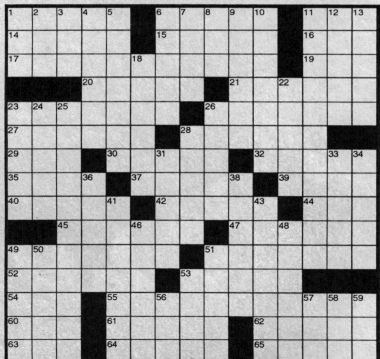

Henry Hook, "Cop-Out," Tough Puzzles, Crossworder's OWN Newsletter, June 1992. Reprinted with permission of Stanley Newman.

# 5 Hollywood Squares
by Donna J. Stone

| WORDS | MINUTES | LETTERS | SCORE | INITIALS |
|---|---|---|---|---|
| | | | | |

Celebrities not found in the Social Register.

## ACROSS

1 Hostile reaction
5 Meat garnish
10 Treats, as flour
15 Life Saver flavor
16 Boss, in Nairobi
17 __ time (singly)
19 Tel __
20 Tony Randall's inept costar?
22 Feet treat
24 Architect Saarinen
25 Porter's kin
26 Biblical ointment
27 Books examiners
28 *thirtysomething* actor
29 Coin
32 Substance in cereals
33 All in
34 Ford followed him
35 Slay
36 Candy shape
37 Line of rotation
38 "You __ heard nothin' yet!"
39 Kojak portrayer
43 *Peanuts'* Lucy Van __
44 Actress Van Vooren
46 "Zip it!"
47 Sylphlike
49 Short exam
50 Help with the dishes
51 Geologic time unit
52 Throw in the towel
53 Exxon mascot
54 Overrun
57 Gave a hint to
58 White weasel
59 "The Swedish Nightingale"
60 Sorority member
61 Get ready, for short
62 Tadpole-to-be
63 E as in "QED"
64 Foolproof
68 Moon Unit's geeky brother?
71 Sound like Simba
72 Islamic greeting
73 Roll with the punches
74 *National Velvet* author Bagnold
75 Battle site of '14

76 *The Threepenny Opera* star
77 Nathan Hale's alma mater

## DOWN

1 Envelope part
2 Not prerecorded
3 In the thick of
4 Geeky *Robin Hood* star?
5 Swear off
6 Grassy surface
7 What leaders set
8 Silk screening need
9 Piece of bakeware
10 Becomes disillusioned
11 __ *the Night* (Pfeiffer film)
12 Moroccan metropolis
13 Hot stuff
14 Yalta attendee
18 Concerning
21 Depend (on)
23 Genesis character
27 Wrote a review of
28 Ineffectual talk-show host?
29 Crisp cookies
30 Video-display dot
31 Napoleon's fate
32 Beethoven's birthplace
33 Bankbook abbr.
35 "New Look" designer
36 *And a Voice to Sing With* author
38 Last word of the New Testament
39 Trump selection
40 Playwright Pirandello
41 Rockies resort
42 Sociologist Hite
45 Piccadilly pound
48 __ Perignon
52 Guatemala's national bird
53 Locust, but not cicada
54 What runners carry
55 Algonquin abode
56 Actress Lansbury
57 Lignite, e.g.
58 Proofreader's discoveries
60 Offense
61 Young boxer
63 Abba of Israel
64 Extend over
65 Island off Scotland
66 Racetrack fence
67 Mahler's *Das Lied von der* __
69 Teacup handle's shape
70 Citrus drink

Donna J. Stone, "Hollywood Squares," *Tough Puzzles,* Crossworder's OWN Newsletter, *February 1992. Reprinted with permission of Stanley Newman.*

boundary-shattering puzzles. The quality and variety of these offerings, along with the work in *GAMES* magazine, far surpassed what the *Times* was then publishing, making evident a substantial groundswell of talent. Maybe even more importantly, Newman's publication engendered a sense of community and mutual support. Rather than the often-cutthroat attitude of puzzle editors at major newspapers, Newman penned encouraging words such as "In many ways, everyone wins in crossword competitions," while also printing honest, straightforward advice aimed at amateurs who wanted to get started writing puzzles. He published playful puzzles in a range of difficulties to accommodate solvers of varying abilities, included constructor profiles that humanized the authors, and even started a "crossword confidential" column so that readers could stay up to date on events and news.

Although indie puzzles would disappear for much of the 1990s after *Crossworder's OWN* ended its run, they returned with a bang around the turn of the century. The first of this next new wave was the syndicated, independent Jonesin' feature, which launched in May 2001. Written by Matt Jones and edited by Matt Gaffney, Jonesin' announced its sensibility through the feature's name—the themes were edgy, the language was fresh and slangy, and very little was considered off-limits. ("Jonesing" can refer to a desire for anything, but it's speculated that it derived from the cravings of heroin addicts.) According to editor Gaffney, the feature was a response to the fact that most alt-weeklies in the U.S. were at that time running the syndicated *New York Times* or other mainstream puzzles, which had little editorial overlap with their own content. Jonesin' intended to fill a gap by providing funny, pop-culture-laden themes about marijuana, tattoos, sex, and other subjects routinely covered by papers in alternative markets. Within a couple of years, Jonesin' had dozens of newspaper subscribers, and was the first successful independent of the young century.

Others followed the lead of Jonesin', including syndicated features by David Levinson-Wilk and Brendan Emmett Quigley. My own weekly puzzle, Ink Well, was the weekly puzzle in the *Village Voice* for a time, before that paper took an assertively libertarian nosedive into irrelevance. Ink Well syndication has had as many as 15 newspapers at a time, all alt-weeklies in North America. In 2006, *The Onion* added a weekly crossword to its non-satirical A.V. Club section, edited by me and constructed by a group of top puzzle makers who wanted to apply their talents to more ambitious and sometimes risqué themes. The content was winking, occasionally politicized, and tuned in to the news in ways that mainstream puzzles could not match. While a major newspaper puzzle generally requires weeks or months of lead-time, the indie puzzles were nimbler operations that could react to the news right away. For example, *The Onion* constructor Byron Walden made an excellent puzzle based on the name Suri immediately after Tom Cruise and Katie Holmes announced their newborn daughter's name; the crossword was proudly embracing its own disposability.

By the late 2000s, the community of independent constructors was once again robust, and offered a diverse and serious alternative to the mainstream. But it was the possibilities of digital distribution that changed the game even more dramatically. Constructor Matt Gaffney launched a site in 2008, and Brendan Emmett Quigley, the sixth-most-published constructor in the history of the *New York Times* and the author of many puzzle books, did the same later in the year. Brendan has a well-deserved reputation for including fresh new words in his grids, and for original themes as well. On the masthead of his new site was a picture of a coffee-stained grid, clues about rappers and synthesizers and *The Wire* conspicuously in view. Few constructors had Brendan's bona fides, and the site was gorgeous. And yet the constructor announced that he would be offering his puzzles for *free*. Moreover, he would create not one but two crosswords each week—three when he began. Brendan saw the site and its original puzzles as a means of advertising his talents that might lead to other gigs, and it did exactly that.

Peter Gordon (no relation to Bernice), former editor of the excellent *New York Sun* crossword, had not been associated with a regular puzzle since that paper folded in 2008, a casualty of the crisis of print media. But Gordon, too, reemerged on the scene in 2010, not long after Quigley's site launched. In a not-so-subtle nod to his former gig, and after a trial period in previous months selling unpublished puzzles that would have been in the *Sun*, Gordon announced a new weekly puzzle called Fireball, which would be sent to subscribers by email for less than $20 a year. Fireball puzzles were to be written by different constructors, and to include both themed and non-themed material. What united them was their high level of difficulty. Gordon wanted to provide a serious challenge with highly inventive gimmicks. Like many of the indie puzzles already flourishing, Fireball also capitalized on the freedom to be edgy when warranted.

Fireball, Matt Gaffney's site, and brendanemmetquigley.com differed even from their recent predecessors in that they were unmoored from the printed page entirely. No news organ granted these puzzles permission to exist. They could not be axed on a whim, nor have their space eyed jealously by publishers in need of more ad space. They did not have to grovel for raises or to contend with overzealous copyeditors. Nor did these puzzles suffer in quality as a result of being unaffiliated with a newspaper. The editors employed their own testers to ensure accuracy and smooth solvability.

As with many things digital, the definition of true "independence" in crosswords can be debated. Modern indie puzzles distributed online or through apps require Internet connections and the mediation of powerful third parties like Apple, Google, and PayPal (which each grab their own pieces of the pie, profitwise). Plus they still need a business model. Discussed further in Chapter Ten *(page 147)*, this now means looking to advertising or solver subscriptions, among other ways of making money. All in all, indie puzzles are not entirely let off the hook by cutting newspapers out of the picture.

Nevertheless, the advantages cannot be denied. Beyond this nimbleness, indie puzzles can afford to be ambitious. Young constructor Neville Fogarty created a project in 2013, supported through the crowd-funding site kickstarter.com, called "The Games People Play." Fogarty envisioned a series of ten puzzles based on classic board games, and set out to raise $1,000 in order to make it worth his while. As he mentioned in his copy for the fund drive, a project like this is not something that many contemporary newspapers or magazines would commission. Those that already have crosswords mostly stick with traditional content, and those that don't have crosswords are unlikely to run them as special features, let alone an entire series. Fogarty ultimately raised two-and-a-half times his initial goal. There are dozens of constructors like him today, who've discovered varying degrees of success.

The rise of indie puzzles in the past decade or so is not without its drawbacks. As the barrier to entry in constructing and self-publishing comes down, the degree of fracture increases. There are now specialty puzzles for every taste, and pop culture specialists creating work for solvers of all persuasions. The tight community of crossword puzzlers is challenged somewhat in a period when not everyone is solving—or even knows about—the same puzzles. However, without question, the era of the independent puzzle has come to fruition in the past decade, and traditional models of distributing and solving the crossword will never be the same.

# YUPPIE RIGHTS OF PASSAGE
## A wry commentary on the "me" generation

**Across**

**1.** Alabama city

**6.** Dance

**10.** Watch over

**14.** Ice-hockey feints

**19.** ___ spades (high card)

**20.** First astronaut's first name

**21.** Spiny succulent

**22.** I.e., for long

**23.** RITE OF PASSAGE #1

**27.** Fair

**28.** Stand for

**29.** Baking-powder additive

**30.** Pre-meal snack

**31.** Recounted

**33.** Dating stars, perhaps

**34.** Difficult situation

**35.** Reserve, as rooms

**37.** Damien's sign

**38.** It may be carved in stone

**39.** New Deal org.

**42.** RITE OF PASSAGE #2

**48.** Shade source

**49.** "The Celtic Twilight" author

**50.** Praiseful poem

**51.** "High ___" (Bogart film)

**52.** Brunei's locale

**54.** Housing-development lot

**55.** Roman romantic poet

**56.** Impoverished

**57.** Punjab princess

**58.** Actress MacGraw

**59.** Greek : Zeus :: Norse : ___

**60.** For one

**62.** RITE OF PASSAGE #3

**69.** Chiding remarks

**70.** French I verb

**71.** The wild West?

**72.** Tidings

**73.** Kind of bull

**76.** Ms. Gardner et al.

**77.** Orion has one

**78.** "Downhill Racer" props

**79.** Bamboozled

**81.** Seating for the masses

**82.** "___ I: Science is We"

**84.** Chemical suffix

**85.** RITE OF PASSAGE #4

**90.** Fixed, as a date

**91.** San ___, PR

**92.** "Somebody bet ___ bay"

**93.** Wear well

**94.** Within reach

97. Caustic substances

98. Fiber source

100. Watches place

101. Rude one

102. Car club: Abbr.

103. Sister of song

107. RITE OF PASSAGE #5

111. "My Friend Flicka" author

112. Porcine palaver

113. Kent State's state

114. Primed the pot

115. Secluded valleys

116. Patch place

117. Queue after Q

118. Archaic exclamations

**Down**

1. Knuckleheads

2. She loved Narcissus

3. Flowery bands

4. Wicked cocktail

5. CIO's partner

6. Played up big

7. Force out

8. Bauxite, e.g.

9. Stabilizes

10. Ryan's daughter

11. Grammar sch.

12. Christie's "___ M?"

13. Priests' subordinates

14. Paul Anka's first hit

15. Icelandic literary works

16. Do a bowling job

17. Salinger title character

18. Farm pen

24. Under the weather

25. Kate Nelligan film of '85

26. Tender touch

32. Give the green light to

33. "Hello, ___ Be Going"

34. Meditated

35. Shampoo ingredient

36. "Your place ___?"

37. Procure

38. Loss liquid

40. Juice extractor?

41. Gumby, essentially

42. "Do I ___ Waltz?"

43. Get ready to go home

44. Cowboys' home

45. Raw recruit

46. Sure thing

47. Makes an ass of oneself

53. Commuter plane

55. Smells

59. Where Mulroney works

60. Raises or praises

61. Vinegary

63. Land-speckled, as oceans

64. Source of the Avon

65. Come out

66. Retirement-village regulation

67. Express pleasure to

68. Henry Ford's son

73. Fraternity letters

74. First-class

75. Verb form

76. Rental listing: Abbr.

77. Rock groups

80. Real-life rerun

83. Room, to Ruiz

86. Go crazy

87. "___ Believe in Magic?"

88. Mistaken

89. Former Chinese capital

95. Ring material

96. Rope sources

97. English empiricist

98. Arm of the Mississippi

99. Modern music

100. Quartet pint

101. Nota ___

102. Working hard

104. Nora's dog

105. Pigeon-___

106. Goes last

107. GQ, e.g.

108. Moral blot

109. Christian abbr.

110. "Norma ___"

## A CURIOUS THING

Before the late 1970s, crossword puzzle people barely knew each other. Other than the crossword fad of 1925, during which time every New Yorker seemed to be solving all the time, and a competition now and then, crosswords were primarily a solitary activity. But in the 1970s, the dedicated hobbyists and the professionals began reaching out to each other and holding get-togethers. These progressed into competitions on the East Coast and eventually the West Coast, as well as casual meet-ups to talk shop. Today, annual puzzle competitions have sprung up all across the country, including Lollapuzzoola in New York City each August, and regional contests in Boston, Chicago, Brooklyn, and Los Angeles, and many more. The 2006 documentary *Wordplay* was filmed at the annual American Crossword Puzzle Tournament, then held in Stamford, which hundreds attend from all over the world every year.

*Eric Albert and Peg Primak, "Yuppie Rights of Passage," Long Island Open, February 1991. Reprinted with permission of Stanley Newman.*

# Stretch Those Quads!
## A hardcore freestyle workout

**Across**

1. Second half of a ball game?
5. Used (to)
15. She uses a bird to sweep the house
17. Computer overhaul
18. Arian Foster stats
19. Little sip
20. Gold, to Guatemalans
21. "Who Wants to Marry a Multi-Millionaire?" network
22. Bodybuilder's units
24. Word before Earth or City, in computer games
27. Drab shade
29. She was Dorothy on "The Golden Girls"
30. Org. that listens for alien signals
31. It's obsolete
35. Jovial question from someone eager to help
36. It covers Miami, Montpelier and Montreal
37. SOPA subject
38. Opera follower?
39. New Year's, in Hanoi
40. Mandolin relative
41. Nancy Grace's network
42. Southwest sch. whose mascot is King Triton
44. Daily grind
45. Homey
46. "___ Ho" (Best Original Song Oscar winner of 2008)
47. The D in OED
50. Easy lunch to prepare
56. Insider's knowledge
57. Viktor Bout or Adnan Khashoggi
58. Dark form of quartz

**Down**

1. Off-kilter
2. Messed with the facts
3. World Series precursor, for short
4. "As I see it," in chatrooms
5. Tack on
6. Shorten nails
7. Smoke
8. Palindromic prime minister of the 1940s-60s
9. Leather sharpener
10. Old rulers
11. Chemist Hahn
12. Oneself, cutely
13. Roxy Music name
14. Room for board games, perhaps
16. Person with a booming voice, often
21. Donut shop option
22. Upgraded
23. Fail spectacularly, like a skateboarder
24. British structure of WWII
25. "No need to pay"
26. Bishops' wear
27. Grain alcohol
28. Put someone in their place
29. Some hats worn on The Oregon Trail
30. Lose your composure, in junior high-speak
31. "Anchors ___"
32. Senator Jake who flew on the Space Shuttle Discovery
33. The plate
34. Ophthalmologist's concerns
42. Implored
43. Richard who played Don Barzini in "The Godfather"
44. Vacation time, in slang
45. ___ the Younger (Arthurian knight)
46. Director Campion
47. Zoologist Fossey
48. Disgusting
49. Cereal with gluten-free varieties
50. Org. that bestows merit badges
51. "Love, Reign ___ Me" (The Who)
52. 420, for 20 and 21: abbr.
53. "Just as I suspected!"
54. "On the Road" protagonist ___ Paradise
55. "Never heard of her"

*Matt Jones, "Stretch Those Quads!" Jonesin', May 9, 2012. Reprinted with permission of Matt Jones and Matt Gaffney. This puzzle is one of the more elegant examples in the history of crosswords of a grid with four adjacent 15-letter entries.*

# Across

**1.** Big letters, for short (and what your answers must be written in to understand the theme)

**5.** Hiking path

**10.** "Which came first?" choice

**13.** Clapton or Cartman

**14.** "The Freshmaker" candy

**16.** Stuff to fix a squeaky hinge

**17.** Aligned correctly

**19.** Pompous attribute

**20.** Stun gun relative

**21.** Jewel

**22.** Amy Winehouse hit

**24.** Complainer's sounds

**26.** 1980s hairstyle that may have involved a kit

**27.** Donut shop quantities

**30.** Cop show with the line "Just the facts, ma'am"

**33.** Cupid's Greek counterpart

**34.** Wire-___ (like some terriers' coats)

**37.** Rowboat propeller

**38.** Send a document over phone lines

**39.** Devices that, when turned, adjust themselves (just like the theme answers)

**40.** Greek vowel

**41.** Biblical verb suffix

**42.** Audrey Tautou's quirky title role of 2001

**43.** Stay away from

**44.** Changed an area of town from residential to commercial, e.g.

**46.** They're collected in passports

**48.** Coffee dispensers

**49.** Cartoonist Guisewite, or her comic strip

**51.** Faith that emphasizes the oneness of humanity

**53.** Rapper ___ Def

**54.** Walkway on an airplane

**58.** Bullfighting cheer

**59.** Neil Armstrong went on one

**62.** Homer's outburst

**63.** It's tossed after a wedding

**64.** Charity benefit, say

**65.** View

**66.** Doesn't eat for a while

**67.** Bridge's length

# Down

**1.** Like some checks: abbr.

**2.** Opera solo

**3.** Sty dwellers

**4.** Crafty plans

**5.** Symbols after brand names

**6.** Rule over a kingdom

**7.** South American mountain range

**8.** Checklist component

**9.** Rawls of R&B

**10.** "Land sakes alive that's awesome!"

**11.** Prefix for byte meaning "one billion"

**12.** Amorphous clump

**15.** Jam, margarine and cream cheese

**18.** Sci-fi film set inside a computer

**23.** Exercise machine unit

**25.** Makes embarrassed

**26.** Class warmup before a big exam

**27.** Postpone

**28.** Make big speeches

**29.** Do the "I am not a crook" thing with the double V-signs, for example?

**30.** Three, in Germany

**31.** Completely devour

**32.** ___ fatty acids

**35.** Troy's friend on "Community"

**36.** Under the weather

**39.** ___ salon

**43.** Well-known quotations

**45.** "Are you a man ___ mouse?"

**47.** Warm up after being in the freezer

**49.** Amounts on a bill

**50.** Liability counterpart

**51.** Physiques, casually

**52.** Lotion ingredient

**53.** Actress Sorvino

**55.** Dove or Ivory

**56.** Hit for the Kinks

**57.** Actor McGregor

**60.** Clumsy sort

**61.** Org. that provides W-2 forms

*Matt Jones, "Adjusted to Fit Your Screen," Jonesin', September 25, 2012. Reprinted with permission of Matt Jones and Matt Gaffney. This puzzle reflects a highly challenging and original theme that requires the solver to reorient their thinking. Jones's puzzle was widely regarded as among the best of the year.*

# Onion A.V. Club
## June 29, 2011

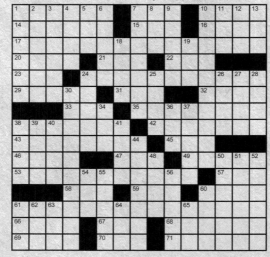

**Across**

**1.** Any piece by Girl Talk, e.g.

**7.** Intensifier after adjectives like big and weak

**10.** "Tony ___: Shred" (skateboarding video game)

**14.** Golf star Sörenstam

**15.** Ocasek of the Cars

**16.** Cartoon character whose name sounds like a drug mishap

**17.** Passed a certain medical school exam?

**20.** Sirens announce their arrival

**21.** ___ stand (college party trick)

**22.** Year that will start seeming retro in 2070 or so

**23.** Driver's ID: Abbr.

**24.** Item used to settle disputes about mathematical connectedness?

**29.** "Chicago Hope" actress Christine

**31.** Pretty big stretch?

**32.** A rat might wear one

**33.** Mendes or Longoria

**35.** Wii maker

**38.** With 42-Across, what people who study living creatures are?

**42.** See 38-Across

**43.** Cozier version of a couch

**45.** Destination of many a fake ID user

**46.** Is in the hole

**47.** Deadbeat ___

**49.** They might be used for daily backups

**53.** Study of how to fight in very low temperatures?

**57.** Sound heard in a Lamaze class

**58.** Cells contributing to the need for a Lamaze class

**59.** Lucy of "Kung Fu Panda"

**60.** Match up

**61.** What the constructor had to do to create the theme entries in this puzzle (boyee)

**66.** He reprised Michael's "Alfie" role

**67.** Bros outrank them, some say

**68.** Romp

**69.** Bed bugs?

**70.** Item that coyotes can purchase via mail, apparently

**71.** "___ nice to be dating someone sane!"

**Down**

**1.** Nickname for an old monopoly

**2.** Condition requiring iron supplements

**3.** Grab

**4.** Frequently downloaded songs

**5.** Instrument featured on Eddie Vedder's new album, casually

**6.** Bread crumbs used to make tempura

**7.** Three-time Viggo Mortensen role

**8.** Take a load off

**9.** Loser

**10.** Tinseltown, to a right-winger

**11.** ___ Annie of "Oklahoma!"

**12.** Part of a drag outfit

**13.** Important

**18.** Muppet prawn introduced in 1996

**19.** "Holy crap!", in a text

**24.** Some Netflix delivery systems

**25.** Secular

**26.** Namesake of many a pizza place

**27.** Language of Pakistan

**28.** "Matrix" protagonist and hopefully someone else someday, so this can be a less dubious crossword entry

**30.** Tools for astronomers and creeps

**34.** Inaccurate info on many online dating profiles

**36.** Pencil on its last legs

**37.** Morgan who is "too sleepy and self-centered to ever hurt another person," per Tina Fey

**38.** Drug that is, ironically, inhaled

**39.** Sioux City's state

**40.** Not cool anymore

**41.** "How ___ Dat" (Master P song)

**44.** Closest to heaven, in a way

**48.** Kill

**50.** Endangered ungulates

**51.** Some grills

**52.** "I can't ___ catch a break"

**54.** Road trip vehicles

**55.** Castaway : raft :: millionaire : ___

**56.** Brand repeated in a Kreayshawn track title

**60.** Jon Bon ___

**61.** You can hear them spin

**62.** Boring pattern

**63.** Queer

**64.** Atomic alternative

**65.** Have

# Onion A.V. Club
## July 20, 2011

**Across**

1. People to hang with
5. Nile risks
9. Fashion designer's asset
14. Punk rocker Tessa Pollitt, e.g.
15. New York's Carnegie ___
16. Prefix meaning "false"
17. Phone button below 7
18. Like Marlee Matlin
19. "Jack and Coke" star Artie
20. Bangkok native into orgies?
23. Home of the National Bunraku Theatre
24. "No returns"
25. ___ chi (meditative martial art)
28. Heavenly figure?
30. Defeat
32. Doofus
35. Wonka candy sometimes stuck to a licorice rope
38. Organization that approves athletic sites: Abbr.
39. Prague native appearing as an extra?
43. Storybook beast
44. Pitch
45. Saturn car model
46. Events
49. H.S. math class
51. Clairvoyance, e.g.
52. Like "Beowulf"
55. Cordial flavoring
58. South African native with a lousy driving record?
61. Billiards bounce
64. Journalist Lisa, formerly of "The View"
65. Julie Christie role in "Dr. Zhivago"
66. Master, in Swahili
67. Penny, perhaps
68. Destination for vacationing whiskey lovers
69. "There's Something About Mary" fluid
70. Word before ring or swing
71. ___ off (pissy)

**Down**

1. "Hey ... over here!"
2. E'en if
3. ABC's "Pretty Little ___"
4. Barely make it across the field?
5. Kool-Aid instruction
6. "___ Little Light" (bio of Hüsker Dü's Bob Mould)
7. Gangsta with game
8. Sorts (through)
9. 1984 romantic comedy starring Tom Hanks and Daryl Hannah
10. Ming ___, of public television's show "Simply Ming"
11. Craving
12. Schlep
13. Eastern Netherlands city
21. Squeezing (out)
22. Sellout, perhaps
25. Stuns, in a way
26. Between ___ and ...
27. Scratchy partner on "The Simpsons"
29. Oscar Wilde's "The Garden of ___"
31. "We ___ robbed!"
32. Dwelling
33. Palms with starchy piths
34. Military money substitute
36. Copy: Abbr.
37. Foul mood
40. Doll who dated Skipper's sister for 43 years
41. Insane
42. Static ___
47. Like Heidi Klum
48. Place for sweaters?
50. Gravy ingredient
53. Muhammad's religion
54. Material for uniforms
56. "___ we dating or what?"
57. Not quite right
58. Ice cream holder
59. Digging, so to speak
60. Think tank unaffiliated with Ayn
61. "60 Minutes" network
62. Amazement
63. Ewe's mate

Deb Amlen, July 20, 2011. Onion A.V. Club, Reprinted with permission of Deb Amlen and Ben Tausig.

# Onion A.V. Club
## August 31, 2011

**Across**

1. March composer
6. "In what way?"
11. Course average
14. Some Italian cars, for short
15. Nymph of the mountains
16. "Pokémon" boy
17. Refinements gained by experience?
19. She lacks horns
20. Unit tracked by the Nikkei Index
21. With 23-Across, what Bridgestone says in response to Goodyear's history?
23. See 21-Across
28. No, to Nijinsky
29. Western apparel store stock
30. Go all out at a party
33. Gp. for people with suits
34. Sedona maker
35. Numbered compositions
39. Limiting one's legal liability?
43. Dissolved substance, in chemistry classes
44. Units marked on a wooden stick: Abbr.
45. Noted gp. of entertainment and sports talent reps
46. Metal projectile in Stooges shorts
48. "Star Wars Episode III - Revenge of the ___ "
49. Half of a Blahnik pair
52. My response to feeling bad about Maynard James Keenan's band?
55. Sticky part of the roof?
58. ___ culpa
59. "Brokeback Mountain" director Lee
60. What Crystal Harris became famous for doing in 2011, and a hint to the theme
66. Chicken ___ Biskit
67. Circumvent
68. Poke fun
69. Sex columnist Savage
70. Full of lip
71. Do a half-___ job

**Down**

1. Test with an essay section
2. Pay stub?
3. Their fights take place in The Octagon
4. Mythical man-beasts
5. Owned property
6. There's one in Canton, OH and another in Springfield, MA
7. Magic board abbreviation?
8. Chinese artist and political activist Ai ___
9. Sound partner
10. Had a bad trip, in a way
11. Rice field
12. In unison
13. Butler who ended with "damn"
18. Thunder Bay's prov.
22. Opinions
23. Casualties of the Iranian Revolution
24. Verboten thing
25. In any way
26. Greenwich Village assent circa 1968
27. GPS ancestor
31. Drags down the street, in a way
32. Station absorbed by the CW
34. Meniscus spot
36. Path opening for nuts?
37. Muse of love poetry
38. "60 Minutes" correspondent Lesley
40. Con man's marks
41. "Is ___, Lord?" (disciples' query)
42. Science magazine started by Bob Guccione's wife
47. They show the Virgin Mary
48. Denial and bargaining, in the grieving process
49. Unsexy
50. Barbera's partner in cartooning
51. Instrument with foot pedals
53. "Why don't you discuss that with your urologist instead of me? Sheesh ..."
54. Nosy person
56. Mid-month time
57. Female megastar, in music
61. Music purchases stored in wallets
62. "Over here!"
63. Is down with
64. -speak
65. Bernanke's group, for short

*Matt Jones*, Onion A.V. Club, *August 31, 2011. Reprinted with permission of Matt Jones and Ben Tausig.*

**Across**

1. They provide holes for leather enthusiasts
5. "The Naked __" (Goya painting)
9. Put on the books, as a law
14. "This might have been a mistake"
15. "Date ___" (MTV matchmaking show involving a mediating parent)
16. Certain "American Idol" viewer
17. Mrs. Nicolas Cage, for 108 days
20. Mrs. Tom Green, for 163 days
21. S&M stroke
22. Pool worker?
26. Robert California, on "The Office," e.g.
29. "The Last King of Scotland" name
32. Language that gives us "banjo" and "gumbo"
33. Frazier downer
34. Mr. Carmen Electra, for 9 days
38. One lap around the track, say
39. How Salt-n-Pepa want you to push it
40. Combustion engine starter: Abbr
41. Mr. Renee Zellweger, for 225 days
43. Wedding page word
44. Emollient plants
45. Suffix with gang
46. Pastoral work
47. Novice bookkeeper, typically
49. Some notebooks
52. Mrs. Kris Humphries, for 72 days
59. Mr. Jean Acker, for 6 hours
62. Overly delicate
63. Crosshairs user, e.g.
64. "___ no thang"
65. Ices
66. Goes out for a little while?
67. Elevation

**Down**

1. "___ Lang Syne"
2. White noise sound
3. Disappoint the coach, perhaps
4. Prayer coverings
5. One gift of the Magi
6. Protagonist of "The Kite Runner"
7. Post-"Friends" flop
8. West Coast convenience store chain
9. Word before "knows," "hurts," and "dance now," in various song titles
10. Bridge protector
11. 2006 T.I. film
12. ___ Lo Green ("Fuck You!" singer)
13. Rugby score
15. "Serpico" author
18. Degree for W.
19. Go bad
23. Under consideration
24. Histrionic
25. See 30-Down
26. Croatian, e.g.
27. 1976 greatest hits album with the track "Evil Woman"
28. Join (with)
29. Fjord, e.g.
30. With 25-Down, interrupts a sentence with a shovel?
31. Actively takes, as meds
34. Accidents dealt with by whisk brooms
35. Old Common Market initials
36. Slangy negatives
37. Sushi topper
42. Beer, in British slang
46. Film that ended Elaine May's directorial career
48. Roadie load
49. Goes nowhere
50. Max of "The Beverly Hillbillies"
51. AOL alternative
53. Iconic cry for Captain Kirk
54. 1987 Reebok acquisition
55. Skatepark fixture
56. Four, on some sundials
57. Taylor and Wilson
58. Staff member?
59. Sixties pol with eleven kids
60. Former Jerusalem mayor ___ Lupolianski
61. Indian lentil dish

*Byron Walden*, Onion A.V. Club, *November 30, 2011. Reprinted with permission of Byron Walden and Ben Tausig.*

## Onion A.V. Club
### August 29, 2012

**Across**

1. Epic ____
5. Capital of Jordan
10. Fake
14. Anvil brand
15. Cause to stir
16. Lessen
17. Chicago basketball team sold to the Vatican?
19. Isn't for some people?
20. Bro's partner
21. J.J. Abrams show filmed mostly in Hawaii
22. Wino
23. St. Louis hockey team sold to a high school?
26. Serious and kind of scary
29. Major video game franchise
30. "Peachy!"
31. "Rocky Horror Picture Show" dance
35. Wheels
36. Lowly workers
38. Take action, legally
39. Teleport, as Harry Potter
42. Toyota brand
44. Pay monthly, say
45. Some Gypsies
47. Minnesota baseball team sold to Thailand?
51. Alfred of publishing
52. Figure in falsified photos
53. Big bird
56. Crucifix letters
57. Philadelphia football team sold to Just For Men?
60. Paul's ticket mate
61. Provide spirit, in a way
62. Quaint, quaintly
63. Vegetables in some risotto recipes
64. Brings in
65. Cold one

**Down**

1. Jacks off, slangily
2. Hip berry
3. Tricksters
4. Ashton's "New Year's Eve" costar
5. Shady places
6. Fluffy chocolate dessert
7. National beginning?
8. Mating call in a chat room
9. 1980s gaming console
10. Spit alternative
11. Poem read in a Zen garden, perhaps
12. Red-headed orphan
13. Doles (out)
18. Grassy plain
22. Fit
23. One returning from the theater?
24. Underfed, maybe
25. Turkey Day tubers
26. Machu Picchu person
27. Tide table term
28. It's pulled out by a groundcrew
31. Little dipper?
32. Major manufacturing continent
33. Texted question of concern
34. Brave crossword solver's tools
36. Gives one star, say
37. Suffix for small rooms
40. Deodorant targets
41. Something for snorkelers to look at but not touch
42. Justice Sotomayor
43. Walgreens competitor
45. European country with a king
46. Pop purchases
47. Pinch pennies
48. Common belly feature
49. Main channel
50. ____, the Creator
53. Character Woods who invented the "bend and snap"
54. Ancient Persian
55. Drug addict
57. Dating letters
58. "Found you!"
59. Bluth brother

Aimee Lucido, Onion A.V. Club, August 29, 2012. Reprinted with permission of Aimee Lucido and Ben Tausig.

# CHAPTER SEVEN

# Mentoring: How Puzzles Move Across and Down Generations

When I began constructing puzzles in 2004, I knew little about the lineage of mentorship of which I was becoming a part. Crossword talent is decidedly not a natural skill, but rather something every constructor has to figure out how to acquire. I say "figure out" because, until recently, the resources for learning the trade were woefully limited, as well as scattered. And even today most constructors are autodidacts to some extent, meaning we teach ourselves, though if we're lucky we may have also had a great mentor at some stage.

My own story is not unusual. I was fortunate enough to become a student of Nancy Salomon, a prolific constructor who volunteers her time to give feedback to newbies. Nancy doesn't advertise her services anywhere. You just have to be lucky enough to find her. After some 20 years, she has directly mentored more constructors than perhaps anyone in the history of the genre.

In the middle of 2004, I sent an email to cruciverb-l listserv to see if any other novices in my situation might want to swap puzzles for feedback. I'd never published anywhere, and in truth didn't especially have plans to do so. I thought it might be fun to write one or two solvable puzzles for friends, and at the furthest reaches of my imagination, I thought about landing a puzzle in a serious daily newspaper and then hanging it on my wall as a novelty after moving on to other pursuits.

Nancy, however, would have none of that. She responded to my email by saying that she would be happy to look at my puzzle, but needed no feedback in return. I sent her a grid I'd been working on using spreadsheet software at work (an ill-advised method attempted by many a constructor starting out), just something I'd thrown together as an experiment. But Nancy took it seriously, replying within hours that "I'm afraid this just doesn't hack it ... I wouldn't be doing you a favor if I jollied you into believing that an editor would accept your fill." Until then, I'd barely considered publishing, editors, and all else that goes into puzzling at the highest level. Nancy, however, immediately began encouraging me to aim for the *New York Times* with every theme idea, and it raised my expectations significantly.

She and I corresponded many times daily, as I practically barraged her with proposals and questions. The utter mess of a puzzle that I started with gradually gave way to decent work with flaws, until my mentor had diligently kneaded every glaring problem out of my grids and themes. All of the bad habits, all of the drifting toward shortcuts and laziness that characterize immature construction, were identified and chased out.

It went on like this for months—she seemed infinitely generous—until one day we had an argument. Nancy can be prickly now and then, and she doesn't mince words. I sent her a theme idea she didn't like, and she explained why in no uncertain terms. However, I disagreed with her reasoning. (She could, at times, be eviscerating even when she was out of her area of expertise. Said one fellow constructor: "My favorite exchange with Nancy was when she lectured me on using plural names when there's only famous person with that name; the entry? PILATES.") In a combative mood myself, I defended the quality of my theme, and moreover told her that she was being unduly harsh. Nancy replied, rather stoically this time, that given how I replied she now knew I was truly ready. She suggested I leave her tutelage and strike out on my own as a constructor, at last. We remain friends, but our mentor-mentee relationship ended exactly then.

A few constructors have taught formal crossword classes, including Caleb Madison and Ian Livengood's Jewish Association of Services for the Aged (JASA) course, which has resulted in multiple *New York Times* publications. However, the great majority of crossword educations read much more like mine—unstructured and idiosyncratic.

Historically, no single figure has been more important in mentorship than the editor. Peter Gordon—particularly when he edited the *New York Sun*—was known for providing voluminous feedback to constructors who sent him puzzles. Constructor Sam Donaldson shared with me one of the long conversations he had with Gordon about an early puzzle idea. "Hopefully the submission below won't completely reek of naïvety," wrote Donaldson in his initial message. Gordon wrote back with a litany of problems about the theme proposal, each of which came with a carefully explained rationale. The correspondence continued through many messages, with the theme evolving each time, until Gordon wrote, "Much better. You're close now." A few tweaks later, and the theme was accepted for publication.

Margaret Farrar, the first editor of the *Times*, also had a reputation as a great source of constructive feedback for aspiring solvers. Those who worked with her have almost universally positive memories. Mel Taub, in an interview from the Pre-shortzian Puzzle Project, says, "Mrs. Farrar was a lovely, caring person. You got a personal note with a critique rather than a rejection slip."

In fact, the rejection letter has a special role in the education of constructors. Though it can sting to receive one, these correspondences from editors are often the ones that truly mold puzzle makers, as opposed to acceptances. The most valuable rejection letters find the smallest germ of a good idea in a newbie's theme concept and extol it, demonstrating to the would-be constructor that they're on the right track after all. Then, the editor's letter catalogs the problems with a theme—inconsistency, unfamiliarity, lack of surface sense—perhaps going on to suggest alternative entries, or at least routes to *finding* alternatives. If these problems were resolved, the letter might say, then the theme would be publishable. And if the editor is especially rigorous, they might pull out a few of the strongest and weakest grid entries, praising colorful phrases and tsk-tsking partial phrases like AMAN or OFLIFE and rarities like ELD (an old-fashioned way of saying "old"). The next time a constructor works on a puzzle, it's a simple step to imagine the voice of an editor in one's head, reminding them not to allow even a single poor entry into the grid. This is a major part of how the best constructors develop self-discipline.

Finally, many constructors today cite books as important sources of information and puzzle wisdom. There haven't been many full-length texts published about how to construct a puzzle, but those that exist are highly revered. The two primary resources are Stan Kurzban and Mel Rosen's *Random House Puzzlemaker's Handbook* (1995) (initially published as *The Compleat Cruciverbalist: Or How to Solve and Compose Crossword Puzzles for Fun and Profit* in 1981), and Patrick Berry's *Crossword Puzzle Challenges, for Dummies* (2004)[9].

Before the era of *The Compleat Cruciverbalist* (which is

---

## A CURIOUS THING

Some of the most useful books for new constructors don't offer direct instruction at all. For example, Michelle Arnot's *What's Gnu? A History of the Crossword Puzzle* demystifies crosswords by explaining the history behind some of their less intuitive conventions, such as rebuses and abbreviation indicators. Moreover, Arnot delves into the personalities and styles of different editors, which casual solvers usually know little about. Meanwhile, Matt Gaffney's brilliant *Gridlock: Crossword Puzzles and the Mad Geniuses Who Create Them* (2006) includes a series of playful chapters on puzzle technology, the puzzle book market, and unique crossword personalities. An illuminating look into the puzzle "scene," Gaffney's book is full of helpful details in spite of giving only limited instructions for how to make a puzzle.

# ROWS GARDEN #32 – HARDER VERSION
## by Andrew J. Ries

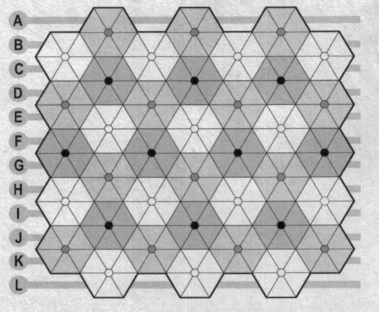

*Andrew Ries, Aries Puzzles, July 2011. Reprinted with permission of Andrew Ries. Ries publishes his Rows Garden puzzles on ariespuzzles. com. The genre was created by Patrick Berry, but Ries today is its most active constructor. Both of these puzzles are clued at the difficult level.*

## ROWS

**A** Annual college football showdowns held in Pasadena: 2 words

**B** Blockbuster 1962 war film that was the highest-grossing black-and-white film until *Schindler's List*, with "The": 2 words

Belmont Stakes-winning jockey a record six times: 2 words

**C** Charles Guiteau, e.g.

"Cogito ergo sum" speaker: 2 words

**D** Dumbfound

Don't waste a second: 3 words

**E** Ecosystem in southern Africa which means "endless plains"

Even-keeled and friendly in nature: Hyph.

**F** Failing to see beyond what's very close

"Foot soldiers" for a retail store: 2 words

**G** *Grey's Anatomy* unit for those on life support, perhaps: 2 words

Getting all gussied up, say

**H** Honor named for the inventor of dynamite: 2 words

Hit 1977 Billy Joel album which features "Only the Good Die Young": 2 words

**I** Items listed on a recipe

Implausibility : gnus :: ___ : larks

**J** Jay-Z and Jamie Foxx, for two: 2 words

Jade is traditional for a couple's thirty-fifth one

**K** Kids who aren't hip, in '50s slang

*Khartoum* co-star, 1966: 2 words

**L** Lover's path indicator: 2 words

## WHITE BLOOMS

"Aw, shucks!": 2 words

Butcher's activity

Emulates Cicero, perhaps

Jimmy Dorsey tune of 1957: 2 words

Least strict, as a disciplinarian

Machine shop tools for making baseball bats, perhaps

Many Leslie Nielsen films

One giving an endorsement?

Places to get a perm

Swirling currents

Title character in a Wagner opera

Turned sharply: Var.

___ Vision (optical chain)

Zone

## MEDIUM BLOOMS

Ancient Balkan land whence Spartacus

Blueprint

"Blue Velvet" crooner Bobby

Bodily metaphor for ill temper

Distress signals

Downfall

Followed orders

Gets into a catcher's position

Hasty writing

Hunter's traps

Legal officer, briefly

___ Pointe, Michigan

Quaint ankle covering

Radio format featuring Sam Cooke, perhaps

## DARK BLOOMS

". . . ___, and the Lord taketh away" (verse in Job)

Bulk cigarette purchase

Casino employee

Female, e.g.

Head of a nunnery

Least batty

Potatoes, slangily

Recoil in fear

Snuggle up

When many stores open: 2 words

# ROWS GARDEN #85 – HARDER VERSION
## by Andrew J. Ries

In the EASIER version, the Blooms clues are listed in the order they appear in the grid, left to right, top to bottom. In the HARDER version, the Blooms clues are listed in alphabetical order.

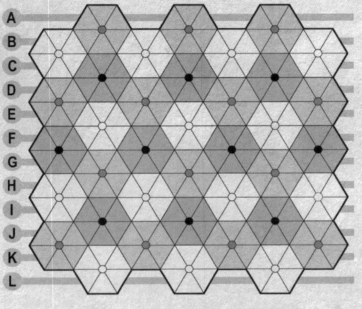

*Andrew Ries, Aries Puzzles, July 2012. Reprinted with permission of Andrew Ries.*

## ROWS

**A** Liquor store sign in place to deter underage drinking: 3 words

**B** Fast time for many Middle Easterners
San Francisco attraction that features the Japanese Tea Garden: 3 words

**C** Renaissance painter nicknamed "Il Furioso"
Play that examined the marriage of Torvald and Nora Helmer: 3 words

**D** Bet between co-workers: 2 words
Monolith known as Wox Niiinon in Arapaho: 2 words

**E** It may include a FICO score: 2 words
Musical group that may include bongos and maracas: 2 words

**F** Acting mischievously: 4 words
Events often facilitated by an auctioneer: 2 words

**G** Current opposition?
Pop-up producer, perhaps: 2 words

**H** Something widely known but not officially recognized: 2 words
The infamous "Make Money Fast" scam, e.g.: 2 words

**I** Stock character in a white coat and frazzled hair, often: 2 words
Under-the-hood enclosure

**J** Rub components
"We should grab a bite sometime": 3 words

**K** Bronx cheers, say
Manhattan section once known as the Silk Stocking District: 3 words

**L** Took another plunge?

## WHITE BLOOMS

Believers in a non-intervening god
Filling station unit
Kanye West or Jay-Z, e.g.
L.A.'s Staples ___
Laura's counterpart during the 2004 presidential campaign
More collected
Obtained
Puts to shame
Short of comedy
*Six Feet Under* star Peter
Skulls
Staunch denial: 3 words
Stylist's application
Walked confidently

## MEDIUM BLOOMS

1968–75 TV police drama starring Martin Milner: Hyph.
Aer ___
Becomes entrenched: 2 words
Carnegie or Mellon
Like many recovery programs: Hyph.
Moved like a snail, say
Party-___ (wet blanket)
Relied, with "on"
Strongbox
Swanky retreats
Tire's grooves
Verizon acquisition of 2008
Washington State hub: Hyph.
"You ___!" (folksy agreement)

## DARK BLOOMS

Bamboo units
Dots in the sea
Drunk as a skunk
If all goes perfectly: 2 words
Lament after a fruitless search: 2 words
Like *Fifty Shades of Grey*
Most unspoiled
Not going up or down
Steve of *Tropic Thunder*
Team that became the Thunder, for short

now out of print but sometimes shows up for sale used) crosswords were arguably a simpler pursuit. Themes were limited or non-existent, intricate "stunt" puzzles were largely unheard of, and the bar for broad recognizability of grid entries had not yet been raised. The pursuit involved little more than arranging words. Of course, there were great constructions in the early years of puzzledom. But there were certainly fewer rules, norms, and conventions to navigate.

*The Compleat Cruciverbalist* uses an archaic variant spelling of "complete" in its title, but there is more to this decision than sounding self-consciously old-fashioned. Since the publication of Isaac Walton's *The Compleat Angler* in 1653, the word "compleat" has been used in many book names to mean "quintessential" or "well-honed." "Compleat cruciverbalist" is therefore a reference to the well-rounded constructor the authors hope to mold. Writing before construction software made filling a grid far simpler, Kurzban and Rosen explain which words to use to produce a friendly grid. An entry like RELATED alternates vowels and consonants, all of which are common in English. It is easy to find words that cross RELATED. The book even includes small blank grids, three squares by three squares, that the solver can practice filling.

The authors give plain-English explanations for basic crossword rules like the limit on black square count, typical word limits for different-sized puzzles, and the arrangement of theme entries in a grid. They also introduce common constructor lingo, concepts like cheater squares, corners, and unchecked letters. Even today, a new constructor reading this book would pick up a lot of the relevant local language. But even beyond technical rules, Rosen and Kurzban offer valuable insight into *style*, that hard-to-describe sense of voice and variety that makes a puzzle sparkle. With regard to cluing: "Imagery is most important. 'Picnic umbrella' evokes thoughts of pleasant outings. 'Shade giver' is lifeless." It is precisely this kind of advice that helped a generation of puzzlers learn not only to construct correctly, but with flair.

More than 20 years later, Patrick Berry published his vaunted *Crossword Puzzle Challenges for Dummies*. The difference between Berry's book, which is exceptionally lucid, and *The Compleat Cruciverbalist*, reveals how much crosswords changed in the interim years. Berry begins his discussion about construction by talking about themes. Themed puzzles had become so much the norm by the early 2000s (and even earlier) that constructors had to develop a theme idea before it was even worth trying to fill a grid. For example, Nancy Salomon wouldn't look at my grids or clues until she had declared my themes up to snuff. So it made sense for Berry to begin there. Moreover, given how many great rule-breaking puzzles had been published in the 1990s and early 2000s, Berry saw fit not only to explain the "correct" way to make a puzzle, but also some of the ways that the typical conventions could be flouted to creative effect.

Today, the web site cruciverb.com is probably the most important resource for new constructors. Cruciverb has many useful free areas, including publisher specifications for various outlets, a "sage advice" section, and "notes from a mentor" by Nancy Salomon herself, as well as a subscriber-only puzzle database with a searchable archive of clues for any word that's ever appeared in a major outlet. In addition to the cruciverb-l listserv, a number of blogs play host to active discussions in the solving and constructing community. American Crossword Puzzle Tournament elite finisher Amy Reynaldo's Diary of a Crossword Fiend (crosswordfiend.com) and Rex Parker's Rex Parker Does the *NY Times* Crossword (rexwordpuzzle.blogspot.

com) are the top two destinations nowadays for insiders, and both sites are excellent places to pick the brains of the top minds in the business. For the most part, they're also friendly communities, to boot.

The Wordplay blog on the web site of the *New York Times* (wordplay.blogs.nytimes.com) features great daily reviews of the puzzle by Deb Amlen as well as conversation from both insiders and casual solvers about the *Times* puzzle in particular. It's another go-to spot. Because of the Internet, the once diffuse process of piecing together information about how to write puzzles has become more centralized and straightforward.

# CHAPTER EIGHT

## Technology

As a constructor, one of the questions I am asked most often is whether I use software to build puzzles and, if so, whether that is considered cheating. As an editor, one of the most common questions I get is whether solving with the aid of a search engine is considered cheating.

Suffice it to say that the answer to both questions, at least from me, is a resounding no. As to the first question, the majority of constructors today work on computers, and as to the second, it's better to learn something new with a hint than to remain mystified and unenlightened. Nevertheless, it is true that new technologies have raised provocative questions in the puzzle world. As with baseball fans, integrity matters a lot to crossword solvers. Digital assistance, like performance-enhancing drugs, requires us to reconsider the rules of engagement, even when we know it's just a game.

Technology has changed puzzles on a number of fronts. We'll begin with construction, and talk about solving a little later. At the most basic level, popular programs like Crossfire and Crossword Compiler allow constructors to lay grids out electronically, obviating any need to pay attention to symmetrical placement of squares. This is a bit of inside baseball, but ever since Margaret Farrar's tenure at the *New York Times*, it has been a rule that black squares in puzzles must be set up with 180° rotational symmetry—in other words, if you spin a puzzle halfway around in any direction, the placement of black squares will be the same as when you began. This constraint can be hard to keep track of when designing grids by hand, because every black square must be matched by a corresponding square in the exact correct position. It is easy to make mistakes that, if not identified early, can ruin a whole grid after hours of work. Software, which places symmetrical squares automatically, eliminates this headache.

Antony Lewis programmed the first version of Crossword Compiler around 1993 (to the best of his recollection). Says Lewis, "There were other (DOS) crossword programs at the time, but they were relatively primitive. It took a few years for computers to have enough memory to make grid-filling algorithms practical (Windows 3.1),

and of course lots of development since then making things more sophisticated and numerous more graphic and export options." Among the primitive programs at the time was a piece of software created by Mel Rosen in the early 1980s, which Rosen claims was the first such program in history. But he did not adapt it for Windows, and Crossword Compiler supplanted it as the industry standard. It has taken the better part of two decades since Compiler was introduced for desktop construction to become the norm, but today it has.

The majority of new constructors choose a piece of software within their first few months of creating puzzles, often after becoming frustrating with the slowness of filling by hand. Of course, there remain many constructors who prefer to grid by hand, and their work doesn't suffer for it. Byron Walden, Merl Reagle, and Matt Gaffney are just three of the crossword megastars whose fill routinely makes me jealous, and they work with minimal if any aid from software. However, for those of us who have come of age with Compiler and other programs, or who have adopted them, there are innumerable payoffs.

Aside from simplifying the process of plotting black squares, software allows a constructor to maintain a personal wordlist, which they can modify and rank as needed. This wordlist tells the program which letter patterns fit into a given space. Imagine the constructor is faced with a sequence like ???EX, where ? represents an as-yet unfilled white square. The built-in wordlist that comes with

**Across**

1 Brunch order
6 Brunch order
12 Bought flowers for the wife, perhaps
14 Colt's sound
15 Dental buildup
16 Result of a bad bike crash
17 Bring to life
18 Arctic bird
19 Money put up front
20 Move by lifting one's finger?
22 "Paradise Lost" setting
23 Holes in one's hands
24 Seal the deal
25 Lost at sea
26 They may be guarded in soccer
27 ___ d'Yeu, France
28 Tool's partner
29 Extremely anxious
32 Paced back and forth over
35 Hummus accompaniment
36 Ireland, in poems
38 Midwestern city with the motto "Smart Choice"
39 "Figures!"
41 Reception rentals
42 Cheer after an olímpico goal
43 Quick glance
44 Debate team stance
46 Expect to happen
47 Big-league
48 "American Pie" actress Mena
49 Give some slack
50 Gin runs

**Down**

1 Celtic Sanders in the Basketball Hall of Fame
2 Breakout systems
3 "Get Back" girl
4 Stomach relief
5 Tight holds
6 World-shaking?
7 "Sein ___ Zeit" (Heidegger)
8 Haaretz employee, probably
9 Moët's partner
10 Party girl?
11 Fruit-ripening gas
13 In a preoccupied way
14 Wine-tasting treat
16 "Good Man, Good Woman" singer
21 "Life of Pi" actor Spall
24 Damson or mirabelle alternative
26 Web page directories
28 It's often acquired with a new house
29 Sports talk radio host whose show is affectionately called "The Jungle"
30 Scoop, say
31 Ballet Russe dancer Léonide
32 Back from the dead
33 Off base, say
34 Active from dawn to dusk
35 Distressed individual
36 Tati's Monsieur
37 Diplomatic compromise
39 Dope sheet's covering?
40 Mila of "Oz the Great and Powerful"
45 #209 on Rolling Stones' "500 Greatest Albums of All Time"

# THEMELESS MONDAY
## #211 in a series

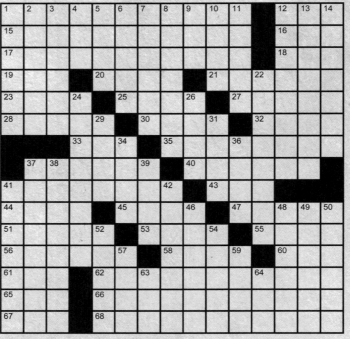

### Across

1  The desire people have to do something good without getting out of their chair
12  "We're trying to watch the movie!"
15  Enjoys one's time off
16  Food fight ammo
17  Tudor dynasty symbol
18  Flub
19  Justin Timberlake's label
20  Second word in "Bohemian Rhapsody"
21  Matched up, as all your mobile devices
23  Offender, to an officer
25  ___ del mono (Spanish liqueur)
27  "How ya like them apples?"
28  "The Little Foxes" nanny
30  Makes a pit stop
32  CNN anchor Bolduan
33  Job listings, for short?
35  Language Thomas More's "Utopia" was written in
37  Northern Illinois University city
40  Some wedding gifts
41  It's often punched at the end of the day
43  "Live Peace in Toronto 1969" performer
44  "Zero Dark Thirty" climax
45  Folk singer Jansch
47  Stockpile
51  Binary star in Perseus
53  Emanuel nicknamed "Murder Mayor"
55  "No doubt"
56  French liqueur
58  Type of tide
60  T-shirt abbr.

61  "I Want More of Everything" author LeShan
62  One just starting out
65  White ___
66  Apple's parent
67  Multipurpose doc, for short
68  '70s project leader

### Down

1  Hillary aide
2  Speared
3  Valhalla's home
4  Jazz vibraphonist Tjader
5  Sweater
6  TV actress Campbell-Martin
7  Classic book with a divination system
8  Software release
9  It's a promise
10  Attitude
11  "Not a chance!"
12  Witness the Super Bowl, say
13  Searcher's cry
14  Pair of fives, in Vegas
22  ___ Plaza ("Die Hard" setting)
24  Rode hard
26  Trickle down
29  Removal by air: Abbr.
31  Lead lines?
34  Big selection of meat
36  Singer Del Rey
37  Telephoned headquarters, say
38  "The Grapes of Wrath" character
39  Rabbit title

41  Spot for a catcher
42  Experienced eagerly
46  Punjab's colleague in comic strips
48  Equipped for
49  NHL All-Star Tyler
50  Wake leaders?
52  Poet Federico Garcia
54  One making deliveries, quaintly
57  "The BFG" writer
59  "My Brother Was An Only Child" co-author
63  Wayne LaPierre's org
64  ___-80

*Brendan Emmett Quigley, Themeless Monday, April 1, 2013. Reprinted with permission of Brendan Emmett Quigley.*

# THEMELESS MONDAY
## #210 in a series

**Across**

1 Return address?
8 Hit the track
15 "The NFL Today" analyst
16 "Pollyanna" author Porter
17 Base head?
18 Strips down
19 Godfather's business
21 22-Across, overseas
22 21-Across, here
23 Sci-fi character who sings "Yub Nub"
26 Philosopher Illich
29 Fender's feature
31 Drum roll drum
32 Cold-weather beverage
33 Actress Ramirez of "Grey's Anatomy"
34 Sea bird
35 "Night"
36 "Whispers of Immortality" poet
38 "___ Banner Over Me Is Love" (hymn)
39 IAMA site
41 Birth control activist Russell
42 Coleridge's "Dejection," e.g.
43 Swiss mathematician Leonhard
44 Trace amount
45 It's seen when you draw the curtain
46 Negligible amount
47 Part of S&L: Abbr.
48 Title in Turkey
50 "Pshaw"
56 Deuterium has one
58 Hit piece?
59 Feature on a meteorological map
60 Crowds
61 Stiffs
62 Express derision toward

**Down**

1 "Little ___?"
2 Morales of "Fast Food Nation"
3 Type of bath
4 "From Dawn to Decadence" historian Jacques
5 Native Georgian?
6 Self-conscious company
7 Hacky sack juggler
8 Loss signifier
9 "All Day Strong. All Day Long" medicine
10 Tropical flyer
11 L on a clothing label
12 Who said "Isn't life a series of images that change as they repeat themselves?"
13 His supposed birthplace is across the street from the Boston Common
14 Early admissions applicants: Abbr.
20 Place for cheap beers in the neighborhood
24 McCain rival
25 Frasier's portrayer
26 Naturally inherent
27 One with a window seat
28 Spirit of '76?
30 42-Across preposition
31 ___ date
33 Mix things up
34 Where to go in a park
37 Bit of a charge
40 Release that's often self-titled
44 "Velvet Goldmine" director Todd
45 Church figure
47 Curling piece
49 Hit the big time
51 Messenger goddess
52 School writing assignments: Abbr.
53 Easter party event
54 "Young Frankenstein" role
55 Make a home, say
56 CNN reporter Robertson
57 That, in Tabasco

*Brendan Emmett Quigley, Themeless Monday, March 25, 2013. Reprinted with permission of Brendan Emmett Quigley.*

# SHINERS

## Across

1 Haughty goodbyes
6 Bazooka, e.g.
9 Beverage
14 Real douche
15 60 minuti
16 ___ art (text graphics used in low-tech emails)
17 Freaky-looking sea predators with sucker mouths
18 Some Echo Boomers
19 Becomes livid
21 "The ___ Pimpernel"
23 "Mike & Molly" channel
25 Classic incumbent campaign slogan
27 Not like in the least
29 Pickle serving
30 Quarters
32 Reason someone might do shots?
38 "Curious George" character, with "The"
41 One of South Africa's capitals, also know as the Jacaranda City
43 Sore point
44 Husbandry student, for short
47 Throw up
48 Place to shed pounds?
53 Mitt Romney's grp.
54 They may come with screwdrivers
56 Mortal Kombat combatant
58 One passed by a sprinter
59 "The French Connection" character
63 Halved
64 ___ journey (traveling)
65 Theater hall
66 Spice (up)
67 Wayne Rooney's jersey number, for Manchester United
68 Feature of toad's legs?

## Down

1 Chess champion of crosswordese
2 "So!"
3 Where you might get the last word in?
4 Hidden Goodness dog food brand
5 Line of text?
6 Ascends
7 Bing thing
8 Campaign marketing strategy
9 First Middle Eastern nation to host the World Cup
10 ___ interface
11 Northeast corridor transportation choice for people with a train fetish
12 Better
13 Dukes?
20 ___ Lonely Boys
22 Apricot alternative
23 Medalist
24 King with a trunk
26 Commie pinko
28 Get your story straight?
31 Musician Brian who uses the pseudonyms Nina Bore and Ben O'Rian
33 Kidz ___ Kids
34 Flock group
35 1992 Robert Altman satire
36 Having a roof overhang
37 Meals made with leftovers
39 Campaign handout
40 Focal point
42 Turkish leader
45 Yoke harness
46 Me Generation problem
48 Exxon partner
49 Muscat resident
50 Hulu or Ustream, e.g.
51 Element #54
52 Furnish
55 "Parks and Recreation" actor Rob
57 "Weird" Al parody based on "Star Wars"
60 Number of Qs in this grid
61 Park place?
62 They're seen around noon

*Brendan Emmett Quigley, "Shiners," July 19, 2012. Reprinted with permission of Brendan Emmett Quigley.*

# MOVING PICTURES

## Across

1. Delivers an address
7. Source of Egyptian lethal injection
10. Smartphone app
13. When Tabitha woke up today
14. Shade trees
15. Cobb's wife in "Inception"
16. Solve, as a puzzle
18. 1981 World Series MVP Ron
19. ___ & Black (clothiers)
20. Birthmark
21. Blossom, Bubbles, and Buttercup, with "The"
26. Highest paid actress of 2011
27. Overseas voter, maybe
28. '70s teen idol now more known for drug troubles
34. Winnebago nation tribe
35. Gloat over
36. Atoms for Peace bassist
40. Kwik-E-Mart town
42. Muscat Stock Market employee, maybe
46. "Mr. Howard" to Jesse James, e.g.
47. "So what!"
53. CivPro student
54. Painter Kahlo
55. Red Roof ___
56. Looping on-line image, and hint to this puzzle's theme
62. "Ice Age" sloth
63. Doo-wop syllable
64. Literally "a set of three"
65. PG Tips product
66. Filthy spot
67. Movie that's tough to stay awake through

## Down

1. Ringer status
2. Saint-Lô sovereign
3. Romance Awareness mo.
4. Robert Morse nickname
5. Van Gogh famously has one
6. Besmirch
7. Not overly friendly
8. Hefty or Brainy
9. Clock setting at Sea-Tac
10. Car co. Obama took over
11. Spanish rice and seafood dish
12. Most ingenious
14. "Even you?," artistically
17. NetZero, e.g.
20. Lemonade ___
21. Greeting card employee, at times
22. Dish with everything
23. Oft-swapped person
24. Producer of head lines?: Abbr.
25. Comprehend
26. Us Magazine's Style Icon of the 2000s, for short
29. "Shirt Front and Fork" painter
30. Play with robots
31. Result of a fielder's choice, mabye
32. One in lederhosen
33. "Star Trek: ___"
36. You send it via YouSendIt
37. Princess with shapely buns
38. Airline whose in-flight magazine is "Atmosphere"
39. Don Draper's creations
40. Richard Branson's title
41. Buttchugging (hopefully)
42. Double-reed player
43. Singer Riperton
44. What's in store
45. Browns grp.
48. "Otherwise ..."
49. Hard to get clean
50. Hobbling walk
51. Lewiston's st.
52. Sharp-dressed
56. They're part of a "six pack"
57. Young number?
58. Industrial Average deviser
59. Meld-making game
60. Steelers cornerback Taylor
61. Where the successful go

*Brendan Emmett Quigley, "Moving Pictures," November 15, 2012. Reprinted with permission of Brendan Emmett Quigley.*

Crossword Compiler could suggest common English words like ANNEX, INDEX, and LATEX. But through years of adding new entries to the list, my version can also suggest, for instance, DUREX, FEDEX, and THEEX. (With a potential clue for the last being something like "Awkward person to run into while with a new girlfriend or boyfriend.") The program is also smart enough to only suggest words that fit subsequent crossing patterns. Filling a grid thus becomes a matter of choosing from a menu of options.

That doesn't mean the art of fill is lost, by any means. Rather, the challenge shifts from playing chess with letter

---

### A CURIOUS THING

Crossword Compiler, in addition to coming with several preprogrammed wordlist options, also comes with a blacklist—words and terms that the average constructor might want to avoid in their grid. The blacklist can automatically alert the constructor if one of these terms accidentally ends up in a grid, either on its own or as part of a longer word. For example, if one were skittish about the presence of the letters ASS in the word SASSY, the blacklist would provide a warning. Although no editor (not to mention solver) today is likely to worry about hidden ASSes in grids, perhaps there are constructors who want to know. However, some of the entries in the blacklist are downright absurd. BREAKING WIND, COITUS INTERRUPTUS, and VENA BULBI PENIS are pretty unlikely to show up in a grid without the constructor noticing. Moreover, I'm not sure who would encounter a word like FORNICATRESSES and feel genuinely offended, rather than laughing at how archaic it sounds.

---

arrangements to optimizing the quality of one's words. There is no longer much excuse for poor or even adequate fill. Today, crosswords are expected to pop with colorful words and phrases, and even valid-but-dull entries like MET can feel a bit "meh." (MEH, for example, would be a much livelier alternative to MET, if you could swing it.) Maintaining one's wordlist entails constant manual updates, undertaken by scanning the news, browsing slang dictionaries, or consulting lists of box office receipts and bestselling books. Soon one's list may swell to 100,000, 150,000, 200,000, and beyond ... the fruits of this rather repetitive labor are borne when filling a grid, as better options show up, enabling cleaner words throughout. The more higher-quality entries in the list, the better one's options will be. Building a wordlist is part careful eye, part brute force. But it is all manual effort.

For this reason, wordlists tend to be hoarded rather than shared. After years of tending a list, certainly, one doesn't feel much like giving it away. Programmer Alex Boisvert, however, has a different take. "It has always bugged me that crossword constructors' word lists remain a closely guarded secret," he writes on his web site. "This led to the following idea: why not create a shared word list that users can update themselves?" This idea became the Collaborative Word List Project, a free, publicly editable database of words and other entries. The project is based on the idea that better wordlists mean better puzzles for *everyone*. Despite my feelings of possessiveness, I confess to finding Boisvert's work compelling. He is using technology to foster community and improve the baseline quality of puzzles, rather than to secure proprietary knowledge.

Boisvert, in fact, has been involved in a number of projects driven by a similar philosophy, including the wonderful Crossword Nexus site, which allows searches of Wikipedia page titles. For example, one can search once again for the sequence ??EX, and Nexus yields hundreds of results, all ranked by relevance, from Ampex to Vitex (OK, so some results are more esoteric than others). Even Will Shortz has admitted that his printed sources are increasingly unhelpful in an era of such robust reference tools. Constructors today are likely to use IMDb, Wikipedia, the Stanford Encyclopedia of Philosophy, AllMusic, and Google Maps (among others) to confirm basic information, and Crossword Nexus, OneLook.com, Cruciverb.com, the database of the National Puzzler's League, and the Internet Anagram Server (among others) to manage letter sequences. Of course, the imperative to confirm facts is also more urgent than ever—rapid information can also be erroneous information.

Wikipedia in particular encourages a certain tone in cluing. This tone is perhaps best described as *trivial*. In the past, crossword clues tended strongly toward the *definitional*. One word synonym clues were the norm until the early 1990s, and at many mainstream papers brevity remains paramount. This resulted, at its worst, in such unthrilling clues as "Girl's name" for JANE. But the times have changed. The *New York Sun* puzzle was a pioneer in the use of long trivial clues like "An automatic one injured Vince Coleman in 1985, forcing him to sit out the World Series" for the answer TARP. This tactic is one way of avoiding repetitive stock clues such as "field shield," and it is seen especially often in digital puzzles that don't have to worry about space constraints.

However, after more than a decade of Wikipedia, triviality has become its own sort of cliché. A clue like "hitting legend who was once traded for infielder Tom Lawless," raises a red flag immediately. First, it reads like a sentence from an encyclopedia. While notable, it's the kind of fact that makes you think "oh …" rather than "wow!" when you find out the answer is PETEROSE. Second, it doesn't require

cleverness to write, which means the solver doesn't get the benefit of having to rearrange his or her thinking. When I spot such a clue, I often go to Wikipedia, just to check, and more often than not my suspicions are borne out. If the clue isn't directly lifted from the site, it's often a matter of just a few words' difference. Wikipedia is a tool for writing fresh clues, but it's not a shortcut.

Solving is another story altogether. Perhaps the first (and most predictable) casualty of the digital era for crosswords was the pay-per-minute crossword answer telephone hotline. Once a large source of revenue for newspapers, who cashed in on the hunger of a desperate solver who *needed* to know the answer to that one last letter in an otherwise finished grid, the puzzle hotline became utterly obsolete with the advent of search engines. Solvers could, with relative ease, find just about any answer they wanted.

However, Google alone proved inadequate for many people, especially when clues were worded in such a way that searching for hints was impossible. And so it came to pass that sites popped up where one could enter a clue and find the precise answer directly. These sites collected years of clue and answer pairs, on the assumption that most puzzle entries are repeats, and therefore can be answered by drawing on data collected from older puzzles. These resources meant that solvers could turn to the Internet much like they used to turn to a friend or coworker to ask, "What's a five-letter word for 'beauty parlor' beginning with S?"

Not all sites that give puzzle hints are so impersonal. At the aforementioned Crossword Fiend, Wordplay, and Rex Parker Does the *New York Times* Crossword blogs, the solutions are an impetus for the real meat: conversation. Every day of the year, Rex reviews the *Times*, while Amy (the Fiend's hostess) and her volunteer staff review just about every quality puzzle out there every day, from the indies to the venerable outlets. Commenters come in droves to rate and discuss the day's puzzles, to pore over minutiae of language, and sometimes to point out errors. The culture of these blogs, while sometimes harsh on the puzzles, is exceptionally intelligent. And usually, when a puzzle gets torn down, it's because the critics have high standards, not out of spite. Will Shortz periodically posts on both sites, either to make special announcements about the *Times* puzzle or to respond to criticisms being leveled by the bloggers or commenters. Crossword blogs have injected a new dimension of community into the solving experience, providing a proud refuge for a certain kind of nerddom.

When both solving and editing, I periodically turn to Google to get through an especially vexing crossing. I don't consider this a failing. In fact, when it happens, I think less of the construction, not of my own skills. I almost never need help with semantic clues, even tricky ones like "Bear's warning" for SELL. But if a clue is a know-it-or-you-don't fact, especially crossing another know-it-or-you-don't fact, then I don't feel guilty at all for consulting Google. To wit: what's a seven-letter word for a "town at the eighth mile of the Boston Marathon"? Don't know? Well, what's a seven-letter answer to the clue "*Treasure Island* illustrator"? Now imagine that you have every letter except the first filled in for both—?ATICK going across and ?CWYETH going down. If you've never heard of a town with 33,000 people, and you don't know who illustrated a 100-year old adventure novel, then you're out of luck. You might fill in an L and get LATICK/LCWYETH, which looks plausible. Or an M to get MATICK and MCWYETH, which seems reasonable enough. But the real answer is NATICK/NCWYETH.

It was precisely this crossing in a 2008 crossword by the extremely brilliant Brendan Emmett Quigley that led to the so-called Natick Principle, a term coined by Rex Parker. The Natick Principle reads: "If you include a proper noun in your grid that you cannot reasonably expect more than a quarter of the solving public to have heard of, you must cross that noun with reasonably common words and phrases or very common names." If a puzzle includes what I would consider a Natick-type crossing, then I have no problem consulting Google as a reference, and neither should you. In any case, there is no right or wrong way to solve a crossword, only the way that feels right (and enjoyable) for the solver. Outside of competitions, you get to make your own rules.

One curious piece of technology that hasn't really changed the experience of solving crosswords, but that might someday, is a program called Dr. Fill. Created (and ingeniously named) by programmer and software developer Matt Ginsberg, Dr. Fill can read and interpret crossword clues, filling the grid as it goes. Although it has trouble with certain kinds of clever themes, it is surprisingly adept in general. In 2012, Dr. Fill entered the American Crossword Puzzle Competition in Brooklyn, finishing an impressive 141st out of 650 entrants. According to Ginsberg, "I'm a terrible solver, and figured this would be a way for me to get revenge on all the folks who are so much better than I am." Ginsberg claims to have written the first filler program as early as 1976, and still sees Dr. Fill as relatively primitive, especially by comparison to the chess-playing Deep Blue and *Jeopardy!*-answering Watson. Themes and difficult clues, both of which rely not only on definitions but on inventive wordplay, remain mostly the province of human beings, at least for now.

The final technological shift in crosswords is one that remains even further from perfection—the digital solving platform. For both desktops and mobile devices, there are a number of programs for doing puzzles without aid of a pen or paper. Many of these are quite sophisticated and flexible, allowing the user to customize how the cursor behaves and how the clues appear. Speed solvers can work very quickly with this software, often even faster than on paper. The interfaces are attractive and every base is covered. However, I notice that when I put my own puzzles online for download, the number of PDFs downloaded far outnumbers the quantity of digital puzzle files.

It appears that paper is still the medium of choice for tackling a crossword. I'm not usually much for nostalgia, but in this case I agree that the older way is better. No program has yet to give me the same feeling of satisfaction I get when solving on paper. In pen, each complete square is a triumph, each part of each letter a visceral engraving. As the grid begins to fill, one senses the heft of the completed portion. The imperfection of handwritten letters speaks of the crooked path every solve takes, through thorny areas with one letter scrawled over another, past one long theme answer filled in one fell swoop and another finished piecemeal, over minutes or hours from different directions. Maybe in different colors.

# CHAPTER NINE

## The Great Constructors

Determining the best crossword constructor, like the best of most things, is a matter of opinion. I wouldn't presume to try to decide conclusively. A recent discussion on this very topic among constructors quickly turned into an attempt to compare great constructors to musicians. With so many worthy candidates, that seems as good an approach as any. However, the bar for inclusion must remain high. Any name mentioned in this chapter is a person of extraordinary talent, not only an all-star but a hall-of-fame candidate (if there were such thing as a crossword hall-of-fame ... maybe someone should get on that?). All musical comparisons are to artists whose names have appeared numerous times in major daily or weekly crossword grids.

Brendan Emmett Quigley famously tried to distill the list of greats by hypothesizing a holy trinity of constructors called the Crossword Jesuses— Patrick Berry, Mike Shenk, and Frank Longo. Brendan wrote: "A 'Crossword Jesus,' simply put, is one whose puzzles are so perfectly formed, their themes so tight they make you go 'wished I'd thought of that'; their cluing is so on target, the overall effect appears as if the puzzle wasn't so much created, but rather it just sort of happened naturally … to achieve the title of 'Crossword Jesus' one has to have performed a few miracles." Brendan, it should be noted, is a clear choice for this chapter himself. As the sixth-most prolific constructor in the history of the *Times*, he automatically receives consideration, but BEQ (as he is known to his fans) also publishes twice weekly on his blog, and for the American Values Club, among other outlets. He is widely known as a connoisseur of contemporary slang and pop culture knowledge, and his authorial voice is unusually present in his creations. From themeless puzzles to brilliant conceptual crosswords, Brendan's nailed them all. Because his success describes a bridge between "major label" and indie crosswords, let's call Brendan REM.

All of Brendan's Crossword Jesuses are frequently named among the best constructors in the business. Frank Longo, discussed in Chapter Two, is known as a digital wizard. He claims to have a wordlist of over a million entries, which if true would be no less than five to ten times as large as nearly any other constructor. Such an immense computerized word list enables Frank to muscle his way into creating wide-open grids without junky entries. Even Will Shortz calls on Frank now and again to help fill a difficult corner in a grid that needs work. Frank does both themeless and themed puzzles with the best of them. His themeless puzzles are remarkably clean given the degree of difficulty he sets up for himself. A

2004 themeless had six 15-letter entries, and all of them were in the language, namely ASSOCIATEDPRESS, THEBACHELORETTE, FIRSTHANDREPORT, LOVEANDMARRIAGE, ELECTRICTOASTER, and TENSEATMOSPHERE. For Frank's peerless technical prowess combined with a human touch, he can be compared to guitarist Jimmy PAGE of Led Zeppelin.

In researching this chapter, no name has been mentioned by more people than Patrick Berry's. The former editor of the *Chronicle of Higher Education* crossword has created over 100 puzzles for the *Times*, most of them memorable even after many years. He has a preternatural aptitude for finding novel themes. One of his rebuses required solvers to put letters in a box in several places. The twist was that the letter pair was read literally in one direction, but pronounced as if aloud in the other. SA thus served as the beginning of the word SALIENT across, while down it was the end of PHOTOSA or, said aloud, PHOTOESSAY. Berry even created a special week-long meta for the *Times* in 2011 in which he wrote every puzzle for six consecutive days, leading up to a special answer that unified all of the week's crosswords. Will Shortz, in explaining why he chose Berry to write the special meta, said, "He's one of the few constructors who can make clean, expert crosswords at any difficulty level." Beyond his versatility in construction, Berry is universally respected as an editor. (Anyway, I've never heard anyone complain.) The *Chronicle* has very high standards, which he maintained and even raised. Berry is CLARA Schumann, transformative pianist (editor) and composer (constructor) alike.

*Right: Brendan Emmett Quigley, Themeless Monday, April 15, 2013. Reprinted with permission of Brendan Emmett Quigley.*

## #215 in a series

### Across

1 Meat and potatoes dish
5 Tilt
9 Military leaders
14 It's passed down in the family
15 Show full of new gizmos
16 Weight watchers marketing term
17 "The Bard's ___"
18 Celtic musical instrument
20 Bon mot
22 Many a save opportunity
23 "However ..."
25 Not totally against
26 Inevitable comparison in reductio ad Hitlerum arguments
27 Chutney fruit
28 ___ control
30 Card carrier
34 Leading up to, in Lit class
35 Bench player?
38 Bouncing baby?
39 Reasons for a cap screw?: Abbr.
41 Their first professional endorser was Ilie Nastase
42 Breakfast stack
44 Café's opening?
46 Spur
47 They'll display your guns
51 Rice, e.g.
52 Assumes
53 Games within games
55 "Remedia Amoris" poet
57 Smarten up?
58 Single numbers?
59 Nevada tourist city
60 Sci-fi setting
61 All knotted up
62 Logical word

### Down

1 James Doakes's rank on TV's "Dexter": Abbr.
2 Split
3 Gave a lift
4 Breaking down
5 The Student Travel Guide
6 Branches out?
7 Sleep lab concentration
8 "Need You ___" (Grammy-winning Lady Antebellum album)
9 Filled pancake
10 Red fruit used in some jams
11 Media workers' union
12 Bordeaux toast
13 WWII gun
19 Those likely to wipe out
21 Leading
23 Pad and pen?
24 Omphalophobia fear, perhaps
28 Ethanol source
29 Smear in a newspaper?
31 Kick around
32 Masseuse's task
33 Recipient of two tablets
36 Classic sleepover game
37 Clipped
40 King's thing
43 Freaked out
45 Danish model Christensen
46 Doesn't leave on the porch
47 Pre-bout psych-out
48 ___ tag
49 State's #2 job: Abbr.
50 Masters accomplishment
51 Six successor
54 Suffix of nationalities
56 Diaper rash cause

# THEMELESS MONDAY
## #213 in a series

**Across**

1 Member
5 "The usual" suspects?
9 Rental property, maybe
14 Programming website?
15 Takeout option
16 "Brusha. Brusha. Brusha." brand
17 Venus, every now and again
18 Facebook action
19 Stellar explosions
20 Question asked by one watching the clock?
23 Maritime: Abbr.
24 Term.
25 Pampered folks?
26 Clears up
28 The A-team
30 Demanding
31 "Caro ___ ben" (Giordani aria)
32 Its third edition is scheduled to be finished in 2037: Abbr.
33 Tranks
39 Like retreads
40 Marked up
41 Home of Jasper Johns's "Flag"
42 Anterior ___ ligament
45 Put a cap on
46 Moving man?
47 Autism Awareness Mo.
48 "J'accuse" writer
49 Actor who voiced Gurgle in "Finding Nemo"
54 Safari game
55 Rial estate?
56 Respuesta en la encuesta
57 Water board?
58 ___-humanité (crime)
59 Low pair?
60 "Must jet"
61 Exam scored between 120 and 180
62 Cuts with combs

**Down**

1 It's a mouthful
2 "That's gonna leave a mark"
3 Stain removers
4 Iconic couple of the '90s
5 One invoked against snakes, for short
6 "Right, right"
7 Goes overboard with
8 Battery recharger
9 "You ___ about that life!"
10 Foresaw well in advance
11 Delivery person?
12 Makes law
13 What to do
21 Nus' preceders
22 Bit of progress
26 Bit of resistance
27 Kobe's teammate
28 ___ James Paul McCartney
29 Ranch tag
31 Highway divider
34 Inc. cousin
35 "Perfectly Imperfect" author Woodruff
36 "Forget I mentioned it"
37 Initialism said in an uncomfortable spot
38 Didn't sell very well
42 Deep dry gulch
43 Update a computer file
44 NCAA ranking list
45 Meme response
46 Manxmen
48 Business technology news website
50 Think about it
51 Operation IceBridge grp.
52 ___ Way (Block on Ninth Avenue in New York between 15th and 16th named after a sweet)
53 Only NL team never to have played in the World Series, briefly

*Brendan Emmett Quigley, Themeless Monday, April 29, 2013, Reprinted with permission of Brendan Emmett Quigley.*

## Across

1 Do a hype man's job
6 Hotmail's co.
9 "Born Free" character
13 Posse's weapon
14 It's said when the lights come on
15 Tonto's "Kemo ___ "
16 Place that serves $28 pints of ale?
18 Obama appointee
19 New Taipei's nation
21 Mancave visitor
22 Jokes about snake eyes?
27 Canine topper
28 Finish off in MMA
29 Dope finale
30 "Cheers" alternative
34 Glass ceilings?
38 Waiting-for-the-test-results feeling
39 Trim
41 Hole punchers
43 "La Traviata" composer
44 Masculine legal process?
49 It's roughly 15% of the world's population: Abbr.
50 "Egils saga" author Sturluson
51 Tag line?
53 What gets cops high?
58 Urban ___
59 Just manage, with "out"
60 Correct
61 Homemade knickknacks website
62 Platform that came with "Duck Hunt"
63 Goes out for a while

## Down

1 Height of a European trip?
2 Deface
3 Abbr. on a tire
4 Sch. that if it were a country, it would rank 12th all-time in Olympic medals
5 Slammer's forte
6 Pump name
7 It's a wrap
8 Newsanchor O'Donnell
9 "Oh fuck" computer key
10 It can give you a leg up
11 Skinny Slice chain
12 Soaring prefix
17 Fourth-tallest NBA player, ever
20 Duke ___ (classic video game hero)
22 System with the REXXDUMP command
23 Basic math word
24 Score marking
25 Major scoldings
26 NASA program that was the first to photograph another planet
30 Opening day pitcher
31 Swell place?
32 Loop vehicles
33 Compete
35 Tech. schools
36 Whatchamacallit?
37 "Soldier of Love" singer
40 ___ whistle
41 He's tied for most-wins at the Indy 500, 4
42 Some brats
43 Said
45 Hard to change
46 "You Send Me" singer Sam
47 Halliburton's founder Halliburton and namesakes
48 "Sixth Day," to Quakers: Abbr.
49 Chuck Jones's company?
52 Bible possessive
54 Insufferable, lovelorn and whiny, in slang
55 Brick-shaped treat
56 Value of the J tile in Croatian Scrabble
57 Brown highlights?: Abbr.

*Brendan Emmett Quigley, "Chilly Reception," March 25, 2013, Reprinted with permission of Brendan Emmett Quigley.*

# THE HUNGER GAMES

**Across**

1 Yankee who had hip surgery yesterday, for short
5 Able to tear a phonebook in half with one's bare hands, perhaps
10 NBA stars Steve Nash and Chris Paul, positionally: Abbr.
13 Mockingjay holding an arrow in a circle for "The Hunger Games," e.g.
14 Pale
15 ___ de France
16 Hunger game #1
18 Satori practice
19 Johanna Mason's weapon in "The Hunger Games"
20 Abbr. on a cul-de-sac street sign
21 Stunned
23 Hunger game #2
26 Make 100% certain
29 Hebrew alphabet opener
30 Celebrate with some fist bumps
31 Taran Killam's show, for short
32 Fertility clinic deposits
35 Hunger game #3
39 Some eggs
40 Remote batteries
41 Man caves
42 Dinner that may be tough to swallow for the guest of honor
45 Hess holder
46 Hunger game #4
49 Go ballistic
50 "Woo-___!"
51 First words of "Anarchy In the UK"
54 Space where programmers work?
55 Hunger game #5

59 Alfonso XIII's queen
60 Balanced bridge bid, briefly
61 Test with a panel
62 Bad manner?
63 Jersey fabric
64 Word on the bottom of many a blog

**Down**

1 "Little Fockers" actress Jessica
2 Gravy thickener
3 Tyrannical boss, say
4 Einstein in "Back to the Future"
5 Seadog
6 Latin stars
7 Literally "life force"
8 The bottom line?
9 Unable to relax
10 Pie-eyed person?
11 Crest rival
12 Mails off
17 Card game played with a piquet pack
22 "Overturned Blue Shoe With Two Heels Under A Black Vault" painter
23 "I don't buy that for a second"
24 Some iPods
25 Penne ___ vodka
26 Real mofo of a puzzle
27 Event where you might rent a booth
28 All-powerful
31 One of India's 28
33 ___ Bradley handbags
34 Lobbying grp.
36 Moveable window part
37 "I didn't mean to blow the whistle"
38 El ___, TX
43 Last half of a slam dunk play?
44 Substitute
45 FDR's boarding school
46 "___ the thing ..."
47 Tabriz native
48 Safari beast
51 Concerning, to a lawyer
52 Netherlands soccer powerhouse
53 ___ liquor
56 Stranded stuff
57 Quick turnaround?
58 It's got a small charge

Brendan Emmett Quigley, "The Hunger Games." January 17, 2013, Reprinted with permission of Brendan Emmett Quigley.

# GIVING THANKS

**Across**

1 See 57-Down
4 Flintstones frames
8 Slides some skin
13 The whole shebang
14 "Well, wow"
15 Comic Sykes
16 Excel specialist, for short
17 Hogwarts job opening?
19 The Partridge Family's manager Reuben
21 Three point line, e.g.
22 Really weird IRS agents?
26 Broke the seal
27 Small work?
28 São ___
31 Clinton or Bush follower
34 Houston hockey pro
37 England's national tree
38 Barricade made of metal thread and pub paper?
43 Obesity meas.
44 Tire (out)
45 Defunct sports org. that replaced the opening coin toss with a scrum
46 Liver ___
48 Mama grizzly, south of the border
50 People see it when the lights turn on
54 The act of gluing corn husks together?
59 Night spot?
60 Stuff burnt at church
61 Volkswagen model that's easy to pop?
66 Windows or OSX display: Abbr.
67 Up to now
68 Warm greeting?
69 Radio talk show host Kinsolving
70 Sleep and a stiff drink, among others, for new parents
71 Holly, to David Petraeus
72 Summer setting for Cleveland: Abbr.

**Down**

1 Amass
2 Kind of skiing
3 Quick once-over
4 Word with food and supply
5 Easter party stuff
6 Garland made in a hipu'u or wili style
7 Tick of the clock
8 Killer bee's bunch
9 Scalpel's kin
10 "___ Farm" (Disney channel sitcom)
11 Hand on your GF's ass, e.g.
12 Bummed
14 Saudi Arabia's neighbor
18 Leg hair remover
20 Military trainee
23 Gallivant (about)
24 Antique maker?
25 It comes before one
29 It's served with cheese, for short
30 Scrape (by)
32 Flo Rida's genre
33 Blood-typing letters
35 NFL coach Ryan
36 Deep Woods Sportsman maker
38 They're worth a shot
39 Speaker on stage
40 Response to the debut of Stravinsky's "Rite of Spring," e.g.
41 Shear fabric?
42 Say "'cause," say
47 Indented
49 Some
51 Irish peninsula near Tralee
52 Followed
53 Like someone looking for young blood?
55 Turns soft
56 Grape drink
57 With 1-Across, being visited by Aunt Flo
58 BCS rankings org.
61 Axe alternative
62 Find a job for
63 "Keep it real"
64 It's dropped when you encounter something shocking
65 Man's name that is an anagram of 6-Down

*Brendan Emmett Quigley, "Giving Thanks." November 22, 2012. Reprinted with permission of Brendan Emmett Quigley.*

Mike Shenk is a consummate professional who is fantastically inventive and who understands crosswords as both art and business. Like Patrick Berry, he is an editor—of the *Wall Street Journal* puzzle, and formerly of *GAMES*—and a constructor, too. He has published cryptic (British-style) puzzles as well as American ones. He co-founded Puzzability, which creates puzzles for corporate and other specialty clients. And he is widely credited as the one who popularized (if not invented) specialty variants such as the "labyrinth" and "marching band" types. Shenk made his name as arguably the greatest constructor of his era in the 1980s, primarily at *GAMES* magazine. He's barely been published in the *Times*, and his editorial work today overshadows his constructions. But his lasting influence, thanks to the invention of so many enduring novelty puzzles as well as his superlative work with themes, make, him the choice of many as the best constructor ever. He is the epitome of a constructor's constructor; Patrick Berry is considered the successor to his talent. Shenk is JAYZ, talented, influential, and an influence to many, while singularly business-savvy.

Perhaps no constructor can be called an artist more than Elizabeth Gorski. It's hard to believe that she's been constructing professionally for only 20 years, as her output feels (and in fact is) enormous. But she began only in the mid-1990s, one of the handful of true greats who came of age concurrent to Will Shortz's early years at the *Times*. Gorski pioneered the grid image, a figure created by connecting the dots in a puzzle after solving it to reveal a visual meta-solution. She's made clocks, horses, a gingerbread man, and a Conga line, among others. The first Gorski puzzle I ever solved was a 2003 grid that required solvers to connect the dots in alphabetical order to draw a Christmas tree. I was floored, not to mention inspired. Liz Gorski has the honor of being the Brian ENO of crosswords, a prolific artist who works across media.

My personal inclination is to call Merl Reagle the greatest constructor of all time, though others disagree, saying he should be second or third. Nevertheless, the task here is not to rank. For my solving buck, Merl satisfies all the requirements to be called a Crossword Jesus. I am frequently awed by his gift for wordplay. Merl is known as a master of puns, but that reputation only scratches the surface of what makes him great. One puzzle reimagined business names in a clever way. The clue for TIMEWARNER was "It doesn't sell alarm clocks"; the clue for BASKINROBBINS was "It doesn't sell birdbaths." This kind of theme is far richer than the usual pun concept. It is an inversion of the standard play on words in that the original phrases are untouched—rather, it is the cluing that makes the puns. This is a difficult move to make without falling flat, but Reagle has the chops to make it happen. Like Shenk, he is known for dabbling in variety puzzles from his days at *GAMES*, but he has done so much since then that it's almost easy to forget. He syndicates a weekly 21x21 puzzle nationally, his major outlet, as well as freelancing now and then for the *Times* and contributing American Crossword Puzzle Tournament puzzles. He is, above all, playful. Merl is ELLA Fitzgerald—popular, clever, seductive (as a constructor anyway), and seemingly never out of ideas.

Henry Hook is a character who interacts rarely or never with the crossword community at large, although there are many opportunities, despite having met many people while working at *GAMES* in the 1980s. Hook is frequently grouped with Shenk, Reagle, and Shortz as a leading light of the New Wave era, especially for his thematic inventiveness, though he was already a prodigious puzzler by his early teens. He now writes fewer puzzles, but still places a puzzle in the *Times* now and then and constructs bi-weekly for the *Boston Globe*. Matt Gaffney was particularly wowed by Hook's work in *GAMES* early in his own career, and

## A CURIOUS THING

Two constructing legends known for the difficulty of their work have similar names—Bob Klahn and David Kahn. The first is known for his brilliantly hard clues, and the other for prominence between Thursdays and Sundays in the *New York Times*, the hardest stretch of the week. Klahn published a compendium called *The Wrath of Klahn Crosswords*, in reference to his reputation for challenges. His clue "Sitting around for years waiting to get drunk?" for AGING captures his humor perfectly. Both are great, but easy enough to mix up by name alone. Kahn and Klahn are XTC and DMX, respectively.

has modeled his meta puzzles after some of Hook's constructions. Gaffney profiled Hook in his own puzzle history/memoir, *Gridlock*, from 2006, suggesting that he is reclusive and misanthropic, not to mention dismissive of his own output. For Gaffney the experience of meeting his idol was powerful and complicated. He writes that Hook now "… struggles financially. He wants his puzzles to speak for themselves, but in puzzles, as in other fields, contacts matter." Matt argued that Henry is the Beatles of crosswords, to Merl's Rolling Stones. But I'll make a case for him as Yoko ONO, an under-recognized, polarizing genius with a sometimes tense relationship with audiences.

Matt, too, though young, is a worthy candidate for the greatest constructor. He was named Constructor of the Year by Crossword Fiend in 2012, and there'll be a strong case for him in a few years as the best of the decade. His incredible work with metas has already been covered in this book. Matt is OTIS Redding; gifted, unparalleled in execution, and lively, but also soulful and serious.

Most of those mentioned so far debuted in crosswords in the 1980s or 1990s, and this is no coincidence. That period was characterized by an ultimately productive feud between the old guard and the New Wave. Stanley Newman, discussed earlier (and who belongs on this list in comparison to THE WHO for his rebellious early style that mellowed with success), Trip Payne (a Hook acolyte worthy of analogy to YMA Sumac for his quirkiness mixed with genuine ability), and Mike Selinker (ETTA James?) each came to prominence in this context. But what about the constructors who came before, as well as since?

We'll begin with the preceding generations. The pre-1980s era is tricky because the constructor as celebrity was rarer. Ruth Von Phul, as mentioned in Chapter Three (*page 51*), was a famous constructor as well as solver. But she faded from view quickly. It's not that puzzles couldn't be good (or even great) back then, but the cult of personality around puzzle makers was all but nonexistent. Still, Frances Hansen, a figure who began in the Margaret Farrer era, is deserving of mention. She is IRA Gershwin; lyrical, poetic, and joyful. Bernice Gordon, inventor of the rebus, who as of 2013 at the age of 99 *continues to construct*, has the honor of being NAS, as prolific and enduring as she is talented. Manny Nosowsky, who began publishing in the *Times* before Shortz arrived, and who excelled at both themed and unthemed puzzles, is the most frequently published crossword constructor in the history of that paper. He is PRINCE, an outsized talent with "hits" across many decades, equally beloved by casual and hardcore solvers, and a true student of his craft. There are also some, like William Lutwiniak, editor of the *Washington Post* crossword, who were greatly admired but fell out of favor as antediluvian when the New Wave ascended. Lutwiniak's somewhat faded reputation should not lessen our appreciation for his work in the Maleska era. Though he might have objected to the popular culture comparison, Lutwiniak is jazz trombonist Kid ORY.

A few seasoned constructors would be profiled more extensively, but for their massive editorial presence. Will Shortz is one of these. Like a great athlete who had their pick of multiple sports, Shortz might well have been a nominee for the greatest constructor of all time had he not assumed editorship of *GAMES* and later the *Times*—he ultimately constructed few crosswords, but his knack for other kinds of word games is well-known. Shortz was at the crest of the New Wave. He could be none other than Dr. DRE, a supreme talent who earned his credibility through hard work and natural talent but always had a mind for his reputation and career. They even align historically, having come up in the 1980s and broken through in the early 1990s with a style otherwise quite alien to their respective areas, which nevertheless succeeded in a huge way. Both, today, are venerable godfathers, generous mentors to subsequent generations. Peter Gordon is similarly a major constructing talent whose editing is more visible. For his commitment to difficulty and virtuosity, Gordon is YES. Rich Norris, editor of the *Los Angeles Times* crossword, is forgotten to many as a constructor, but he too was a noteworthy talent in his day. Norris is ANI DiFranco, whose great creative heyday is bygone, but who remains something of an impresario—and whose older work is worth revisiting.

Nancy Salomon, my mentor, has a quiet role as one of the greats. She is an expert at solid early-week puzzles, and her grasp of the fundamentals of crosswords cannot be doubted. She remains often in the background, but her influence is felt. Her work may seem lite, but on examination it reveals many layers. Nancy Salomon is ABBA. (Lynn Lempel has a similar story, and might fit as ELO for similar reasons.)

Some have cited Jordan Lasher, who died in 1995 at far too young an age, but who was decidedly ahead of his time in his punning approach. According to his obituary, "in [the puzzle] 'Lack of Composure,' his punning entries were based on composers' names: 'gift for a composer' was a 'Bach scratcher,' and 'a composer's cache' was a 'Haydn place.' In 'Riddle, Riddle,' the answer to the clue, 'What's worse than raining cats and dogs?' was 'hailing taxis,' and 'the Grand Canyon' was a 'hole of fame.' " He is SYD Barrett, of early Pink Floyd fame, a brilliant figure who left the trade before his time.

The aforementioned Maura Jacobson has been described as from the old school although her work resonates quite powerfully with contemporary construction. She is a giant who is closely associated with one outlet, *New York* magazine. She wrote an extraordinary number of puzzles, even for a long career, and rarely broke from the approach that she perfected early and pulled off as well as anyone has. Like AC/DC, Maura Jacobson was consistently entertaining for decades.

A.J. Santora published under every *New York Times* editor, from Farrar in the 1950s through to Shortz in the 1990s. Shortz said his puzzles had "timeless elegance." He primarily wrote Sunday crosswords—85 in total. Santora is BONO, having had success in the largest arena of puzzledom across an unusually wide range of eras.

Moving to the present time, Byron Walden writes some of the most wonderful, idiosyncratic, and occasionally difficult puzzles around. He dabbles in the unique and somewhat dirty (a 2009 *The Onion* puzzle featured synonyms for a certain male body part), but he has the approach of a true craftsman. Walden absolutely packs his grids with theme material, and uses fill that might be considered contrived if others included it. With Walden, however, a brilliant clue usually saves the day (and the entry). And his work is so solver-friendly, even when difficult, that one tends to forgive him his excesses. Perhaps more than anyone else at their peak today, Walden might qualify as a Crossword Jesus, bringing "wished I'd thought of that" ideas to his puzzles again and again. He is most often seen in the *Times* and American Values Club, though he's also contributed to the American Crossword Puzzle Tournament. Byron is RUSH—imaginative, unusual, and impossible to get out of your head.

Francis Heaney and Patrick Blindauer have often collaborated, and so I'll write about them together. They share an eccentric sensibility and can be sarcastic now and then.

Both are especially adept at late-week difficult themes, and have a reputation on this basis. One recent collaboration showed "food pyramids," or foods like COBBSALAD broken up in the grid into triangular stacks. Puzzle stars largely for the past decade or two, both may be just getting started, but they are extraordinary among their peers, and possess the very rare ability to be laugh-out-loud funny in a crossword. Are they not men? They are DEVO.

# 6 DOWN by Mike Shenk

## ACROSS
1 Prepared cherries jubilee
9 Board's dread
15 Movie whose hero was Ted Striker
16 More than touched
17 Is composed
18 Farmers' market units
19 Serpent's tail?
20 Fool's gold
22 Federation, for short
23 L. Sprague De Camp's ___ *Darkness Fall*
25 Truth alternative
26 Where President Fujimori rules
27 If's alternative, in programming
28 Venice's La Fenice, for one
31 Kings' followers
33 Trumpeter
34 Base contacts make it blue
37 Montana colleagues
38 Come into
40 Midasized?
41 Soother's words
43 Greek avenger
47 Gunpowder et al.
48 Clash participants
49 TV setting
50 Midback muscle, for short
51 *Breaker Morant* setting
54 *The Sultan of Sulu* playwright
55 50-50
57 Member
59 Least exceptional
60 Entirety
61 Attacks
62 Deighton title

## DOWN
1 Shallow
2 Company known for making tracks
3 Graves' brother
4 Brig tenders
5 Jet, to controllers
6 "Careful!"
7 Bags
8 Fancy
9 Issue
10 *The Naked Jungle* threat
11 "Life ___ Song"
12 Tallchief, for one
13 Check name
14 Disney's Bianca and Bernard
21 '52 Sugar Bowl player
24 Haul monitors?
26 Specify, rudely
29 Fabled cheering section
30 Cumulonimbus creation
32 Sound maker?
34 Grand Slam winner in '58
35 Site of Clapton's "Tears"
36 Show places
39 Friendly address?
40 Bar patron
42 P.T. Barnum "attraction"
44 Grand Canal island
45 Win over
46 Hard
51 Reach 22
52 Expresses a preference
53 Falls apart
56 Originally called
58 He said "Up, get you out of this place"

Mike Shenk, "6 Down," Tough Puzzles, Crossworder's OWN Newsletter, December 1993. Reprinted with permission of Stanley Newman.

# AMAZEMENT 2 ★★★

BY MIKE SHENK

This puzzle is both a crossword and a maze. To solve, first complete the crossword in the usual manner. Then, starting in the first square of 1-Across, wind your way one square at a time (left, right, up, or down, but not diagonally) to the last square of 114-Across, traveling only through squares containing one of the letters in the answer at 63-Across (shaded). Watch for twists, turns, and dead ends, and don't get lost.

ANSWER, PAGE 58

### ACROSS

1 High points
6 Nancy's chum
12 Skedaddles
18 Read incorrectly, perhaps
19 Line
20 Bodily
21 Olympics awards music
22 Jessica's TV portrayer
23 Marked down
24 Stamp letters?
25 Knifes
27 Famed London gallery
29 Cacao seed site
30 Part of West Point's motto
32 Moved from memory to disk
33 Morse E
34 Loose talk?
36 Asparagus unit
38 Pronoun type: Abbr.
39 Baseballer Rod
41 Gaelic
42 Votes from the antis
44 Urgently
46 MPG raters
48 Leg-of-mutton sleeves
51 Pinballer's worry
52 Petal pusher?
56 Brick carrier
57 Spy in the organization
59 Like some gowns
61 Porter's "Miss ___ Regrets"
63 SEE INSTRUCTIONS
65 Poi source
66 Some vaccines
68 Female rabbits
70 Alternate spelling: Abbr.
71 Canadian capitalist?
72 The Godfather, familiarly
74 Took a snooze
76 Zing
77 Coops
79 1988 Dennis Quaid movie
80 Faux pas
83 Character actor Arnold
85 RN's forte
87 Hiker's route

91 June awards broadcast
93 Dunderhead
94 Rodeo janglers
96 Neutral color
97 S.A.T. relative
98 King Lear character
100 Frugal
102 Preschooler
103 Longtime puzzle editor Margaret
105 Beethoven opus
107 Like most yodeling
109 Shows scorn for
110 Creator of many a fine mess
111 Annoyances
112 Six-line stanza
113 Breakdown cause, perhaps
114 Made dresses

### DOWN

1 Hangs on the bulletin board
2 Twelve Oaks or Tara
3 Pipe clogger
4 Castle's core
5 Big rigs
6 Babushkas
7 Galahad's dad
8 Drove
9 Turns right
10 Shampoo type
11 Speaking skill
12 Burns, e.g.
13 Fixes chairs
14 Surgery settings, for short
15 Roughly equal
16 Hawk's grabbers
17 Spike-driving aid
18 Actress Adams and others
26 Husking bee unit
28 Pigged out
31 The masculine side
33 Moore's 007 replacement
35 Mastered
37 Part of a Clue accusation
39 Casals and Ma
40 Smart, in a way
43 Makeshift solutions
45 Mixing the deck
47 "Tamerlane" author
48 "Oh, I understand"

49 Simpleton
50 Done in
52 Ozone menace
53 "___ at the office"
54 Fine fiddle
55 Thunderbolt hurler
56 King of the road
58 Series finale, often
60 Bizarre
62 Comedian White
64 Safe ports
67 Have unpaid bills
69 Primer pooch
73 Maintains a faster speed than
75 Ready the apples for pie
77 Easter colors

78 Men and mice
80 Hires a crew for
81 Neighborhood
82 Prefaces, briefly
84 Shade from the sun
86 Dernier ___
88 On the go
89 Had pressing business?
90 Mandolins' kin
92 Compete in a roller derby
94 Steeple point
95 Velcro forerunners
99 Once, once
100 Bad-tempered
101 Exultation
104 Everyday grind
106 Scoundrel
108 Parishioner's perch

Mike Shenk, "Amazement 2," GAMES, 1989. Reprinted with permission of Kappa Publishing. Instruction for solving: Moving up, down, left, and right, but not diagonally, find a route from the upper left square to the lower right using only letters in the central entry.

# SEMI-FINAL [Easier Clues]
## A THEMELESS MIXTURE LIKE THE USUAL PLAYOFF PUZZLE, BUT NOT NEARLY AS TOUGH.

**Across**

1. Folksy concert
9. Diamond weights
15. San Antonio landmark
16. Funicello's frequent co-star
17. Sistine Chapel worker
18. Perfumed cream
19. Kitty starter
20. National park in California
22. Espionage org.
23. Debate side
24. Countless
25. Unpleasantly humid
26. Damascus' country
28. Baseball's Red or White
29. Carried
30. Gun-owner's org.
32. Pitcher's dream game
34. Auks' kin
38. ___ bones (old calculator)
39. Gulf Stream setting
41. Moon buggy
42. "Just ___" (antidrug slogan)
43. Deteriorate
45. Bat Masterson's hat
49. "___ Championship Season"
50. Cone homes
52. Shade
53. Unprocessed
54. Paperback publisher
55. Tower town
56. Fancy marbles
58. Fixes deeply
60. Ari of "Kate & Allie"
61. "Stop that!"
62. Out of one's tree
63. Mad's espionage strip

**Down**

1. Gown features
2. Porter's pen name
3. Sage Greek general
4. Modern scandal suffix
5. Ziegfeld
6. Before the deadline
7. Fingerpaints
8. Mechanical twisting
9. Like many superheroes
10. The Bard's river
11. Fish-Bull go-between
12. Individually from the menu
13. "Guess Who's Coming ___?"
14. Basketball wear
21. Anglo-___
24. Quarterback Dan
25. Serve a sentence
27. Stroller occupant
29. Humans, e.g.
31. Strong insect
33. Linden or Holbrook
34. Deli offering
35. Theater actress/teacher
36. Gymnastic dismounts
37. Warning sound
40. Ancient Egyptian languages
44. Join forces
46. Horned chargers
47. Break into pieces
48. Frothy
50. Cup: Fr.
51. Gas gauge reading
54. Swiss capital
55. Greets Fido
57. Source of Thomas Lipton's fortune
59. Actress Ullmann

*Mike Shenk, "Semi-Final" Long Island Open, 1987.*

# CAPITAL INFUSION
## by Elizabeth C. Gorski © 2011 Crossword Nation

**Across**

1 Thickener used by candymakers
5 Dread
10 "May I ___ favor?"
14 Hershey's caramel candy
15 Magna ___
16 Lover's quarrel
17 Swashbuckling trio of Oman?
19 Be a sore loser
20 Thread holder
21 So-so grades
23 Bollywood star Aishwarya ___
24 Alternative healing system of Egypt?
28 2:00, give or take a few minutes
30 Hesitant sounds
31 Golden, in Giverny
32 Director Wertmüller
35 Cut up, as carrots
38 Predict the future of the Czech Republic?
42 Two cents
43 "Extra virgin" Italian product
44 Cape Town's land: Abbr.
45 ___ Lanka
46 Formal
49 Undergraduate degree from the University of Azerbaijan?
54 Rhyming fighter
55 Opposite of exo-
56 Sun Devil Stadium locale
60 Nest egg protector
62 Euphoria in South Sudan?
65 William's bride of 2011
66 Maine college town
67 Last name in spydom
68 NRA segment
69 "___ next time . . ."
70 Pub sign shorthand

**Down**

1 Folded body parts
2 Increase in value
3 To boot
4 Highly-decorated art style
5 Play the part?
6 Rob Roy's "no"
7 ___-Roman wrestling
8 Scarlet fever cause
9 Handheld stunner
10 Indiana Jones' fear
11 Jaguars in the garage
12 Lush Hawaiian island
13 Dusty storage area
18 Jai ___
22 OPEC participant
25 Frequent "Survivor" setting
26 Horned critter
27 Tony
28 Unable to decide
29 Overlapping women's garments
31 Printer spec.
33 Cambodian leader Lon ___
34 Stage whisper
36 Handcraft-selling site
37 Narc's employer
39 Wizard
40 Of value
41 Afghanistan's ___ Bora
47 Miss Kett
48 Be boiling mad
49 Sweet and yeasty Polish cake
50 Wanted poster name
51 Pear tart ingredient
52 Stunt driver's move
53 Poker-faced bomb squad member
57 Hamm and Farrow
58 Stop during a storm
59 Oklahoma city
61 Room with comfy seating
63 "Fuel" singer DiFranco
64 Jokester's text message

# Orange Alert
## by Elizabeth C. Gorski © 2011 Crossword Nation

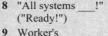

### Across

1 Winery barrels
6 Salty waters
10 Flabbergast
14 Not miss ___ (stay on course)
15 "Gone with the Wind" estate
16 "Now I understand"
17 Cocktail made with peach schnapps and fruit juice
19 Walnut's center (it's vegan!)
20 "Is it a boy ___ girl?"
21 Quaint "Omigosh!"
23 State leader?
24 "Take a hike!"
28 Pizza spice
30 Manning with two Super Bowl rings
31 Mark Harmon's TV drama
33 Knitter's ball
34 Stand up
36 Go for ___ (swim)
38 Cuba's Castro
41 Lucy's hubby, on- and off-screen
42 "Chicago" actress Zellweger
44 Prefix for legal or medic
45 Surmise
47 Not fake
48 Big time periods
49 One who's in the make-up business?
51 Svelte person's nickname
53 British verb ending
54 "My bad!"
57 Bar code reader
59 Reverend's address: Abbr.
60 Props for golf balls
62 Follower of Carol or Paul?
63 Hawaiian necklaces
65 Stallone played Rambo in this 1982 action thriller
70 "The King ___"
71 Feminizing suffix
72 Former Oldsmobile model
73 "Underboss" author Peter
74 "Gangster Squad" actor Gosling
75 Savory Greek sandwiches

### Down

1 Half-___ (Starbucks coffee order)
2 "Aladdin" critter
3 Expresses, slangily
4 Instrument with a shallow learning curve
5 "Sophie's Choice" writer William
6 NYC subway stop
7 Roof overhang
8 "All systems ___!" ("Ready!")
9 Worker's compensation
10 America's "Uncle"
11 "Iron Man 3" supervillain played by Ben Kingsley
12 Track star Bolt, aka the world's fastest person
13 "I beg to differ!"
18 Racing suit logo
22 Not able to hear
24 "Rigoletto" composer
25 Martian, for one
26 Beauty pageant contestant from a panhandle state
27 Down from a duck
29 Kvetch
32 Trig class ratios
35 "Old MacDonald" refrain
37 Church bell sounds
39 Use a delete button
40 Surgical beam
43 Draw out, as a response
46 Huck Finn's transport
50 "___ Madness" (1936 film)
52 Tote designed for a guy
54 Muslim faith
55 She played Thelma in "Thelma and Louise"
56 Athena or Hera
58 "Pimp Juice" rapper
61 Spanish miss: Abbr.
64 Venus, to Serena
66 Capitol Hill VIP
67 "___ the ramparts ..."
68 Conquistador's gold
69 Hair styles

# ON EASY STREET
## By Henry Hook
### ★★★

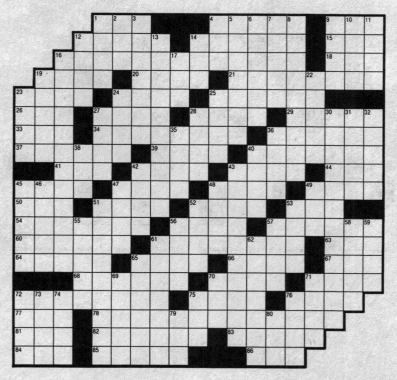

<ACROSS>

George Burns role
Ile St.-Louis's location
Quid pro ____
Greek architectural order
McCarthy's mouthpiece?
Berlin connection
Biased judge's street?
Versailles agreement
Baseball Hall-of-Famer Johnny
Jeopardize
Take a shortcut
Obedience school command
It's off-target
Long green
R.S.V.P.
Two for the show?
Indonesian paddle boat

29 Bulletin board items
33 Nonsense
34 From Nineveh
36 Five iron
37 Sign of nervousness
39 With frills
40 "____ see"
41 "A mouse!"
42 Spondulicks
43 Fictional rafter
44 ____ U.S. Pat. Off.
45 Track
47 Beaver's mom
48 Hoodoo
49 Stone Age discovery
50 Like Abner
51 *Soleil* 's counterpart
52 Wiggler or bucktail
53 Understand
54 The makings of a dull boy
56 Spitz's cousins, for short

57 Barman or barmaid?
60 Like cumulus clouds
61 Trashy literature
63 Rotation duration
64 Doctor's request
65 Years and years
66 Parishioners' place
67 Stocking scuffer
68 So to allow life
70 Reunion group
71 Screen
72 Part of "PG-13"
75 *Grapes of Wrath* surname
76 Golfer Ballesteros
77 Carry Nation's prop
78 Attila the Hun's street?
81 Poorly
82 Tickled
83 Conclude
84 Susan, of *L.A. Law*
85 Takes ten

86 Looker's leg

<DOWN>

1 "____ fishin' "
2 Assn.
3 Logs of a sort
4 Jiffy
5 It's losing ground
6 Tennessee Williams lizard
7 Chutzpah
8 Put on an act?
9 *Je ne sais* ____
10 One, on a one
11 "Garfield" dog
12 Stupefy
13 Gospel singer's street?
14 Harvard prexy Derek
16 *Cheers* actress's street?
17 CIA forerunner
19 "If My Friends Could See ____"
22 It may be eaten or drunk

23 Rice was his downfall
24 Cry to the huskies
25 Low cart
27 Actor Rambo of *Dallas*
28 Guitarist's gadget
30 Fund-raisers' street?
31 Pirates slugger Ralph
32 Marsh plant
35 Purse pursuit
36 Tailless tabby
36 Mideast hill
40 Sommelier's suggestion
42 Hong Kong harbor sight
43 Winner's street?
45 Five kings of Norway
46 Rural estate
47 People who might be hung?
48 Checkers move
49 A handful

51 *Marmion* hero
52 What a shark might make
53 Interstices
55 Emulate Arachne
56 Contrivance
57 Bowling green
58 ____ cologne
59 Sandberg of the Cubs
61 Casals or Ma
62 Library activity
65 You can count on it
69 "Once upon ____ . . ."
70 Funnyman Bill, to fans
71 '65 Beatles movie
72 Clerk's stamp
73 Spindle
74 Depend
75 *Oklahoma!* baddie
76 Undesirable masses
79 Danish island whirlwinds
80 Vitamin dosage: Abbr.

Henry Hook, "On Easy Street," GAMES, 1988. Reprinted with permission of Kapp Publishing.

# Moving Day
## by Elizabeth C. Gorski

## Across

1 Online address starter
5 Biblical brother
9 Easy ___ (piece of cake)
14 Is overly sweet
19 Old electronics brand
20 Ticket dispensers
22 Triple Crown winner
23 Stinger who's next in line?
25 Historic English county
26 More up to it
27 Easily recognized
28 News org. article on the Drudge Report
30 Computer mavens with unibrows and beards?
33 Some Deco works
35 Gallery display
36 Plant bristle
37 Hilariously-funny girl?
43 Washington Irving's Crane
47 Showstopper by The Three Tenors
48 Adhesive-backed komodo dragon stickers?
54 Seek advice from
55 "This Old House" carpenter Norm
56 Scribble (down)
57 Texter's "I think"
60 Cook under intense heat
61 Professional wrestling duo
64 One who calls at night?
68 Puzzle theme (look for the anagrams!)
75 ___ schedule (early)
76 "Eiffel Tower" and "The Models"
78 Remove mist from a car windshield
83 Proof-of-age items: Abbr.
84 Pub drink
87 "Enough, Carlo!"
88 Classic skirt styles
90 Intermittent sheepish response?
95 "Miscellaneous" items?
98 "Lordy!"
99 Carrier used by a handyman?
101 Furry TV alien

103 Nashville sch.
106 ___ Rica
107 Duds seen at a coming-out party?
111 Tipper, when she was Second Lady
115 View from a rope bridge
118 Volleyball star Gabrielle
119 Sphere
120 Harry Chapin song about felines tangling with Alexander's sculpture?
124 "___ Days" (Schwarzenegger flick)
125 Subway line?
126 City in New Jersey or California
127 Hat rack item
128 Speaks with Marlee Matlin
129 Winged love god
130 Land in W. Europe

## Down
1 "Ver-r-ry funny!"
2 Father's Day gift
3 Aglow at dusk
4 Chef's knife
5 "I love," in Latin class
6 Jump into a pool?
7 Moral principle
8 Little sucker
9 ___ Goeth ("Schindler's List" character)
10 New Delhi wedding dress
11 Lobster claw
12 Chemical suffix
13 Gated properties
14 Place to do some checking?
15 In need of directions
16 Guesstimate phrase
17 River of Flanders
18 Hot, like a hunk
21 Frat house characters
24 "___ Little Tenderness"
29 '90s Presidential candidate H. Ross ___

31 Chang, to Eng
32 Pkg. insert
34 "Bringing Up Baby" studio
37 ___ anglais (English horn)
38 Unmatched
39 Mr. Beethoven
40 "You Know ___ Good" (Amy Winehouse hit)
41 Huge name in banking
42 Menthol cigarette brand
44 Alphabet trio
45 Dye type
46 Got into some hot water?
48 Thug's weapon
49 Letter-shaped brace
50 Sudden impulse
51 "I could ___ horse!'
52 Biblical measure
53 In ___ (unmoved)
58 N. African nation
59 Possesses
62 Southern constellation
63 When repeated, it's a fish
65 "Deep Space Nine" role
66 Not broadcasting right now
67 Whopper
69 "Mallet Concerto" composer Rorem
70 React in horror
71 Nashville great Ernest
72 Russian range or river
73 Tear down, British-style
74 "At Last" singer James
77 Posed for a portrait
78 Loony
79 Fashion designer Fiorucci
80 Yahoo! co-founder David ___
81 Scott Turow memoir set in Harvard
82 Snuggles into an overstuffed chair
85 "Wild Thing" rapper Tone-___
86 Ice cream maker Joseph
89 Rich flavor
91 Comic Philips

92 Stimpy's pal
93 Apple desktop computer
94 Jail unit
96 Cuts in half
97 Boot camp VIP
100 Cattle marker
102 ___ song (inexpensively)
103 Market Watch subj.
104 Withdraw from the Union
105 Log-on access info
107 Force
108 ___ nous (confidentially)
109 Joy on "The View"
110 Tattles
111 Talking horse on classic TV
112 Belgian painter Magritte
113 Baghdad's ___ City
114 Serving of Marshmallow Fluff
116 Speller's clarifying words
117 French wines
121 "Exodus" hero
122 Friendly opener
123 Certified bank products: Abbr.

Elizabeth Gorski, "Moving Day," 2013. Reprinted with permission of Elizabeth Gorski, Crosswordnation.com.

# Plane Geometry
## by Elizabeth Gorski

## Across

1 Unit of loudness
9 Pertinent
16 Slurring one's speech, say
17 Sushi bar soups
21 Call home from the office
22 Households
23 Love, Italian-style
24 Indonesia's capital
25 Once-___ (quick appraisals)
26 Like a sidewalk cafÈ
28 Encrypt?
29 Longtime N.Y. Yankees captain
32 Nonverbal communication syst.
33 Antique shop items
36 Bambi's aunt
37 Agreeable guy
39 Lifestyle expert who appears on "Today"
41 Wanna-___ (copycats)
42 ___ Darya (Asian river)
44 Swedish auto
45 Conger-like
46 Kidnapping org. in '70s headlines
47 Virile: Abbr.
49 At the helm
53 Taunt
54 "Quiet, the baby's sleeping ..."
56 "Taste!"
57 ___ anglais (English horn)
58 High-altitude airflow
62 German car that's a cousin of the "Beetle"
63 Canon printer type
67 "___ chicken walks into a bar ..."
68 Sailor's greeting
70 That, in Mexico
71 Gentle "Little Women" character
72 Surgery sites, for short
73 Flying zones that may be restricted
76 "Super Mario Galaxy 2," for one

78 Southwestern flats
79 "Get Smart" enemy gp.
81 Creditor's concern
82 Diet food term
83 World's fastest-flying military demonstration squadron -- it's the puzzle theme!
87 Actor's role
90 Central point
91 Orchestra's conductor
95 Flamenco concert shout
96 "You're oversharing!" in a text
97 83-Across' signature flying formation depicted by six puzzle squares
98 Stumble
99 Narrow estuary
100 Fertilizer choice
102 Nutmeg State Ivy Leaguer
104 "The Waste Land" monogram
105 Destroyed, as a battleship
106 Russian villas
108 With 116-Across, uplifting song lyrics (it's the puzzle soundtrack!)
114 Least inhibited
116 See 108-Across
119 "¿ ___ santÈ!"
120 Type of "steak"
121 Accustom
122 Woolf's "___ of One's Own"
123 Online tech review site
124 Zaire's Mobutu ___ Seko
125 Memory "outage"

## Down

1 No longer in fashion
2 Late morning hour
3 Wide-screen motion picture process
4 "___ you!" (challenger's cry)
5 Montana's nickname, with "country"
6 Austin-to-Boston dir.
7 Some HDTVs, brand-wise
8 Astro's Space Age family
9 Modifying word: Abbr.
10 Zadora of "Butterfly"
11 Debonair
12 Warner who played Charlie Chan
13 Apt to be carried away?
14 Canal zone entrance?
15 Begins
17 Navigation aid
18 "___ business!"
19 Tooth brush brand
20 Six, in modern Rome
26 Financial guru Suze ___
27 Ladies' man
30 Ballet class jumps
31 Morales of "NYPD Blue"
34 Monthly mailing
35 Floating dock
38 "Dancing With the Stars" airer
40 Mattress brand
43 Sputnik launcher: Abbr.
46 Belgrade resident
48 Low blow
50 "We Will Love ___ Will Perish" (Pete Seeger)
51 NFL team that plays in MetLife Stadium
52 Bandleader Puente
53 Working person
55 "Oh, that's rich"
57 Like baby dachshunds
58 Debris from the sea
59 Parisian silk
60 Hands on deck
61 Mixed bar drink with no alcohol
63 Occasions for storytelling
64 Banana bread unit
65 Witty Bombeck
66 Wealthy frequent fliers
69 "Amen!"
71 Lettuce variety
74 Pre-college exams
75 Squeak or creak
76 Vice ___ (the other way around)
77 Former CIA chief Porter ___
80 NFL guard Chris
81 O.T. book
84 Tangle, as in a net
85 540, to Caligula
86 Reduce the density of
87 Mariah Carey, for one
88 First Lady before Bess
89 Get angry about, say
92 Aligned
93 Suds-removing car wash devices
94 Acorn, some day
101 Complete, in brief
103 Dubuque citizen
104 Museum offerings
105 Medicinal tea
107 ìLemme ___!î (fighter's cry)
109 Fingernail shaper
110 Dart here and there
111 OED terms
112 Flows out
113 Liquid adhesive
115 Agitate
117 PC bailout key
118 Seeing thing

*Elizabeth Gorski, "Plane Geometry," 2013. Reprinted with permission of Elizabeth Gorski, Crosswordnation.com.*

# POST-DOCTORAL WORK
## Physicians who went on to other things.

**Across**

1. Painter Chagall
5. Come apart at the seams
9. Vacuum-tube gas
14. ___ close to schedule
15. Italian resort
16. ___ Haute, IN
17. Physician-turned-dictator
20. Actor McQueen
21. "Eat ___ eater" (law of the jungle)
22. Not ___ many words
23. Baldwin of "The Hunt for Red October"
25. Bit of legalese
27. IOU
30. Physician-turned-revolutionary
35. Young fellow
36. Movie-chain name
37. Israeli money
38. Greet the day
40. Even the score
42. Skilled
43. Hid away
45. Workers' rights org.
47. Southeast Asian language
48. Physician-turned-synonymist
50. Sunbeams
51. Seeing things
52. Presidential prerogative
54. Aid in wrongdoing
57. Water, to Juan
59. How some daters go
63. Physician-turned-educator
66. Sort of stew
67. Aroma
68. Handy bit of Latin
69. Crimean country house
70. Scale starters
71. Something owed

**Down**

1. Kitchen cleaners
2. Med. school course
3. Rodeo prop
4. Neckwear
5. Ziegfeld's nickname
6. Bullet bounce
7. ID info
8. "Leave him alone, ___ bully!"
9. ___ glance (quickly)
10. No longer worried
11. Look of contentment
12. Metals in the rough
13. Wolfe the detective
18. ___ Monte
19. Aphrodite's equivalent
24. Author Umberto
26. Kind of therapy
27. Envelope attachment
28. "Outcasts of Poker Flat" writer
29. Knucklehead
31. "Dallas" family name
32. Cub scout leader
33. Satisfy, as a mortgage
34. Some singers
36. Suspicious
39. Sort of sugary
41. Car in a building
44. Wild fancy
46. Hwy.
49. Rhyming newsman Charles
50. Stirred to anger
53. QB's stats
54. In the center of
55. Theda of silent films
56. Leif's pop
58. Bring to naught
60. Big bag
61. Bellyacher
62. To the ___ (completely)
64. "Now I get it!"
65. Prior to

*Manny Nosowksy,*
*"Post-Doctoral Work,"*
*Long Island Open, 1991.*
*Reprinted with permission of*
*Stanley Newman.*

# YOU CAN SAY THAT AGAIN!
## The father of modern-day crossword tournaments works this side of the street for the first time.

**Across**

1. Sicilian rumbler
5. Can't stand
9. Pythias' pal
14. Diver Louganis
15. Controversial arms buyer
16. Scientific discipline
17. Elvis Presley flick of '62
20. Kiss
21. "___ We Got Fun?"
22. Wedding-announcement word
23. Streetcorner sign
25. "And ___ Goes" (Linda Ellerbee book)
27. Mont Blanc, for instance
30. Unexpressed
32. "Mary Tyler Moore Show" spinoff
36. Fifties bombshell Diana
38. Kvetch
39. Fishing nets
40. Song from "The Student Prince"
43. Slot-machine fruit
44. Seven, on a sundial
45. 10 cc, perhaps
46. Follow
47. Madonna's in-laws
49. Actor Beatty
50. Place for a chapeau
52. A long time
54. Comments from the hard of hearing
57. Butter bits
59. Old wine in new bottles
63. Large national sorority
66. Used Elmer's

67. It may be hit or raised
68. "Terrible" Russian
69. World War I battle site
70. Dick and Jane's dog
71. Starr and Kyser

**Down**

1. Grade A purchases
2. Fit
3. Pianist Peter
4. All lit up
5. Scottish scenery
6. Onassis' nickname
7. Scarlett's mansion
8. Volunteer
9. Pooped
10. "Arabian Nights" first name
11. "Rise up so early in the ___ ..."
12. Girl-watch
13. Wall St. org.
18. Jazz singing
19. ___-Cone (summer snack)
24. 1980 Chrysler debut
26. Show place?
27. Confuse
28. "Sophia" author
29. Puts on a proper face
31. "Uncle!"
33. Peel it and weep
34. Not too clever
35. Tried to find out
37. Pig's nose
39. Hospital recovery?
41. Cagers' protection

42. Pinta's partner
47. Actress/singer Bernadette
48. Tournament ranking
51. Little bit
53. Role for Valentino
54. Nervous
55. Shortest-titled #1 Beatles tune
56. Libel
58. Be messy
60. Thomas ___ Edison
61. Hang around
62. Brinker of fiction
64. Start of a drive?
65. Overmuch

Will Shortz, "You Can Say That Again!" Baltimore Open, 1987. Reprinted with permission of Stanley Newman.

# CHAPTER TEN

# Puzzle Economies

Puzzle economies are, no pun intended, something I'm personally invested in. As editor/owner of the American Values Club crossword, which became independent from *The Onion* in 2012, I am responsible for determining constructor compensation. The standard system for crosswords nowadays, while more humane than it was in the past, remains distinctly unfriendly to constructors. While I might have made the same claim as other publishers, and offered industry-standard payment, I regard the current system as fatally unequal. My hope is that by giving the constructors who work for me a stake in the success of my feature, I will attract top-quality puzzles. Before getting into the details, I'll outline a brief history of what constructors have earned for their craft over the past 100 years or so.

The money in the puzzle business was middling, to put it mildly, in the old days. One publication's spec sheet from 1953 offered $4 for a standard puzzle, the equivalent of about $35 today, according to the Consumer Price Index. Even more remarkably, that rate was the same for 13 x 13, 15 x 15, *and* 17 x 17 puzzles, even though there is a substantial difference in the amount of time it takes to make those respective sizes. Meanwhile, a so-called "jumbo" puzzle, at 25 x 29 squares, paid $8.50, or around $75 in contemporary money. That size is more like gargantuan than jumbo; the largest seen in most newspapers today is 23 x 23. Not only does the word count increase, but so does the complexity of fitting everything together without repeating entries. A puzzle that large could therefore easily take several days to finish. Tellingly, the 1953 spec sheet also offered a rate for a 500-word puzzle story: $15. The modern equivalent of $130 isn't too shabby for a short piece of writing, and it demonstrates just how devalued crosswords were as a form of content by comparison.

Another sheet called "Rules for Constructing Crosswords" went so far as to warn "Never give your puzzles gratis to any publication. If it is worth printing it is worth buying. Though the constructor derives enjoyment and education in creating original puzzles, the market should not be glutted with free contributions. Many people depend on crossword puzzles for an income. Don't destroy their source of revenue." Perhaps $4, then, was actually generous—it must have been a buyer's market indeed, if constructors were giving their work away for free.

By 1993, the rate at the *Times*, the most generous in the country among dailies, was $50, or around $80 in contemporary dollars. Today the rate at that paper is $200 for a daily puzzle and $1,000 for a Sunday-sized (21 x 21). Under Will Shortz, who has advocated for better constructor pay, the rate has thus not only kept up with inflation, but far surpassed it, moving closer toward what most would consider fair. Undoubtedly, competition has helped spur this trend. While ho-hum themes can be repeated ad nauseam, clever and original ideas are rare, and puzzle editors covet them. The *New York Sun* continually raised its rates during Peter Gordon's editorship to encourage constructors to send their A-grade work to him. It worked, and the *Times* was compelled to respond by raising its own rates. But since the *Sun* folded, the *Times* has not budged from $200—a period, now, of six years and counting. Other outlets, such as the *Chronicle of Higher Education* (edited by Jeffrey Harris), have more or less kept pace, raising their daily pay to $150. Others, such as the *Los Angeles Times* ($85), *USA Today* ($65), and *GAMES* magazine ($50), continue to pay 1990s rates well into the second decade of the 20th century. Typically, this is less the fault of the editor than the publisher. Given the current state of print media, the rate freezes are not exactly surprising.

Despite the generally upward direction of puzzle compensation during the past 100 years, rates remain out of whack with what constructors could reasonably be demanding. I am often asked whether anyone can make a living as a constructor, and with perhaps two or three exceptions in the United States, the answer is no. These lucky few must, moreover, pump out book after book to earn money, as freelancing alone could never be enough. Editors, on the other hand, receive salaries or royalties, which can amount to a steady living. But freelance constructors are beholden to the severely limited terms of the agreements they sign. These agreements offer a low rate given the time commitment of writing a puzzle, the scarcity of theme ideas, and the prominence of the venues. But this is only the beginning. Papers also buy first rights *and* future rights, meaning

## A CURIOUS THING

There are many potential niche markets for puzzle makers, from high-paying corporate gigs to alumni magazines, from educational crosswords to advertisements. But few opportunities offer the allure and fun of a marriage-proposal puzzle. At their most involved, proposal puzzles will actually run in the newspaper, so that the person proposed to won't be suspicious. Of course, then everyone who solves the puzzle is in on the joke, at least once they finish. The idea is that the couple will do the crossword together, as if everything is normal, and slowly the unwitting party will recognize that their name at 1-Across was no coincidence—the central entry might read WILLYOU/MARRYME as a final payoff. My greatest dream, however, is to construct a breakup puzzle for someone in need of an innovative way to tell their soon-to-be-ex that things are over. To my knowledge, no such puzzle has ever run in a major puzzle outlet, but drop me a line if you'd like to make history.

that the constructor relinquishes all ownership of a puzzle once he or she signs it over. The *New York Times*, published by St. Martin's Griffin, releases as many as five or six new books a month. All of the crosswords in these books are recycled from the pages of the newspaper. This is a lucrative secondary market, and the rows and rows of books with Will Shortz's picture on the cover in bookstores are testament to their popularity. The publisher does not publicly release details, but a quick Bookscan check reveals that sales are robust. There are many millions being made in crossword books each year. However, for books republished from newspapers, with rare exceptions, precisely none of the profits go to the people who wrote the puzzles.

The most common reason offered for this inequity is the difficulty of accounting. But one imagines that, if constructors were to collectively demand a greater share of puzzle profits, newspapers would be forced to figure it out. As the sole administrative figure involved with the American Values Club, I've made it my job to be accountant as well as editor. This doesn't come easily, but the alternative seems preposterous. There is no other creative industry where content providers would agree to sacrifice so much of their potential earnings. Perhaps I am sympathetic because I've been a constructor as well as an editor for ten years. Regardless, our agreement is and has been that constructors receive, first, a fixed minimum rate of $100 per puzzle no matter what. In addition to this, 25 percent of all income (derived from subscriptions, syndication, etc.) is divided among constructors, who thus share proportionally in the feature's success. Finally, this agreement holds not only for regular revenue sources, but for books, apps, and all other secondary revenue sources. The constructor effectively retains ownership over their work. Perhaps something along these lines will be the future of crossword markets—a number of very prominent editors privately think so.

When crosswords were safely ensconced in newspapers, they were supported by advertising. For a company running a print spot, appearing on the same page as the puzzle meant proximity to a feature that readers were likely to spend serious time with—perhaps an hour or more, with their ad in view. What happens today when, as discussed in Chapter Six, puzzles increasingly go independent? Advertising is a much less viable option, so one must pursue other strategies. The American Values Club followed the Fireball puzzle by charging an annual subscription. Even $15 a year strikes some people, who are accustomed to solving the puzzle for free in the newspaper, as too high. But for others, just over 25 cents per puzzle feels justifiable. Many high-profile crossword outlets have crowdsourced funding since 2012, raising money on sites like kickstarter.com. No less than six crossword puzzle projects have raised multiple thousands of dollars.

Of course, subscriptions aren't a new invention. The *New York Times* charges $40 a year for online access to its puzzle, and as of several years ago had at least 50,000 subscribers. Combined with the harder-to-calculate value of having the crossword in the paper, and revenues from books, the crossword is a hugely valuable venture for the *Times*. Even those who get the physical newspaper must pay for digital access. Naturally, the feature has significant expenses to cover as well, but the puzzle remains one of the few profitable arms of an otherwise struggling media empire. Subscriptions are no small part of this.

Crosswords, as with many creative industries, are in a time of economic turmoil. Things have improved for constructors since the days when publishers exploited the idea that making puzzles was fun, and therefore not worth paying for. But we're not entirely out of the shadow of that idea. Hopefully the future will bring cooperation among constructors to ask for fair compensation for their work. There is more than enough money in the crossword industry today to justify it. I leave you, at last, with a few of my own crosswords (sign up for them at inkwellxwords.com).

# Onion A. V. Club
## June 9, 2010

**Across**

**1.** Rockies, e.g.: Abbr.

**4.** Mushroom makers

**10.** Vex

**14.** "That hurts!"

**15.** Leader of the band the Medicine Show

**16.** Like some sources: Abbr.

**17.** Snicker segment

**18.** Yoga pose

**20.** French articles

**22.** Gang leader of the 70s and 80s?

**23.** Moves quick, archaically

**24.** With 26-Across, "Mad Men" creator

**26.** See 24-Across

**28.** Overwhelm with, as homework

**29.** Bird that apes

**31.** "Shame on you!"

**32.** More devious

**33.** "___ Money" (2008 Busta Rhymes hit)

**34.** Regarding

**35.** Fashion designer who created Julius the Monkey

**38.** Problems that may result from screwing studs without using some kind of barrier device: Abbr.

**41.** Lowly laborer

**42.** Duck down?

**46.** Anthemic preposition

**47.** He played Charles

**48.** Porous pyroclastic

**49.** With 51-Across, 1976 Ramones hit

**51.** See 49-Across

**52.** "Bull Durham" setting: Abbr.

**53.** "ROFLMAO!"

**55.** Survey opción

**56.** Party with too many dudes... or a hint to this puzzle's theme

**59.** Simpson trial judge Lance

**60.** Eye provocatively

**61.** Stands on a soapbox, perhaps

**62.** Unagi or anago

**63.** Año, to Andrew

**64.** Float event

**65.** Feed format for blogs

**Down**

**1.** 2005 song with the lyric "I mix your milk with my cocoa puff"

**2.** Polish place

**3.** In a winsome way

**4.** Ritalin target: Abbr.

**5.** Word before arrow or heart

**6.** "That's so cool!"

**7.** "The kissing disease"

**8.** Emulate the Dude

**9.** ___ punk (The Mighty Mighty Bosstones' genre)

**10.** Pie cuts, essentially

**11.** Hits the tab key

**12.** Most appealing, as casino slots

**13.** ESL part

**19.** Daughter of Uranus, in myth

**21.** Immerses

**25.** Dance done after Birkat Hamazon

**26.** Lisa Leslie's org.

**27.** "The Lusty Men" studio

**29.** Character voiced by George Clooney in 2009

**30.** It's twisted

**33.** "A Clockwork Orange" narrator

**34.** With hands on hips

**36.** Aware of

**37.** Opposite of alte

**38.** ___ story

**39.** Like some who can't vote

**40.** He sucks a lot

**43.** Like "Fritz the Cat," vis-à-vis "Felix the Cat"

**44.** Trick-taking games

**45.** Updates

**47.** Historical meeting places

**48.** Ended incrementally, with "out"

**50.** It's purpose is stunning

**51.** Geometric symbol for an angle

**53.** Oft cheated-on goddess of Greek myth

**54.** Way off

**56.** Salty sauce source

**57.** Arlen Specter's party, once

**58.** Half of a deadly fly

*Caleb Madison,* Onion A.V. Club, *June 9, 2010. Reprinted with permission of Caleb Madison and Ben Tausig. The* Onion A.V. Club *crossword became the independent American Values Club xword in 2013. You can subscribe to it at www.avxwords.com.*

# Onion A. V. Club
## July 13, 2010

**Across**

**1.** Small amounts of sunscreen

**5.** Farmers' market letters

**8.** Mess up, as an owner's furniture

**14.** Comforting words after a fall

**15.** Detroit-based labor gp.

**16.** Pressed sandwiches

**17.** Mobile crosstown, e.g?

**19.** Sniff and then some

**20.** Really, really beautiful

**21.** Really, really big

**22.** DMV employee?

**24.** Alternatives to Levi's

**27.** Headed for the morgue, perhaps

**28.** Sugar suffixes

**29.** Hardware store binful

**32.** Pass over

**35.** Vegetarian's motto?

**41.** Character retired by Sacha Baron Cohen

**42.** Words before shoppe, often

**43.** " ... long walk ___ short pier!"

**47.** California ball club, briefly

**49.** Try to get a rise out of

**50.** Airport security measure that's getting old?

**55.** Soundtrack to many a lighting up

**56.** Safety devices used during acts of congress?

**60.** On the fence

**61.** Term for what happens when your phone wrongly predicts the word you want to type, and what shows up in 17-, 22-, 35-, and 50-Across

**62.** PBS "Newshour" host

**63.** Compass dir.

**64.** Soaks

**65.** Most like a fox

**66.** They're figured into a QB rating

**67.** Casual refusals

**Down**

**1.** "___ do that?" (Urkel catch phrase)

**2.** In the center of

**3.** Like the Honda Element

**4.** Employee's assets

**5.** Three-dimensional

**6.** Pickled

**7.** Chorus around babies

**8.** Word after Old or Scary

**9.** Underwear brand that recently ended their relationship with Charlie Sheen

**10.** Paint with a saintly ring

**11.** Ross and Frances

**12.** Not prerecorded

**13.** Barbara and Jenna, to Jeb Bush

**18.** "The Book of ___" (2010 Denzel Washington picture)

**21.** City with a Suntory Museum

**23.** Small bouquet originally used to mask rotten smells

**24.** Mind-expander of a sort

**25.** Prefix with friendly or conscious

**26.** Direction ender

**30.** "Eh?"

**31.** Narrator Paradise in "On the Road"

**33.** Unfriendly

**34.** Famously dark mystery author

**36.** Squiggly Spanish diacritic

**37.** Like pencil nubs

**38.** Style manual publisher

**39.** Chisel cousin

**40.** Pince-___

**43.** Non-alcoholic beer choice

**44.** Frat party drinking prop

**45.** Full of pulp, as fruit

**46.** Magnetism

**48.** Climb up

**51.** Loses the attention of

**52.** In plain sight

**53.** Navigates a racing boat

**54.** Creature with a queen

**57.** Top draft status

**58.** That masturbation causes blindness, e.g.

**59.** Some mobile communiqués

**61.** "We Know Drama" channel

*Ben Tausig, July 13, 2010.* Onion A.V. Club. *Reprinted with permission of Ben Tausig.*

## Across

**1.** Sea-___ Airport

**4.** He said "The revolution is not an apple that falls when it is ripe. You have to make it fall."

**7.** Not getting any, by choice

**13.** "The Piano" heroine

**14.** Losing line in a children's game

**15.** Big name in lock-changing

**16.** Space station that had a supply of vodka

**17.** Jagger in rare form?

**19.** Political tract holder?

**21.** "Just like me"

**22.** Greenskeeper's roll

**23.** Arthur ___ Sulzberger, Jr. (New York Times publisher)

**27.** Cousin of t'aint

**30.** Make a Halloween costume, say

**32.** Little chuckle

**33.** Unruly crowd

**34.** Cracklin' ___ Bran

**36.** Tool carried by a sherpa

**38.** One who might have to drop the line to perform salah?

**42.** Chatted

**43.** Spy device dropped into each of the theme entries

**44.** Budgetary guess: Abbr.

**45.** ___ moment's notice

**46.** Previously, in a 19th century literature class

**49.** Green

**51.** "If you don't mind ...?"

**53.** Free throw's path

**55.** Monteverdi opera

**58.** Owl food trade?

**62.** Tiny organism in the tub?

**65.** "Next round's on me"

**66.** Parched

**67.** Sharp turn

**68.** "___ needs food, badly" (Classic line from the video game Gauntlet)

**69.** Iron Maiden, nowadays

**70.** That, in Tegucigalpa

**71.** Leia, to Luke, casually

## Down

**1.** Home to the NHL's Lightning

**2.** "Later, muchacho"

**3.** 1993 Al Pacino gangster movie

**4.** Universe

**5.** Pueblo sun god

**6.** WSJ reader, perhaps

**7.** Main character in "Hair"

**8.** Clue room

**9.** Intend on

**10.** ___ Lanka

**11.** It has a lot of chapters: Abbr.

**12.** Stuffed head on a wall, perhaps

**15.** Overseas farewells

**18.** Duane Reade competitor

**20.** Ready to be taken down?

**24.** Poutine relative

**25.** Internal pumper

**26.** Activity with positions

**28.** ___ de puzzle (crossword writer's pseudonym)

**29.** Unhip "Clueless" girl

**31.** Gov. Walker's st.

**33.** Classic Mazda

**35.** "Getting shit done," initially

**37.** Goat milk treat

**39.** Fruit-flavored drink

**40.** Grins

**41.** "Hometown Proud" supermarket

**42.** Spread out in the morning

**47.** Das ___ ("Combination Pizza Hut and Taco Bell" rappers)

**48.** Happy to see someone, perhaps

**50.** Zip drive maker

**52.** Paintball player's cry

**54.** "Have You Ever Seen the Rain?" band, for short

**56.** Source of some food poisoning

**57.** French eggs

**59.** Hungarian leader Nagy

**60.** Leak

**61.** Advanced degs.

**62.** ___-relief

**63.** Put away some bowties

**64.** "Much appreciated," in a txt

*Brendan Emmett Quigley, April 6, 2011.* Onion A.V. Club. *Reprinted with permission of Brendan Emmett Quigley and Ben Tausig.*

# Onion A. V. Club
## September 16, 2010

**Across**

1 Players Ball attendee
5 Host who sells vowels
10 April number crunchers, for short
14 One of Pittsburgh's rivers
15 "I Feel for You" singer Khan
16 Political diatribe
17 Paranoid feeling while standing in a cornfield?
20 "Lost" actor Somerhalder
21 Small Federal Reserve Notes
22 Greek letters
23 With 53-Across, poison corn fed to a hot girl?
27 Eases (off)
29 "I could go on ... "
30 Gun, as the engine
31 Weakness
33 Pac-10 sch.
35 Booted grounders, e.g.
37 Corn body wraps?
43 Submit, as a contest entry
44 Soft drink since 1924
45 How a steep slope rises
48 B-F linkage
51 Bunch of bills
52 Smart crowd
53 See 23-Across
55 Capital of Can.
56 Apply non-lethal force to, supposedly
59 Aurora, to the Greeks
60 Intimate experience in raising corn?
66 Persian's place
67 Prefix with financing or economics
68 "Mitla Pass" author Leon
69 "Uh-unh"
70 Back of a skipjack
71 They're *supposed* to be corny...

**Down**

1 "The Masque of the Red Death" author
2 Guitarist James on "Siamese Dream"
3 Russian space station
4 Assume for argument's sake
5 Torch holder
6 Ice-T's "Always Wanted to Be ___ "
7 Bob Dylan's youngest son
8 Of the same family
9 "Citizen ___ "
10 Computer monitor part: Abbr.
11 EBay bought it in 2002
12 Name, as a successor
13 Clothing brand name with an umlaut
18 "If I only had a heart" singer Bert
19 Teeming
23 God, in Latin
24 Use acid to make art
25 They often sue the U.S. govt.
26 Too
28 Sportscaster Rich
31 Highly successful Hollywood actor James presently on "General Hospital"
32 Become maggot-infested, perhaps
34 High points
36 L.L. Bean rival
38 Kicking and screaming activity?
39 Up to, briefly
40 Icky creature
41 Pad ___
42 Half of an argument
45 Really attractive, in slang
46 Straight, casually
47 Tempt into crime
49 Tapped, as experience
50 Green sci.
53 Sell stolen stuff
54 Exhaust
57 Funds for the less fortunate
58 "MADtv" bit
61 How some Mexicans travel to the USA: Abbr.
62 Bobby or Benjamin
63 "All the King's Men" actress Joanne
64 Victorious shout in a card game
65 Suffix with baron

# Clubhouse Division

## Across

**1.** Finished the cake, say
**5.** Roasts
**9.** Safe space
**14.** Word in absorbency
**15.** Little on "The Wire"
**16.** Tequila source
**17.** Acknowledged guilt, perhaps
**18.** What an electroencephalograph shows
**20.** At-a-loss utterance
**21.** Big ___ of OutKast
**22.** It's a lot less slimy if you roast it, actually
**23.** A-lists, hopefully
**27.** BBC competitor
**30.** Like some credit in school
**31.** At-a-loss utterance
**32.** "Call of Duty: Black Ops II" desert setting
**33.** Heat meas.
**35.** "Nobody wants to see you slobbering all over each other"
**38.** Certain spring training matches, and a hint to this puzzle's theme
**42.** Extremely goofy duck-billed creature
**43.** Quick moment, quickly
**44.** Character who literally "jumped the shark"
**45.** "___ like I said ..."
**47.** Golfer Cheyenne Woods, to Tiger
**51.** Source of some private pain?: Abbr.
**52.** They match for residency
**55.** Swiss jet magnate
**57.** Tennis's Ivanovic
**58.** Spice amt., perhaps
**59.** Ironically titled Lennon/Ono album
**63.** They might make you scratch your head
**64.** Chemical warfare chemical
**65.** Mountain man's tool
**66.** Cutting line?
**67.** Confuse
**68.** Historical autocrat
**69.** Lions' arenas?

## Down

**1.** Like most cocaine, to some degree
**2.** Hybrid west coast cuisine
**3.** Not on the hook, as for taxation
**4.** "Which way ___ they go?"
**5.** 1970s funk dance, with "the"
**6.** "Triple sevens! Triple sevens!"
**7.** Ovine exclamation
**8.** ___ Lanka
**9.** Strike supporters?
**10.** Gelatinous dessert ingredient
**11.** "So sexy!"
**12.** Biblical woman whose name means "life"
**13.** Contra platform, briefly
**19.** Go to sleep, with "off"
**21.** Spoiled, maybe
**24.** Kayak alternative, transportation-wise
**25.** Frequently hot and sticky months
**26.** Perlman on the rocks with Danny DeVito
**28.** Certain reed
**29.** Uses a sight
**32.** Mr. Burns's wife?
**34.** Pill-bottle letters
**36.** They may be celebrated after throwing bombs: Abbr.
**37.** Sheet at a meeting
**38.** They're often higher for the fair
**39.** Burial unit
**40.** One who may charge a flat fee
**41.** Pound, in British slang
**46.** Poetic subunit
**48.** Draw in
**49.** X-ray type
**50.** Telepaths
**52.** State that divides its Electoral College votes
**53.** Write well as hell, say?
**54.** Chief Wayne ___ ("Sons of Anarchy" character)
**56.** Complimentary adjective for a metal band
**59.** Org. that enforces liquid regulations
**60.** Spitball shape
**61.** Piece, in '90s hip-hop
**62.** Young people may carry fake ones
**63.** Subject of secret Cold War military experiments

Ben Tausig, "Clubhouse Division," Ink Well, March 14, 2013. Reprinted with permission of Ben Tausig.

# Doubly Fun

**Across**

**1.** Durable textured wall material
**7.** Word said while wearing a sexy cat costume
**11.** Thing on a cat's paw
**14.** Persist
**15.** Currency recently in crisis
**16.** Band with a trippy jukebox/spaceship logo
**17.** TV show about a Trojan War hero's early years as a mobster?
**20.** Strip on a mountain?
**21.** Bond in "License to Kill"
**22.** Pacific island getaway
**23.** Mostly female punk band of the 1970s, with "the"
**25.** Note above C
**26.** Director who had to have "Life of Pi" explained to him over and over before he agreed to adapt it?
**31.** Bathtub drink
**32.** Dr. Eric Foreman portrayer, on "House"
**36.** Clinton-era space station
**37.** Louisiana sub
**39.** Lightning ___ bottle
**40.** "Spaced Cowboy" yodeler
**43.** Wear the right clothes and such
**45.** Clique of cows who totally knew about this patch of grass before anyone else?
**48.** Curse associated with Joe Pesci
**51.** Scale
**52.** Deep feeling
**53.** Consumes quickly
**56.** Johnny ___
**59.** Particularly pisslike cheap drinks?
**62.** Put down a dog?
**63.** Tree with nuts used in pesto
**64.** Puncture with silly-looking cleats, as a lawn
**65.** Was in first place
**66.** Charon's river
**67.** Getting buzzed, say?

**Down**

**1.** Places to seek wellness
**2.** "Nip/___"
**3.** American naturalization test subject
**4.** Team that lost to MIA in the 2013 NBA playoffs
**5.** Like some spring days
**6.** Like infomercials, often
**7.** Remainder
**8.** Commercial prefix with -Tune
**9.** Wee warbler
**10.** Sashimi topper
**11.** Spin one's wheels?
**12.** Hello, to Ku'uipo
**13.** One may be turned in a lot
**18.** Lioness profiled in the book "Born Free"
**19.** Like some apartment listings
**24.** Jean-___ Godard
**25.** "Yeah, obviously"
**26.** Electrical impedance units
**27.** Prepare, as pasta
**28.** "Check," in poker
**29.** Insect-resistant plant, e.g., briefly
**30.** Sexual partner
**33.** It may scoop up baba ghanoush
**34.** Nabokov novel about a Russian literature teacher
**35.** Sex on the beach component?
**37.** Prosecco-opening sound
**38.** Strap-___ (sex shop items)
**41.** Emulate Steve Vai
**42.** Pharmacist's abbr.
**43.** Flying disc on the beach
**44.** Tech company headquartered in Armonk, New York
**46.** Nude cousin?
**47.** Danny who wrote the "Simpsons" theme
**48.** Like some Bach works
**49.** Authored
**50.** Looked at libidinously
**53.** Huff
**54.** "Down by the River" supergroup, initially
**55.** "I'll take 'Before & After' for $200, ___"
**57.** One-named Deco designer
**58.** Talked above one's pay grade
**60.** "Come on Pilgrim" and "Interpol," for two
**61.** Prior to, poetically

# Let the Right One In

**Across**

1. Respond to, as a tip
6. Dodge SUV
11. "Science Friday" host Flatow
14. Olive Oyl suitor
15. "Channel Orange" musician
16. Queensbridge rapper
17. Proctologist's "time to go to work!"?
19. Devices in front of treadmills
20. Hunk's display
21. Fit
22. Healthy seed also used for kitschy figurines
23. "My plan is to hide inside John's piano and jump out at him"?
28. Level a flat, say
29. Jaunty trip
30. Bath sitting spot?
33. Animal yelling like a human in a recent viral video
34. Indian goddess after whom an actress is named
36. Transgender modeling school that promises quick results?
41. Response to a detailed story about a UTI
42. Incur extra cell charges, perhaps
43. Footwear alternatives to Roos
44. Go back over, as a story
46. Canceled
49. Hamster's exercise bestie?
52. Bones in a cage
53. Site that was super fun before they had rules; once I sold a deed to the moon on it
54. Loan shark's note
57. Treat as a plaything
58. Navy computer programmer's project?
62. International Space Station precursor
63. Presidential nickname coined by Molly Ivins
64. Patty and Selma, e.g.
65. Gif alternative
66. "God ___ this mess"
67. Careful scrutiny

**Down**

1. Fifteenth best-selling artists of all time
2. Sandwich type similar to a BLT
3. "Hotel Rwanda" ethnicity
4. The Senators, on the scoreboard
5. 2008/2012 campaign portmanteau
6. "Search me"
7. Harold in the Roosevelt administration, or his son in the Clinton administration
8. Recent notable Couric get
9. Analyzed, as the numbers
10. Strap-___
11. Out of gear?
12. Beside oneself
13. Dictator who trained as an ophthalmologist
18. Flows' partners
22. Technology that brought us Jar Jar Binks
24. Space
25. Sound that might scare a mouse
26. Polynesian party
27. Suffix for relatively small things
30. Installation, say
31. Häagen-Dazs option
32. Director whose work has been nominated for 123 Academy Awards
33. Potential pick-up spot with bars inside
35. Old-timey cries of distress
37. Compound in pee
38. Sit on the couch
39. Hindu island in Muslim Indonesia
40. Viking's drinking word
45. Defaces, as a yard on Halloween
46. Rich, important people
47. Highland scotch brand
48. The Stonewall, famously
49. Many a Jack Nicholson character
50. Google smartphone
51. Sixth-century Chinese dynasty
55. ___ von Bismarck
56. Whence the villains in the original "Red Dawn"
58. Link for a drive, say
59. Org. for Sid the Kid and Alexander the Great
60. Pissiness
61. Pre-French 101 word

*Ben Tausig, "Let the Right One In,"* Ink Well, *February 28, 2013. Reprinted with permission of Ben Tausig.*

# Nothing Major

**Across**

**1.** Came back from the beach?
**6.** Lesbos lyrist
**12.** Fawn (over)
**15.** Wine taster's consideration
**16.** Like tape, e.g.
**17.** Penguin-looking bird
**18.** Junior members of a lodge?
**20.** ___ Moneypenny
**21.** Hippie's trip, perhaps
**22.** Time killers on a device
**24.** Long-distance hauler
**25.** Manager of oral hygienists of ill repute?
**31.** Ruler divisions: Abbr.
**33.** Boo-boo
**34.** It's not hard rock
**35.** Aluminum giant
**38.** Like Munch's "The Scream," in 1994 and again in 2004
**40.** Puppy Bowl at which the Puppy Cam debuted
**41.** Certain independent, and an apt title for this puzzle
**44.** One might be bowled over
**45.** Masses
**46.** Sierra ___
**47.** Noodle in tempura soup
**49.** Prime draft status
**50.** "What it do?"
**51.** Arthur Sulzberger, e.g.?
**54.** Modern Nintendo consoles
**58.** Nintendo rival
**59.** Noted Barbadian pop star
**61.** Sn, on a table
**62.** Try to trademark your new invention?
**67.** Brad Paisley's "___ de Toilet (The Toilet Song)"
**68.** Cover with diamonds, as it were
**69.** Tint in some nostalgic images
**70.** Home for un poisson
**71.** "Crocodile" of film
**72.** Equally influenced right

now by Nam June Paik's video work and Bedouin poetry, say

**Down**

**1.** Charles or Ray of modern design
**2.** Knee supporter
**3.** Bust
**4.** Typed expression
**5.** Paul of "Little Miss Sunshine"
**6.** "___ bleu!"
**7.** "I don't care which one"
**8.** Kung ___ chicken (Americanized Chinese dish)
**9.** Grocery store sticker letters
**10.** Very attractive
**11.** Ancient Irish alphabet
**12.** Site of the 2012 G8 Summit
**13.** Moniker for Jesus
**14.** Approves
**19.** Certain guards against babies
**23.** Bro
**26.** Still competitive, potentially
**27.** Pod contents, in an analogy
**28.** Fox's Roger
**29.** Look like a horndog
**30.** Its state berry is the blueberry
**32.** Road safety org.
**35.** Get hyped
**36.** Saved
**37.** Church key, e.g.
**38.** River to the Rhone
**39.** SeaWorld orca name
**42.** Word before comic or plane
**43.** Sink stuff
**48.** Pos.'s opposite
**50.** Word to denote the deleted portion of an email
**52.** Without warning, say
**53.** Hold forth
**55.** Ham-handed
**56.** Civil rights leader Roy
**57.** Grilled meat from Indonesia
**60.** "Andre the Giant ___ Posse"
**61.** Everyone's first Myspace friend
**63.** Where a post-ER patient might go
**64.** Pearl Jam album with "Alive" and "Jeremy"
**65.** The oil in its liver is a source of omega-3 fatty acids
**66.** Coloration

*Ben Tausig, "Nothing Major," Ink Well, July 4, 2013. Reprinted with permission of Ben Tausig.*

# Switching Sides

## Across

**1.** Jacket summary
**6.** They deal with the UAW
**9.** Portmanteau for a piece of eye broccoli
**14.** Heard
**15.** Craft for the paranoid
**16.** Erotica author Nin
**17.** Popular image manager
**19.** Watch-crystal holder
**20.** Reality show about Botoxed Shakespearean actresses?
**22.** Active Japanese volcano
**23.** It might get you into more underground stuff
**24.** Band on Butt-head's shirt
**27.** Middle school insult
**31.** Pesters
**35.** Hand model's appeal?
**38.** Maintain, as blades
**39.** Corleone enforcer Luca
**40.** Influential play for the genre of sci-fi
**41.** Tim Rice musical with absolutely no influence on sci-fi
**43.** 1,000-pound Yellowstoner
**44.** Cargo headed to a dragon's factory?
**47.** Kept track of
**49.** Low voice in opera
**50.** June Carter ___
**51.** Drive letters
**53.** Hotel extra
**55.** Dentist?
**63.** Company with a penguin mascot
**64.** Record of dad getting hit in the crotch, perhaps
**65.** Hypocritical pejorative when used by millionaire senators born into political families
**66.** Org. that opposed Medicare in the '60s
**67.** Page partner
**68.** Curses
**69.** Prefix with fire
**70.** Ho Chi Minh Mausoleum city

## Down

**1.** Something you might be out on
**2.** Debussy's "Clair de ___"
**3.** Major in astronomy?
**4.** Working people's routines
**5.** Ennui
**6.** Expert, slangily
**7.** Creative writing degs.
**8.** Release tension, in a way
**9.** Old Spice spokesman
**10.** Like the haircut I just got from this old Polish dude that then I had to fix
**11.** Look wistfully
**12.** Claims to have a nonexistent girlfriend, say
**13.** Bag letters
**18.** Start ranting
**21.** Grammarian's correction
**24.** "Who's Afraid of Virginia Woolf?" playwright
**25.** Not straight
**26.** YOLO popularizer
**28.** Heart parts
**29.** Weds follower
**30.** Uses Prodigy, say
**32.** Commodore computer introduced in 1985
**33.** Certain high school outcasts
**34.** Strip on the lawn
**36.** Prevent from squeaking
**37.** Sterile female worker, e.g.
**42.** Technics SL-1200 ancestor
**45.** Common caveat in crossword clues
**46.** Valium manufacturer
**48.** Minnesota's fourth-largest city
**52.** Once-again fashionable soulful rock instruments
**54.** Punch
**55.** Kunis who voiced Meg Griffin
**56.** Taking care of something
**57.** Single-minded captain
**58.** Roberto Baggio or Gianluigi Buffon, e.g.
**59.** IRS agent, casually
**60.** Big name in bloodthirsty sixteenth-century empire building
**61.** Martinez who won four World Series rings with the Yankees
**62.** Big white dude in Tibet
**63.** Constellation shaped like a coat hanger

Ben Tausig, "Switching Sides," Ink Well, *February 7, 2013. Reprinted with permission of Ben Tausig.*

# Triple Features

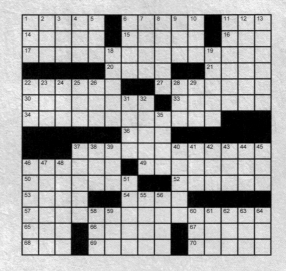

## Across

**1.** Gem

**6.** Places for piercings

**11.** Flight coordinators in a union busted by Reagan: Abbr.

**14.** 2011 hurricane that hit New York City

**15.** Submit an April return, the modern way

**16.** "___ Carter" (Lil Wayne's fourth record)

**17.** With 34-Across, petulant dynast of Rebecca Black's empire?

**20.** Discharge

**21.** "Dies ___" (Day of Wrath)

**22.** "Keep your pants on"

**27.** Each of the titles in this puzzle's theme answers, e.g.

**30.** Her image was stolen in 1911 and recovered in 1913

**33.** Military academy freshmen

**34.** See 17-Across

**36.** Leader who was born in Burma and who died in Myanmar

**37.** With 50-Across, renegades working for a network of backpacking lodges?

**46.** Line on a check

**49.** Game that required the Zapper

**50.** See 37-Across

**52.** Gem surfaces

**53.** Gernreich who designed a scandalous monokini

**54.** Sound of laughter

**57.** Weapon recovered from a preserved body at Area 51?

**65.** The Wings, on the scoreboard

**66.** "I can have this?"

**67.** Test outcome that once might have classified someone as a "moron"

**68.** Dreyer's partner in ice cream

**69.** Late-night host with a self-titled show

**70.** Hamlet's cousins?

## Down

**1.** Brand that's not for peanut allergy sufferers

**2.** "Uhh ..."

**3.** Twice, Chinese dissident artist Ai's given name

**4.** Doors classic, with "The"

**5.** Agriculturalist's field?

**6.** Member of the inaugural class of inductees to the National Toy Hall of Fame

**7.** "The Wizard ___"

**8.** One may help you clean up your junk

**9.** 2003 Will Ferrell holiday movie

**10.** Deep body, often

**11.** Palpitating

**12.** "The Work of Art in ___ of Mechanical Reproduction"

**13.** Drew and Mariah

**18.** "#!*@% paper cut!"

**19.** Like many a bathroom floor

**22.** Mischievous World of Warcraft figure

**23.** Neither partner

**24.** ___ Nuevo (Spanish New Year)

**25.** Morvan of Milli Vanilli (i.e., the one who's still alive)

**26.** Leader of leaders?

**28.** Tech school for crossword champ Tyler Hinman

**29.** Skilled at something, in slang

**31.** Hentai, e.g.

**32.** Having broken out as a teenager?

**35.** Streaming TV site

**37.** Sportscaster and NBA Hall of Famer Brown

**38.** Musician who's probably going to end up in your grid when you've got 33 3-letter words

**39.** Babe's milieu

**40.** Protagonist in the highest-grossing film of 1985

**41.** Letters for the wanted

**42.** Chemical featured at some modern dispensaries

**43.** French street

**44.** Pick, briefly, in football

**45.** Cadillac luxury vehicle introduced in 2013

**46.** Chafe

**47.** Torn to bits, as by a lion

**48.** David Bowie's "Space ___"

**51.** Reject rudely

**55.** Austen novel adapted by the BBC in 2009

**56.** "Right on, preacher"

**58.** Org. where Dallas is in the East and St. Louis is in the West, for some reason

**59.** Remark while on grass?

**60.** Noted three-ingredient sandwich

**61.** Head across the pond?

**62.** "The otters are holding hands!"

**63.** Aural affront

**64.** Messes with the bass, say, as a DJ

*Ben Tausig, "Triple Features," Ink Well, April 11, 2013. Reprinted with permission of Ben Tausig.*

# Video Circuits

**Across**

**1.** Company that bought the naming rights to Boston Garden

**7.** Stroked

**15.** Sales limit for rare items, say

**16.** Australian city where News Corp. was founded

**17.** -

**18.** "Praise Citizens United! Praise Citizens United!"?

**19.** Very common Muslim name

**20.** American bike company, oddly enough

**22.** Take, as a shot

**23.** "The art of making guests feel at home when that's really where you wish they were"

**25.** Add some color to

**27.** 1989 James Cameron film, with "The"

**30.** Falls in line

**32.** IV

**34.** "Fin" Tutuola portrayer

**35.** Smoker's action

**37.** Respond to Lasik surgery, say

**39.** She might work with Quentin on "Kill Bill 3"

**40.** -

**43.** Personal lubricant for a druglord?

**45.** "Past Life Martyred Saints" musician

**46.** Keystone ___

**47.** "Grey Gardens" first name

**48.** CBS maritime drama

**50.** Online expression of shock

**52.** Wedding registry tableware brand

**56.** Aloe, e.g.

**58.** Walk on water?

**60.** City associated with Francis

**61.** "Little Women" woman

**63.** U.S. Green Building Council rating system

**65.** Palindromic abbreviation in industrial music

**66.** -

**69.** Music fan concerned with expanding his mind as well as his body?

**71.** Early 1950s presidential campaign slogan

**72.** Area of concern to the FCC

**73.** Fubu alternative, in urban clothing

**74.** Arcade game in which characters can pass through tunnels to get to the other side of the screen

**Down**

**1.** Projectile hurled at Fozzie Bear

**2.** "CSI" facility

**3.** "There's no need for sarcasm"

**4.** On point

**5.** Big name in unnervingly militaristic toys

**6.** Fermented frank topper

**7.** Place where lots of money gets lost on the floor

**8.** Former soccer phenom Freddy

**9.** Squat count

**10.** Kagan of the court

**11.** Simba's mom

**12.** Vessel for young drinkers

**13.** LeShan who wrote about children

**14.** Mo. known for lights

**21.** Orville Redenbacher's rival

**24.** Put down words, in a way

**26.** Historically black university in Alabama

**28.** Rig on the road

**29.** Persian for "place"

**31.** Keep being mad, perhaps

**33.** Majority Leader since 2007

**36.** No. that Bloomberg's soda ban would have limited

**38.** Sooner State city

**40.** Burns and Jennings

**41.** Village People classic

**42.** One in a juvenile court?

**44.** Equipment

**49.** Liquor with futuristic sexy robot ads

**51.** Bathroom mold

**53.** Corporal or sergeant

**54.** Character with a "sense of snow" in a 1997 thriller

**55.** Marathoner Geoffrey Mutai, e.g.

**57.** Old-time anesthetic

**59.** Fix a sloppy cartographer's work

**62.** Will name

**64.** Commercial prefix meaning "dependable"

**66.** Insult, or enjoy

**67.** Tall Ernie of pro golf

**68.** Letters before a pen name

**70.** LSU's conference

*Ben Tausig, "Video Circuits," Ink Well, May 9, 2013. Reprinted with permission of Ben Tausig.*

# One Plus One

**Across**

1. Band-Aid maker, briefly
6. Officer of the future
11. Orientation tool
14. Multiple choice choices
15. Gayle's bestie
16. As (so-and-so) cooks it
17. Brothers on a classic Nick show
19. Media org. with lots of soothing voices
20. Nocturnal emission?
21. Visual
23. Bust
26. "No problem"
29. Likely to fail, as a student
31. Gas from beans, e.g.
32. Send out
33. Racer Protasiewicz or ex-prime minister Jaroszewicz (or a variant spelling of Tchaikovsky's first name)
35. Blended whisky cocktail
41. Like Vikings
42. Roughly
44. Late
48. Half of a series couple
50. Consecutive games between two teams in their respective stadiums
53. Alternative to JFK or LGA
54. Conveyances generally only ridden downward
55. Blunted swords
57. One gone cray-cray, as it were
58. Coffee shop freebie
64. "Is that true about me?"
65. Jean Stapleton's "All in the Family" role
66. Utah's ___ Mountains
67. Delt neighbor
68. Some stereos
69. Place with mandatory communal meals, sometimes

**Down**

1. Slur you just kind of hope won't come out when hearing WWII stories
2. 2012 Best Actor-winning role for Daniel
3. Sarcastic negation
4. ___ Scott v. Sandford
5. Paper inserts in cassette tape cases
6. Gene part
7. Cook's corp.
8. "It's On (Dr. ___) 187um Killa" (Eazy-E EP)
9. Fill up, in a way
10. Simon follower
11. Chinese steamed bun served with dim sum
12. French mountain goat
13. Unit of land
18. Barnes & Noble e-reader
22. Adobe image file
23. Scot's uh-uh
24. Certain hold-up sites
25. Wheel brought to many a party
27. Dwelling
28. Minor quibbles
30. Rumored Xbox competitor from 7-Down
33. Removed the peel from
34. Networking connections
36. Minus signs
37. Spit or swallow, e.g.
38. 2012 Channing Tatum/Rachel McAdams drama, with "The"
39. Lake next to Cedar Point amusement park
40. Warning before a sexy clip
43. Twelfth-to-last word before "play ball"
44. "You gonna let her talk to you like that?"
45. Knob on an amp
46. What alcohol works as, if you drink enough of it
47. Sore, say
48. Counterfeiter catchers
49. Hippie's bus, casually
51. Full-figured
52. Colorful food fish
56. He plays Sam in "Transformers"
59. Craziness
60. Jeremy of a predictably brief media craze
61. Raggedy doll
62. Inc., abroad
63. Surviving Milli Vanilli member

*Ben Tausig, "One Plus One," Ink Well, June 27, 2013. Reprinted with permission of Ben Tausig.*

# Sorting Letters

**Across**

**1.** Brownish photo tint
**6.** See 51-Down
**10.** Classic British sports cars
**14.** Omega-3s, e.g.
**15.** Sin for one who's gone green?
**16.** Chakra cousin
**17.** Bugs's question
**19.** One-named singer of "The Wanderer"
**20.** Sectional, say
**21.** "The Stand" hero Redman
**22.** Foul
**23.** "We're screwed ..."
**27.** Popular rave drug, briefly
**30.** Rapper associated with Queensbridge, Queens
**31.** Broadcaster
**32.** Vioxx maker
**34.** Kenan Thompson's sketch show
**35.** "Black Is the Color of My True Love's Hair" singer Simone
**38.** 1980 ZZ Top hit
**42.** Salty bodies
**43.** Org. with shows in theaters?
**44.** Creepo
**45.** Fracking rock
**47.** Pandemic during World War I
**49.** Delta in-flight magazine
**50.** Transformer who leads the Autobots
**54.** Places for casual conversation
**55.** "Pacific ___" (2013 summer flick)
**56.** Device produced by Carl Zeiss
**60.** Person holding the cards?
**61.** Exposes oneself?
**64.** Away from the wind, on the water
**65.** Recess
**66.** Genre for Weird Al
**67.** Gp. with a key and a martini glass in its logo
**68.** "Got it"
**69.** "Dope"

**Down**

**1.** They've got teeth
**2.** Sound return?
**3.** Subject of the biopic "La Vie en Rose"
**4.** Pound neckwear
**5.** Pompous person
**6.** What one might sink to
**7.** Provide, as with a quality
**8.** Bolivian president Morales
**9.** City where BHO graduated from college
**10.** Was lucid
**11.** Axe wielders
**12.** Cook in the bottom of the oven, say
**13.** Financial institution of '80s-'90s crisis infamy
**18.** Nutrition.gov org.
**22.** Controversial coat material
**24.** Peeling potatoes, stereotypically
**25.** Helmut of Fashion Week
**26.** Drug unit
**27.** Some SUVs
**28.** Mild chuckle
**29.** Put your kid in a position to suck
**33.** Scanned the goods, say
**34.** ___ Balls (erstwhile Hostess treats)
**36.** It helps you keep your head up
**37.** Dry, as skin
**39.** George Takei character
**40.** Plays for a sucker
**41.** Someone who went somewhere
**46.** Morns
**47.** Playful
**48.** Drag one's feet, say
**50.** Philosopher known for his "razor"
**51.** With 6-Across, big name in bad taste, in more ways than one
**52.** Like some trans people, briefly
**53.** Push aggressively, as through a crowd
**57.** Fashion mag with an "Ask E. Jean" column
**58.** LeBron's shoe company
**59.** Skedaddle
**61.** Purveyor of barely legal dietary supplements, often
**62.** XXX's opposite
**63.** Company "sorted" in this puzzle's circled squares

*Ben Tausig, "Sorting Letters," Ink Well, July 18, 2013. Reprinted with permission of Ben Tausig.*

# Flicks Off

**Across**

**1.** Having poor taste?
**6.** John of the Velvet Underground
**10.** Buy
**13.** Glue bull
**14.** Broken up
**16.** Crossword regular Sumac
**17.** Podiatric policeman?
**19.** 1985 Akira Kurosawa film based on "King Lear"
**20.** Stuck
**21.** Musician on whom Gus Van Sant's "Last Days" is based
**23.** 2012 Seth MacFarlane film about a talking bear
**24.** Wrestler with a "shell shocker" finishing move?
**27.** Marked a loss, in a way
**30.** Crime Alley-to-Wayne Manor dir., in Gotham City
**31.** Maya Angelou works
**32.** Get close without being close
**34.** Honda SUV
**36.** Six games, if one player loses all six
**37.** "The eating of omelets is hereafter punishable by death," e.g. [See byline]
**41.** Mix-A-Lot title
**44.** Lust, e.g.
**45.** Lust after
**49.** Battery connection
**52.** Faulkner's "___ Lay Dying"
**54.** Many a neo-ska group
**55.** Heated discussion about crabs?
**58.** 2001 Michael Mann biopic
**59.** Large sea ducks
**60.** Of Old Scratch
**63.** 2004 James Wan horror film that launched a franchise
**64.** Sound of fright that lasts all through Hanukkah?
**67.** Prefix with tard or form
**68.** Bond market buy
**69.** Probe (into)
**70.** Omelet-maker's need

(back before the 37-Across, of course)
**71.** [The horror!]
**72.** Thus far

**Down**

**1.** Catch the fancy of
**2.** Cowboy in Simón Bolívar's army
**3.** Band featuring Rush Limbaugh
**4.** Jay-Z's team
**5.** Take, as acid
**6.** Cult leader's robe, I imagine
**7.** Bee: Prefix
**8.** Lakers' local rivals, on the scoreboard
**9.** Ready for action, in a way
**10.** Goes for a spin?
**11.** "Hit up my Yahoo! account"
**12.** Most evidently just back from a Miami vacation, say
**15.** Bobby on the '70s medical drama "Emergency!"
**18.** Well-dressed fellow
**22.** "Dog"
**25.** Hippie's odor
**26.** Role-playing game player, stereotypically
**28.** Scratch (out)
**29.** Got super into
**33.** Mild movie ratings
**35.** YouTube clip, for short
**38.** Thailand, until 1932
**39.** Fivescore yrs.
**40.** General who countered the Taiping Rebellion, which was waged over access to sugary fried chicken
**41.** Prepares for a big purchase
**42.** Michael Jackson's home state
**43.** Victory in front of a hostile crowd
**46.** How athletes tend to speak in post-game interviews
**47.** Lessen, as pressure
**48.** Paperless pass
**50.** Rapper who mentored Kendrick Lamar, casually
**51.** Bird with a wide wingspan
**53.** Cobbler's measure
**56.** Only with for the money, say
**57.** Wee bit
**61.** "Amazing, right?"
**62.** Voting affirmations
**65.** Indian province once colonized by Portugal
**66.** Seaside ___, N.J. ("Jersey Shore" setting)

*Ben (1972 Phil Karlson horror film with a theme song by Michael Jackson) Tausig, "Flicks Off," Ink Well, June 11, 2013. Reprinted with permission of Ben Tausig.*

# SOLUTIONS AND NOTES

Reflecting on 100 years of crosswords reveals quite a lot. It's a story of Americana that arcs through several wars, the volatile history of print journalism, culture clashes over knowledge and taste, and much more. It is, as they rightly say, only a game, but still an awfully rich one.

So often centennial retrospectives are written in nostalgic moments when the present is seen to pale in comparison to a vibrant past. But we're all fortunate to be living in a boom time for puzzle creativity here in the early 21st century. We are well beyond the point when the *New York Times* could claim to be the only game in town. The past ten to 20 years have arguably witnessed the greatest advances in quality and variety in the history of the pastime. And the future promises to be even brighter.

PAGE 4

PAGE 12   STEPQUOTE

PAGE 16 LEFT

PAGE 16 RIGHT

**PAGE 17 BOTTOM**

```
A V E R T S   A L T E R S
V E L U R E   P E A N U T
E N A T I C   P A L T E R
N I P S   E W E   L I F E
G A S   R E A   C U E
E L E V E N   R E M E L T
      I N     N O
M O N A D S   A S P I R E
E R E   E L M   N I L
T I E R   V I I   S H O D
I O D I D E   D E L E T E
E L E M I N   S T A R E R
R E D A N S   T A P E R S
```

**PAGE 17 LEFT**

```
S Y Z Y G Y   C H A S T E
I C I E R   B R E V I E R
P L O W   R O E   E V E R
H E N   R E L A Y   A P O
O P   R E S U M E D   O R
N E M E S I S   A I M   S
  D A M O N   A R M E D
P   N I L   S I N E W E D
A S   T E N U R E S   M R
S P A   D O M E D   L E A
S I R E   M A D   P E R I
E L E G I A C   B E G I N
S T A G E D   F E A S T S
```

**PAGE 17 RIGHT**

```
D I S F E L L O W S H I P
E N T E R E D   A L O N E
S N E E R S   S V E L T E
K E E L S   S P E E D E R
  R L S   M I I   P U R L
R   D I A N E   P I E
E T   E L M E R   M S
H O Y   B E E T S   S
A R E T   A S S   D A M
S T O R A G E   L E V E R
H U M A N E   P A L A T E
E R E C T   B E S T I A L
S E N T I M E N T A L L Y
```

**PAGE 18 LEFT**

```
A B S I S T   Q U I D   F O S S I L
P R E S T O   U N D E   A M P E R E
P O N T O N   I T E M   G E Y S E R
E A T   P I   D I M E   O N   A N I
A C R E   C O D E   N O T   A M I D
R H Y M E   O L   I T S   A R E C A
      N B   E D N A   A M
M E A N D E R   E F T   S E P T I C
A S E A   D I T T I E S   S A R C O
D O R I C   B E A R D E D   N E E D
E X O D U S   R I M   T R A G E D Y
      L O   A L E S   Y R
S C E N T   I T   D I G   C L A I M
E L S E   P O O R   D O T   A N N A
P I T   M A   G A M E   H E   O D S
S E A L E R   E M I R   R A D I U S
I N T E N T   N I N A   U S A N C E
S T E A D Y   Y E E L   M E L T E D
```

PAGE 18 RIGHT

PAGE 19

PAGE 20 UNO

PAGE 21

PAGE 26

PAGE 27

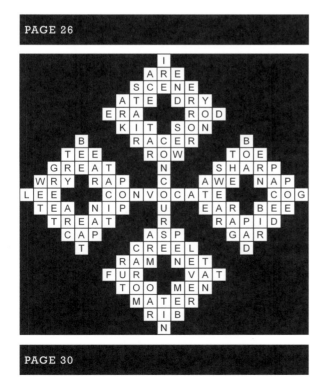

PAGE 30

PAGE 31 LEFT

PAGE 31 RIGHT

PAGE 34

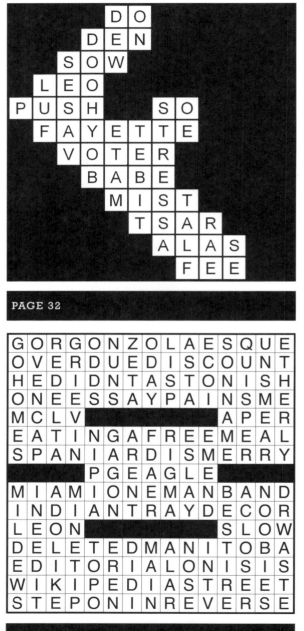

PAGE 32

PAGE 35 CUCKOO CROSSWORD 2

ANSWER: A, which you must put in the central black square of the grid to dig the PANAMA CANAL, formed from PANAM and CANAL. The clue for PAN AM works for both it and PANAMA CANAL [It revolutionized 20th-century global transportation] and the clue for SHIPS works for both it and SHIPS ACROSS [Transmits, as to the other side of a body of water]. Also you connect the PACIFIC and ATLANTIC by digging the canal (PACIFICA RADIO and TRANSATLANTIC). Also note that no letter is actually missing from the grid since it's a pangram, so the solver must look elsewhere for the answer.

```
S T L L T S R V C S ■ J S T T
N R S G H T D N S S ■ C H R R
F N N C L N T R S T ■ C T T N
F N D N G D R C T R ■ N L M T
D M S S N T C K T S ■ C N N S
■ ■ ■ D L R ■ T H S N D T H
W T C H F L ■ P P P S T P P R
D C L R Z ■ S X S ■ G R N T D
W H L B R R W S ■ S N T S N S
N N N R R T V ■ N P M ■ ■ ■
D C G M ■ R L S T C N V N N C
Q L T S ■ N C H R C T R S T C
N D Q T ■ P H N C N S L T T N
T T T R ■ T R N T T H L G H T
T R S S ■ H S S C R T S T T L
```

**PAGE 36   VWLLSS CRSSWRD**

```
D I S P E L ■ O N E ■ E R E
I M P A L A ■ N O R ■ G E L
S P I C E R ■ S E T I T O F F
M A G I C K ■ H U M E R I ■
A L O F T ■ P I P E ■ A D D S
Y E T I ■ B O P S ■ S N E A K
■ C A R E S ■ M A S A D A
■ P A N A M ■ C A N A L ■
C O U R T S ■ C A R E T ■
V I T A S ■ P R I X ■ L A F F
S C U D ■ M U O N ■ Q A T A R
■ P I S A N S ■ A U N T I E
A D J O U R N S ■ M A T U R E
W O O ■ E N E ■ I S I N T O
E B B ■ Z E D ■ N I C E O F
```

**PAGE 37   CAN YOU DIG IT?**

```
N O T M E ■ S I M P S ■ T O S
A B H O R ■ E B O O K ■ I R T
W E E W I L L I E W I N K I E
S Y L ■ C E E ■ ■ O K B Y
■ A G A I N A N D A G A I N
A S K A ■ A L I E N ■ ■
S H E R P A ■ P L A N ■ P S U
T U R N E D T H E T A B L E S
O N S ■ S H O O ■ H O R A C E
■ C O R R S ■ A N T S
C H I L I C O N C A R N E ■
O A T Y ■ ■ O R E ■ T W A
H U B E R T H H U M P H R E Y
E T A ■ B A U E R ■ L O I R E
N E D ■ S P E W S ■ Y I P E S
```

**PAGE 38   QUIET QUAINT QUINTET**

```
S E E M O K ■ A T O M ■ P P S
I L L I N I ■ T O N E ■ A L I
E B A Y E R O T I C A ■ V E G
M A L A ■ S T Y L E N O L A N
■ ■ Z I T S ■ ■ R O S A
L I T A N Y ■ S E A L E V E L
O S A K A ■ L O R C A ■
M A R I J U A N A C I N E M A
■ A R B Y S ■ D O V E S
N E A R M I S S ■ L O R E N A
O L I E ■ ■ I O N E ■
M A R M O T R I N G ■ A B I T
A I M ■ T O A D V I L L A G E
D N A ■ T O T O ■ N E L S O N
S E N ■ O L E S ■ S A Y E R S
```

**PAGE 39   ACHY BREAKY HEART**

ANSWER: WATCH. Each of the theme entries is a three-word phrase where each of the three words starts with the same letter. Those initial letters spell out WATCH.

Notes: This is a typical trick for an easy meta, where the theme entries spell the meta out in some way.

ANSWER: SEA LEVEL. Each of the five theme entries conceals a brand of pain reliever: E(BAY ER)OTICA, S(TYLE NOL)AN, MARIJU(ANA CIN)EMA, MAR(MOT RIN)G and TO(AD VIL)LAGE. The hidden sixth entry is SE(A LEVE)L.

**PAGE 40**

```
H O O P   P L A T   G I F T E D
U N D O   E U R O   O N L I N E
G O D S H A V E T H E Q U E E N
    S O B   E I S   N O S Y
S H M E A R C A M P A I G N
T O O   R A U L   S T L
E L M S   I S I N   L A M B S
R E M A I N S T O B E S H E E N
N S Y N C   O V A L   A R G O
    E G O   A R I A   C A R
  S H E L F R E S T R A I N T
A S I A   A M A   I C U
M O Z Z A R E L L A S H T I C K
S L E E V E   L E S T   O B O E
O O D L E S   Y A P S   S E X Y
```

**PAGE 41   HELL'S KITCHEN**

```
C O L A   I R A Q I   A M S
H A I R I N A B U N   S P O O N
C A K E S O F S O A P   L I L L I
U S E   N O H   L E N D O N
T E N A M   O O H E D   A N T
  R A K E I N T H E D O U G H
F I L L I N G W I T H J O Y
I D E O   I G O T O   G L A Z E
E O N   F T S   A D S   X E D
F L O U R   C O S M O   D E A D
  P E T R O L E U M J E L L Y
V A N I S H I N G C R E A M
O R E   C O M E A   N O D O Z
D M A J O R   U T E   A B E
K A T I E   T O U G H C O O K I E
A D A M S   R O L L S O F F A T
  A S S   I P A I D   T A R S
```

**PAGE 42   CATCHING THE 6:15**

```
S T A R T I N G P I T C H E R
N A T I O N A L A V E R A G E
A U T O M O B I L E T I R E S
C R U S T   O D E   O P A R T
K I N   H E B E   O N E S
  C E D A R   S S S S S S S
    E L A P S E S   E A T
J E W E L   R O N   T A S T Y
A L A   H O W D A H S
S K I D R O W   S E I S M
  N E H I   T A P S   H A I
H A S T O   G I L   H E R O N
I N C O M P A T I B I L I T Y
F O O T B A L L D E F E N S E
I S T H I S S E A T T A K E N
```

**PAGE 43   THE SKY'S THE LIMIT**

```
C A S T L E   P A S T E L S   S A S H E S
A R T I E S   E S C A P E E   T U P E L O
F L Y M E T O T H E M O O N   A R A R A T
E E L E R   T R O N   S S E   R A T E
  N E D S   T O T E M   C A L   C I A
    C O L   A S T A R I S B O R N
P R O B E R S   R E D Y E   S T E A M E D
R O N E L Y   I A N   N A B   E L K E S
O M E N S   P L U T O C R A T   M E S
C A T S   B A L L E T   S T O L A   T R I
O N O   W O N   R H O   W A S   H E R
L O U   H A D E S   E B B I N G   M E T E
  C H I   A S T E R O I D S   M A S O N
W H A T S   S O P   E T A   M O D U L E
V I O L E T S   R E U S E   D E P E N D S
O F F O N A C O M E T   C I D
N E V   M I R   A S C O T   A L V A
  E D A M   A C T   T H A T   L E E D S
C A N A P E   T H E D A I L Y P L A N E T
E L U D E R   E A T A B L E   R E S A L E
E A S E R S   S P E N S E R   E Y E L E T
```

**PAGE 44 COLORIZING**

```
G A T   S I P S   A D A G E     T R A M
R A N I   T O I T   B E V E L   C H A S E
H U G E   A U R A   O M E N S   L E N T O
E C L A I R   A L I V E   S A W A   C O W
T H E   B R I C K R O A D     O R S O N S
T E R R E   M I E S   N E C K W E A R
    I R O N E D   H O B O E S   G O A L
  L I B I D O S   F A R I N A   D E U C E
B O M B A S T   H O N   T I T L E   S E T
O R I O N     P A R K A   C O O L
P E N N   J O L L Y   G I A N T   R O S A
    L A D A   A B E L L   D O M E S
P E I   A N D C O   E E K   T I E B A C K
M M M D X   L A D E R S   T O R M E N T
S U P E   D O T I N G   B E A V E R
  R E M O T E S T   E O N S   S T I L E
L A U P E R   T H E B O S T O N   S O X
O L D   E Y E S   R A B B I   D E F O R E
B L E S T   R A Z O R   O O Z E   O B E R
E I N E S   A L O N E   O N I T   R A N T
S E T A   S T E E D   S S T S   D R S
```

**PAGE 45 FOOD STOP**

```
B L A S T   D O G S   E Q U I P
A O R T A   M O O R E   D U N C E
G R E E N P E P P E R   S A D I E
G R I M   O N E S E L F   K E E P
Y E N   P I U S   C I A   E R R S
    S O S     B E N D E R
P I C K L E J A R   G E E   G E M
A S H E   S I R E E   S L E E V E
S H E E R   F E A S T   S L E E T
S O F T E R   A T S E A   I N N O
E T S   A O K   H O T P O T A T O
    S P O N G Y     O W E
D I A L   F O R   S E L L   H E E
A T M E   S T O I C A L   M A N X
R A B A T   T O M A T O P A S T E
E L I Z A   E V A N S   A S T E R
D O T E D   D E N T   S H O R T
```

**PAGE 46 EASY AS ABC**

```
J A M B S   R O B I N   R E F S
A R A I L   E V A D E   E X I L E
B A S S O   C E L L S   V I L E R
  T H E S C A R L E T L E T T E R
    C H I L D     S I R   E V E
S L O T   A L O H A   T I E R E D
T A N   S O S   E L A T E D
I D E A S   T R I T E   I L I E
F L I P S I D E O F A R E C O R D
F E N S   C A N I T   S T A K E
  O N E T O N   M I T   T E N
B A L S A M   R E M U S   P H D S
O R E   T E E   O S T E O
O N E H U N D R E D T O N E R O
T O W A R   G O R E S   I T E M S
S L A V E   A T I M E   D I N A H
  D Y E S   R E E S E   S C O R E
```

**PAGE 47 NAME-DROPPING**

```
R E A P   A L O H A   P R O V   I S A T
A L L I   L E M O N   P I A N O   T A C O
J O A N N E W A R D   E T H E L B A R R Y
A N S W E R E R   D E N T S   C E L I E
    H A T S   L E A N S   C A D I
S A W E R S   P I E C E   M O N O C L E D
A B I E S   H U M P H R E Y B O G   I V E
N E L L   D O N E   M A R S   C L I N
D E L   R O C K Y M A R C I A   T O L L S
S T I M U L U S   A S E E D   B R A I S E
    E A S E S   B Y O N E   W A I T A
P U M P E D   C L O N E   B A S S I N E T
O V A L S   G E O R G E G E R S H   H U R
L U K E   C A R T   U N T O   D E B I
I L E   J A M E S E A R L J S   B E L I E
C A R O U S E S   C H I L I   S E L L E R
    U N T S   T A I L S   T A T I
  G O T T A   F O R T E   A U T O G I R O
R A H F A W C E T T   D U S T I N H M A N
I I I I I   A L L I E   U N I O N   T A M E
P L O T   Y U L E   P E A R Y   S T A R
```

PAGE 48   SPEECH! SPEECH!

PAGE 50   CLEF NOTES

PAGE 49   HOW SWEET!

PAGE 53   HANDYMAN'S SPECIAL

## PAGE 56 PUZZLER AT WORK

```
. C U P I D . C A R A M E L . . L E M O N .
M U R I N E . E L E V A T E . S A L U T E
A B I T T E N L I P A K N O T T Y B R O W
P A S T O R A L . . L E A . R E T A K E S
. . . N E T . A T O M S . A P O . . . .
C R O N E . . B R I N Y . A L P . C L E M
L A D E . . P O O L . K N E E . A I M E
A T I E T H A T S T W E A K E D A S K E W
R E S . R U C H E . A U R A . I C E R S
A S T A I R E . A D L E R . A L A D Y
. . S T O R M E D . E N A B L E D . .
. U P T O N . A R D O R . L O R E T T A
S H O R N . L A I N . I D A H O . O H S
W H O I S T H I S S O L V E R A N Y H O W
A U L D . R A C E . I O L E . M E S A
T H E E . U N E . B A S R A . C A R E Y
. . S A N . L U S T Y . S P A . . .
S T R A I N A . A N T . F O R T I E T H
W H A T S T H A T Y O U S A Y I T S Y O U
A R N E S S . C H A R L E S . A L L E G E
N O T M Y . T E N S E S T . M E A R A .
```

## PAGE 59 SHAKESPEARE USES A COMPUTER

```
A M I D . G O A D S . N E R D . . W R I T
T O B E . E N S U E . A L O U D . H E R E
T H E C O N S T A N T I M A G E . E D E N
A A R . R U E H L . O V E R . B R E A D S
C V I . L I T E . B O E R . A R I L . .
K E A T O N . . C U L . . S H I N B O N E
. . S P E E C H L E S S M E S S A G E S
D A M P . A R A B . A T O M . E R R I S
A R I . S O R E R . F L A G S . R E L O
B A N D A N N A . A I R . . S H O . .
. T H E R E S M A G I C I N T H E W E B
. . M I R . S U N . A H O R S E O F .
T A R A . B E S E T . I C E R S . L O B
A L O R S . E R A S . B A R R . A S T I
P L U C K F R O M T H E M E M O R Y . .
A S T A I R E S . A N A . C H E A T S
. . T E U T . B A I T . A S T O . B O A
S Q U I R M . D U C T . A N T O N . U R N
A U T O . P R I N T I N G T O B E U S E D
G I A N . S I N C E . I R E N E . M E R E
E T H S . . M O O D . L A S E R . A R O D
```

## PAGE 60 I COME FROM IOWA

```
O A T H . A D O . . S E R U M . A R B O R
O B O E . D R S . A S M A R A . M O I R A
M A M I E E I S E N H O W E R . I N L A Y
P S A L M . B I N G . . E A R N . A L T O
H E R . B O B F E L L E R . I O R . Y E N
. N E A R L Y . E A R . N A V I E S . .
A N O D Y N E . G E O R G E G A L L U P
D E L I . E S T E . . A G E . L I N E S
M A D T V . H A S . S T E . S A D A T
. . H E R B E R T H O O V E R . A C U
D O G S T A R . A O L . R E L A Y E D
I S L . J A M E S V A N A L L E N . .
C H E W S . A A H . R E X . A G G I E
T E N E T . M I R . T E A L . E R N E
. A N D Y W I L L I A M S . V I O L A T E
. M O R A S S . R D A . T I E D O N .
O B I . O I L . D A V I D R A B E . T H D
B U L B . L A T E . N O I R . L O W E R
I N L E T . B U F F A L O B I L L C O D Y
E N E R O . E B E R L Y . A S I . T O G A
S Y R I A . L E R O Y . L T D . O D E S
```

## PAGE 61 IT'S IN THE GENES

```
O R C S . U T I L E . H A R E M . R A H
P O L O . L U N A R . E D I N A . A I D A
A L O T . T R A I L B L A Z E R . S N A G
L E G H O R N . . E E L Y . S T I G M A
. . D E R A I L S . F A I T H H E A L E R
S C A R E . P O E T . S N E E . A N E .
M A N N A . . L A B . . T R A . S A M E
A R C . D R I L L S E R G E A N T . D O A
S P E N S E R . M A O . T A T E R S
H E R O . A M P . S O T T E D . P U R E E
. . S T R A I G H T S H O O T E R . .
U P P E R . S T E R E O . N R A . O F F S
P E R S I A . A E R . . A R T W O R K
T R E . O X F O R D S C H O L A R . R O I
O U S T . E R R . A O L . . I R E N E
. S H E . I S O N . D U D E . F A C T S
S M A R T C O O K I E . R E G A L I A
L E G A C Y . A M A H . R E E L S I N
A L E E . B O D Y B U I L D E R . I T S A
B E E N . E L I E L . P I U S I . N E E R
S E T . R A N D Y . S E N S E . G R E Y
```

**PAGE 62  REJECTED OLYMPICS EVENTS**

| T | O | B | E | | P | E | T | R | A | | S | A | N | T | E | | F | E | L | T |
| E | B | A | N | | E | T | H | E | L | | O | R | E | A | D | | O | D | O | R |
| R | O | L | L | | S | H | O | P | L | I | F | T | I | N | G | | O | N | C | E |
| M | E | D | I | A | T | O | R | | N | A | I | L | | I | N | T | A | K | E | |
| | E | S | T | E | S | | M | I | T | R | E | | M | E | A | N | | | | |
| P | O | R | T | E | R | | S | O | S | O | | A | I | R | B | O | R | N | E | |
| A | L | D | E | N | | M | O | O | N | W | A | L | K | S | | S | T | I | E | S |
| R | E | A | D | | M | A | C | R | O | | B | A | I | T | S | | E | A | R | S |
| K | O | S | | P | I | C | K | E | T | F | E | N | C | I | N | G | | L | V | E |
| A | S | H | T | R | A | Y | S | | R | E | E | K | | A | R | I | S | E | N | |
| | | I | H | I | S | S | | S | K | I | T | S | | S | P | O | T | | | |
| A | B | L | O | O | M | | P | I | L | L | | S | H | O | W | E | R | E | D | |
| C | R | O | | R | A | C | E | R | E | L | A | T | I | O | N | S | | U | L | A |
| T | A | S | S | | S | A | N | E | R | | P | O | L | O | S | | G | M | E | N |
| U | V | E | A | S | | B | A | N | K | V | A | U | L | T | | P | E | R | C | S |
| P | O | R | T | U | G | A | L | | E | R | R | S | | C | A | N | U | T | E | |
| | | I | D | O | L | | D | E | N | T | S | | R | A | V | E | N | | | |
| E | L | P | A | S | O | | B | E | N | D | | M | A | T | E | R | N | A | L | |
| D | I | E | T | | B | A | I | L | J | U | M | P | I | N | G | | O | I | S | E |
| A | N | N | E | | E | R | A | T | O | | B | A | N | T | U | | U | N | I | T |
| M | E | N | D | | R | E | S | A | Y | | A | N | E | S | T | | S | G | T | S |

**PAGE 63  WORDIES**

| T | H | E | M | | P | R | I | M | A | | O | S | S | I | | | F | A | D | E |
| O | O | Z | E | | H | O | N | E | S | | T | O | W | N | S | | I | M | A | S |
| T | U | R | N | B | A | C | K | T | H | E | C | L | O | C | K | | R | A | P | T |
| O | R | A | T | E | S | | S | E | E | S | | | R | A | I | S | E | T | H | E |
| | | | H | E | E | P | | | S | T | A | N | D | S | I | N | L | I | N | E |
| G | A | M | E | S | | A | T | M | | M | O | S | | N | O | I | S | E | | |
| A | L | A | | | A | L | A | I | | S | A | T | | | G | O | G | | | |
| D | O | U | B | L | E | O | R | N | O | T | H | I | N | G | | P | H | O | N | Y |
| S | U | I | T | O | R | | A | N | K | A | | E | R | S | | T | R | U | E | |
| | | U | F | O | S | | O | I | L | | E | M | O | T | E | | E | D | S | |
| | J | U | S | T | B | E | T | W | E | E | N | Y | O | U | A | N | D | M | E | |
| F | E | R | | S | I | L | O | S | | M | O | E | | T | I | D | E | | | |
| L | E | N | D | | C | I | D | | A | M | B | I | | N | U | A | N | C | E | |
| U | P | S | E | T | | G | O | A | F | T | E | R | T | H | E | P | R | I | Z | E |
| | | | P | A | M | | L | E | E | | O | B | A | D | | | C | A | R | |
| S | E | R | T | A | | D | O | T | | W | E | T | | E | N | E | R | O | | |
| T | I | M | E | A | N | D | A | G | A | I | N | | | S | A | R | A | | | |
| E | M | I | S | S | A | R | Y | | W | O | R | E | | M | O | T | O | R | S | |
| M | I | G | S | | N | O | T | W | O | W | A | Y | S | A | B | O | U | T | I | T |
| P | A | R | E | | A | V | O | I | R | | H | A | S | T | E | | R | I | C | E |
| O | N | E | S | | | E | N | T | R | | S | N | E | E | R | | E | C | O | N |

**PAGE 64  WHAT'S BLACK AND WHITE AND RED ALL OVER?**

| A | P | A | C | E | | S | P | O | T | | A | R | M | | E | R | A | S |
| L | E | M | O | N | | C | A | P | E | | D | O | A | | M | E | E | T |
| P | R | A | M | S | | E | V | E | N | O | D | D | S | | B | A | S | E |
| S | U | N | B | U | R | N | E | D | S | K | U | N | K | | A | L | O | T |
| | | | R | A | T | S | | | A | P | E | | T | R | I | P | S | |
| A | M | A | Z | E | R | S | | T | A | P | | Y | E | A | R | S | | |
| R | E | C | E | D | E | | O | A | S | I | S | | S | T | A | T | U | S |
| T | O | M | B | | R | A | N | C | H | | O | P | T | | S | I | S | I |
| E | W | E | R | S | | C | A | K | E | | F | O | O | L | S | C | A | P |
| | | A | E | G | I | S | | | T | E | P | E | E | | | | | |
| F | O | R | W | A | R | D | S | | S | H | E | S | | A | D | R | E | M |
| A | L | A | I | | A | S | I | | T | O | N | Y | S | | N | O | V | A |
| D | E | N | T | E | D | | S | H | O | P | S | | P | A | U | P | E | R |
| | C | H | E | S | S | | E | W | E | | M | A | N | N | E | R | S | |
| E | T | H | A | N | | E | O | N | | H | O | S | T | | | | | |
| T | I | E | R | | A | N | G | R | Y | D | A | L | M | A | T | I | A | N |
| T | A | R | A | | P | O | L | Y | M | E | R | S | | C | A | S | I | O |
| E | R | O | S | | O | R | E | | C | A | P | O | | I | C | A | M | E |
| S | A | S | H | | D | A | S | | A | N | O | N | | D | O | W | E | L |

**PAGE 68  COMMENTARY**

| D | I | S | H | | P | E | L | T | S | | O | N | T | A | P | | C | A | V | E |
| O | N | L | Y | | O | T | E | R | I | | C | H | I | L | L | | A | L | E | X |
| D | E | E | M | | P | R | I | O | R | | A | L | C | O | A | | R | E | N | E |
| O | P | E | N | Q | U | E | S | T | I | O | N | | K | E | Y | W | O | R | D | S |
| S | T | P | A | U | L | | | H | U | N | A | N | | S | T | I | L | T | S | |
| | | | L | I | A | N | A | | S | I | D | E | S | | A | T | E | | | |
| C | L | O | S | E | C | A | L | L | | C | A | T | C | H | P | H | R | A | S | E |
| R | O | M | | T | E | S | T | A | T | E | | T | A | O | S | | C | A | V | |
| O | K | A | Y | | H | O | B | O | | E | E | L | S | | P | A | I | N | E | |
| P | I | R | A | C | Y | | S | T | A | N | D | I | N | G | O | R | D | E | R | |
| | | C | H | I | E | F | | E | N | T | | A | I | N | G | E | | | | |
| O | F | F | H | A | N | D | R | E | M | A | R | K | | P | O | N | D | E | R | |
| T | O | O | T | S | | E | I | N | S | | E | N | I | D | | A | R | L | O | |
| I | C | U | | A | M | A | D | | S | E | A | M | O | S | S | | E | A | U | |
| C | I | R | C | U | L | A | R | S | A | W | | P | U | N | C | H | L | I | N | E |
| | | O | N | O | | S | U | M | A | C | | S | T | A | R | E | | | | |
| | F | E | L | I | P | E | | P | U | M | A | S | | N | U | G | G | E | T | |
| F | U | L | L | T | E | R | M | | S | I | G | N | L | A | N | G | U | A | G | E |
| R | E | L | O | | C | O | U | P | E | | N | I | O | B | E | | M | Y | R | A |
| A | G | E | D | | I | D | I | O | M | | E | D | G | E | R | | E | L | E | C |
| T | O | N | I | | A | E | R | I | E | | Y | E | S | E | S | | S | E | T | H |

**PAGE 70  ELEVENS**

**PAGE 71  SUPERGROUPS**

**PAGE 72  WACKY READINGS**

**PAGE 74  TWENTY UNDER THIRTY**

PAGE 75  TWENTY UNDER THIRTY

PAGE 82  HOW'S THAT AGAIN?

PAGE 81  X-SPELLED

PAGE 83  WEEKEND WARRIOR

## PAGE 84 COMMON SORT

```
A C I L M   L O O W   B E H R
H H M O U   A R W Y   A L U U
A A B L S   C D E E F I I R T
B D E   C D E E   L O S S T
  C D O R   R S T U   E T Y
E F I R V Y   E E I N S
D L L O Y   B D E E G H I N T
D E I N   A E F K S   A N O R
A A C E I L L R S   A D N N O
  D D E L O   B D E O O T
A N Y   A C E M   A E S V
D E E G H   A F G N   A C M
A I L N O R S T U   I N T U Y
G L P U   I L O T   N O O P S
E L S S   O Y Z Z   E M R S T
```

## PAGE 87 SATURDAY STUMPER

```
O C E A N S T A T E     T A P
N A V R A T I L O V A   O S U
O R A N G E S O D A S   L I P
U N D O   W A N D   I D E A S
R E E L     E L I N O R
    D A N   L E N   N A S H
R E P R O   Y R S   K N E E
H O T A I R     I C E C A P
O P E L   O T B   D O Y E N
P E R M   O R E   E E K
  N E W M A N       O H N O
S H A R I   L A M P   N A I L
E E L   C R A Z Y E I G H T S
A L L   K I L I M A N J A R O
S P Y   G A R Y L A R S O N
```

## PAGE 88 B MOVIES

```
A B A S H   O R C A   N A R E S     G I B
M A R I A   S E L L   E N O C H   S H O O
T H E B L A S T O F T H E M O H I C A N S
    F R I E D   O R N E   N A Z I S
S N O C O N E S   B O U T O F A F R I C A
T O R I N O   T E E N   O R O
P R A T E S   X E S   T O R T   B E E P
A T T Y   A T I T   Q U A K E   E N N A
T H E B R I G H T S T U F F   L A L O S
  L A R U E   H I T   C E S A R S
B R A I N M A N   A R K   B R A G T I M E
B O R G I A   W Y E   L A R G O
G O T H S   T H E W I Z A R D O F B O Z
U N I T   J O K E S   M O U E   E R N E
N E S S   A N O N   T A O   E D D I E S
  A D E   I G L U   C R E D I T
T H E S T O R Y O F B O   S E R E N E L Y
I O W A N   E R I E   L O T U S
T H E B O W L A N D T H E P U S S Y C A T
L U R E   T A H O E   A G E D   E A V E S
E M S   S Y S T S   H O N E   S P I R E
```

## PAGE 89 CIRCULAR REASONING

```
M O P P   O O R T     O D D S
S C H O O L R O O M   B O R O
S H O R T S T O P S   S N O W
  S O T T O   T O G O   J O N
    H O N K   F T R O O P
T O D O S   O F F   N T H
W H O S   W H O   S O O N G S
O N O   S O L O M O N   S O O
B O R N O N   L O T   C O N N
    T O D   S S T   J O N G G
  C O H O R T   S T O L
P O D   M O R O   R H O M B
O N O R   C O M M O N R O O M
O D O R   S L O O P J O H N B
H O R S   L O C O   F O G S
```

**PAGE 90   COP-OUT**

```
B O X E R . A P E A K . T W O
A R E N A . S A N T E . H E X
G O D I S M Y I L O T . . E M E
. . S H E E N . O C A S E Y
R E E L E C T . A T H L E T E
A F R E S H . S C H U S S .
I F A . T A R O T . P A T T I
D I N S . M U S E D . B R E T
S E R U M . L A D Y L . I L E
. . U N U S E D . N A P A L M
I N S U L T S . P A Y O L A S
C A S P A R . D A M O N .
I C I . T O B A C O U C H E S
E R A . T H I N E . T H E G O
R E N . O S C A R . S O N G S
```

**PAGE 91   HOLLYWOOD SQUARES**

```
F L A K . A S P I C . S I F T S
L I M E . B W A N A . O N E A T A
A V I V . J A C K K L U T Z M A N
P E D I C U R E . E E R O . A L E
. N A R D . C P A S . O L I N
S P E C I E . B R A N . S P E N T
N I X O N . D O I N . B A R
A X I S . A I N T . S A V A L A S
P E L T . M O N I Q U E . H U S H
S L E N D E R . Q U I Z . W I P E
. E O N . Q U I T . T I G E R
S W A R M . C U E D . E R M I N E
L I N D . C O E D . P R E P
E G G . E R A T . S U R E F I R E
D W E E B I L Z A P P A . R O A R
S A L A A M . A D A P T . E N I D
. M A R N E . L E N Y A . Y A L E
```

**PAGE 94   YUPPIE RIGHTS OF PASSAGE**

```
S E L M A . H O O F . T E N D . D E K E S
A C E O F . Y U R I . A L O E . I D E S T
P H I L L I P S E X E T E R A C A D E M Y
S O S O . L E T . A L U M . C A N A P E
. T O L D . I T E M . M O R A S S .
. B O O K . O M E N . R U N E . C C C
H A R V A R D B U S I N E S S S C H O O L
E L M . Y E A T S . O D E . S I E R R A
A S I A . P L A T . O V I D . N E E D Y
R A N I . A L I . O D I N . E A C H
A M E R I C A N S T O C K E X C H A N G E
. T S K S . E T R E . M A E . W O R D
P A P A L . A V A S . B E L T . S K I S
H O A X E D . P E W . A R T I S . I N E
I N S I D E R T R A D I N G S C A N D A L
S E T . J U A N . O N D E . L A S T
. T O H A N D . L Y E S . B R A N .
. G E N E V A . B O O R . A A A . K A T E
M I N I M U M S E C U R I T Y P R I S O N
A L S O P . O I N K . O H I O . A N T E D
G L E N S . K N E E . R S T U . E G A D S
```

**PAGE 96   STRETCH THOSE QUADS!**

```
A L A I . A C C U S T O M E D
W I L M A F L I N T S T O N E
R E C O N F I G U R A T I O N
Y D S . N I P . O R O
. F O X . R E P S . S I M
E C R U . B E A . S E T I
A T H I N G O F T H E P A S T
W H A T C A N I D O Y A F O R
E A S T E R N T I M E Z O N E
I N T E R N E T R E F O R M S
G O E R . T E T . L U T E
H L N . U C S D . R U T
. B R O . J A I . D I C
B O L O G N A S A N D W I C H
S E C R E T H A N D S H A K E
A R M S D E A L E R . O N Y X
```

## PAGE 97 — ADJUSTED TO FIT YOUR SCREEN

```
C A P S   T R A I L     E G G
E R I C   M E N T O S   O I L
R I G H T S I D E U P   E G O
T A S E R   G E M   R E H A B
      M O A N S   P E R M
D O Z E N S     D R A G N E T
E R O S   H A I R E D   O A R
F A X   T A B L E T S   E T A
E T H   A M E L I E   S H U N
R E Z O N E D   S T A M P S
    U R N S   C A T H Y
B A H A I   M O S   A I S L E
O L E   N O I S S I W N O O W
D O H   G A R T E R   G A L A
S E E     F A S T S   S P A N
```

## PAGE 98

```
M A S H U P   A S S   H A W K
A N N I K A   R I C   O D I E
B E A T E N P A T H O L O G Y
E M T S   K E G   M M L
L I C   T O P O L O G Y G U N
L A H T I   E R A   W I R E
      E V A   N I N T E N D O
B I O L O G Y   C U R I O U S
L O V E S E A T   B A R
O W E S   D A D   C D R W S
W A R C R Y O L O G Y   H E E
      O V A   L I U   J I B E
D R O P S C I E N C E O N E M
J U D E   H O S   C A V O R T
S T D S   T N T   I T I S S O
```

## PAGE 99

```
P A L S   A S P S   S T Y L E
S L I T   D E L I   P S E U D
S T A R   D E A F   L A N G E
T H R E E W A Y T H A I
  O S A K A   A S I S   T A I
      K I T E   T H W A R T
A S S   N E R D S   U S O C
B A C K G R O U N D C Z E C H
O G R E   S P I E L   S K Y
D O I N G S   T R I G
E S P   E P I C   A N I S E
    C R A S H I N G B O E R
C A R O M   L I N G   L A R A
B W A N A   A N T E   E R I N
S E M E N   M O O D   T E E D
```

## PAGE 100

```
S O U S A   H O W S O   P A R
A L F A S   O R E A D   A S H
T A C T S O F L I F E   D O E
      Y E N   W E D I D N T
S T A R T T I R E   N Y E T
H A T S   D O I T U P
A B A   K I A   O P U S E S
H O L D I N G D O W N T O R T
S O L U T E   M M S   C A A
      P I E P A N   S I T H
S H O E   I P I T Y T O O L
T A R S I D E   M E A
A N G   D I T C H I N G H E F
I N A   E V A D E   T E A S E
D A N   S A S S Y   A S S E D
```

**PAGE 101**

```
A W L S · · M A J A · E N A C T
U H O H · M Y M O M · V O T E R
L I S A M A R I E P R E S L E Y ·
D R E W B A R R Y M O R E · · · ·
· · · L A S H · · T Y P I S T · ·
B O S S · · · I D I · B A N T U ·
A L I · D E N N I S R O D M A N ·
L E G · R E A L G O O D · · I G N
K E N N Y C H E S N E Y · N E E ·
A L O E S · S T A · · I D Y L · ·
N O N C P A · · I B M S · · · · ·
· · · K I M K A R D A S H I A N ·
R U D O L P H V A L E N T I N O ·
F R A I L · A I M E R · A I N T ·
K I L L S · N A P S · · R I S E ·
```

**PAGE 102**

```
F A I L · A M M A N · · S H A M
A C M E · R O U S E · · W A N E
P A P A L B U L L S · · A I N T
S I S · L O S T · · A L K I E ·
· · V A R S I T Y B L U E S · ·
I N T E N S E · H A L O · · · ·
N E A T O · · T I M E W A R P ·
C A R · P E O N S · · · S U E ·
A P P A R A T E · · S C I O N ·
· · R E N T · S L O V A K S · ·
S I A M E S E T W I N S · · · ·
K N O P F · · Y E T I · E M U ·
I N R I · B A L D E A G L E S ·
M I T T · C H E E R · O L D E ·
P E A S · E A R N S · B E E R ·
```

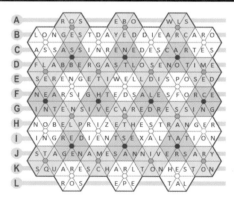

**PAGE 106**

| LIGHT | MEDIUM | DARK |
|---|---|---|
| DARN IT | THRACE | GIVETH |
| BONING | SCHEMA | CARTON |
| ORATES | VINTON | DEALER |
| SO RARE | SPLEEN | GENDER |
| LAXEST | FLARES | ABBESS |
| LATHES | DEMISE | SANEST |
| SPOOFS | OBEYED | TATERS |
| SIGNER | SQUATS | CRINGE |
| SALONS | SCRAWL | NESTLE |
| EDDIES | SNARES | AT NINE |

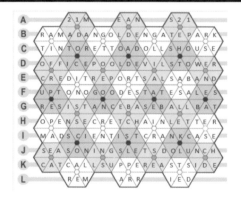

**PAGE 107**

| WHITE | MEDIUM | DARK |
|---|---|---|
| GALLON | ADAM-12 | SHOOTS |
| RAPPER | LINGUS | ISLETS |
| CENTER | SETS IN | LOADED |
| TERESA | LEANED | AT BEST |
| CALMER | ANDREW | NO LUCK |
| KRAUSE | 12-STEP | EROTIC |
| GOTTEN | INCHED | PUREST |
| DEISTS | POOPER | STABLE |
| ABASES | COFFER | COOGAN |

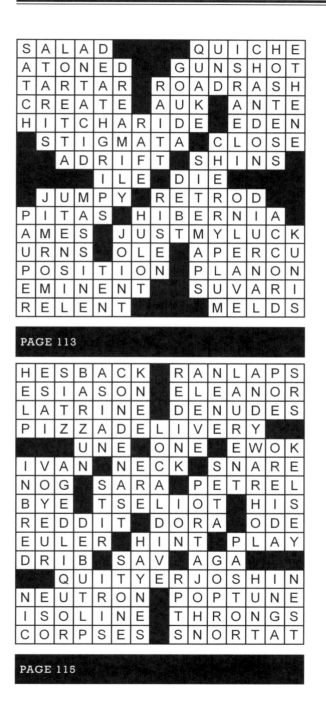

PAGE 113

PAGE 115

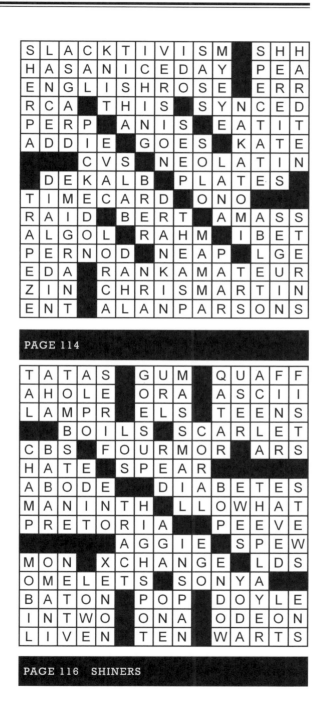

PAGE 114

PAGE 116 SHINERS

Crossword grid:

| O | R | A | T | E | S |   | A | S | P |   | G | P | S |
| F | O | U | R | A | M |   | E | L | M | S |   | M | A | L |
| F | I | G | U | R | E | I | T | O | U | T |   | C | E | Y |
|   |   | A | S | T | O | R |   | M | O | L | E |   |   |
|   | P | O | W | E | R | P | U | F | F | G | I | R | L | S |
| J | O | L | I | E |   |   |   |   | E | X | P | A | T |
| L | E | I | F | G | A | R | R | E | T | T |   |   |
| O | T | O | E |   | R | U | B | I | N |   | F | L | E | A |
|   |   | S | P | R | I | N | G | F | I | E | L | D |
| O | M | A | N | I |   |   | A | L | I | A | S |
| B | I | G | F | R | I | G | G | I | N | D | E | A | L |
| O | N | E | L |   | F | R | I | D | A |   |   |
| I | N | N |   | A | N | I | M | A | T | E | D | G | I | F |
| S | I | D |   | B | O | M | P |   | T | R | O | I | K | A |
| T | E | A |   | S | T | Y |   | Y | A | W | N | E | R |

**PAGE 117 MOVING PICTURES**

Crossword grid:

| S | T | E | W |   | L | E | A | N |   | B | R | A | S | S |
| G | E | N | E |   | E | X | P | O |   | L | O | F | A | T |
| T | A | L | E |   | T | I | N | W | H | I | S | T | L | E |
|   | R | I | P | O | S | T | E |   | O | N | E | R | U | N |
| H | A | V | I | N | G | S | A | I | D | T | H | A | T |
| O | P | E | N | T | O |   | N | A | Z | I |   |   |
| M | A | N | G | O |   | M | I | N | D |   | P | A | L | M |
| E | R | E |   | P | I | A | N | I | S | T |   | R | O | O |
| S | T | D | S |   | N | I | K | E |   | E | G | G | O | S |
|   | C | H | E | Z |   | A | R | O | U | S | E |
|   | S | L | E | E | V | E | L | E | S | S | T | E | E | S |
| S | T | A | P | L | E |   | T | A | K | E | S | O | N |
| E | A | S | T | E | R | E | G | G | S |   | O | V | I | D |
| P | R | E | E | N |   | S | O | L | I |   | R | E | N | O |
| T | E | R | R | A |   | E | V | E | N |   | E | R | G | O |

**PAGE 125**

Crossword grid:

| C | O | C | K |   | S | O | T | S |   | A | S | S | E | T |
| H | U | L | U |   | T | H | A | I |   | I | P | A | N | A |
| A | C | E | R |   | P | O | K | E |   | N | O | V | A | S |
| W | H | A | T | M | A | K | E | S | I | T | T | I | C | K |
|   | N | A | U | T |   | S | T | N |   | T | O | T | S |
| O | P | E | N | S |   | S | T | A | R | T | E | R | S |
| H | A | R | D |   | M | I | O |   | O | E | D |   |   |
| M | U | S | C | L | E | R | E | L | A | X | A | N | T | S |
|   | O | L | D |   | X | E | D |   | M | O | M | A |
|   | C | R | U | C | I | A | T | E |   | L | I | M | I | T |
| G | O | E | R |   | A | P | R |   | Z | O | L | A |
| A | U | S | T | I | N | P | E | N | D | L | E | T | O | N |
| E | L | A | N | D |   | O | M | A | N |   | O | T | R | A |
| L | E | V | E | E |   | L | E | S | E |   | F | E | E | T |
| S | E | E | Y | A |   | L | S | A | T |   | F | R | O | S |

**PAGE 126**

Crossword grid:

| A | M | P | U | P |   | M | S | N |   | E | L | S | A |
| L | A | S | S | O |   | O | H | O |   | S | A | B | E |
| P | R | I | C | E | Y | B | A | R |   | C | Z | A | R |
|   |   |   | T | A | I | W | A | N |   | B | R | O |
| D | I | C | E | R | O | L | L | H | U | M | O | R |
| O | N | L | A | Y |   |   | K | A | Y | O |   |   |
| S | T | E | R |   | A | S | E | V | E | R |   |   |
|   | O | F | F | I | C | E | L | I | M | I | T | S |
|   | U | N | E | A | S | E |   | N | E | A | T |
| A | W | L | S |   |   | V | E | R | D | I |   |   |
| J | U | S | T | I | C | E | F | O | R | M | E | N |
| A | F | R |   | S | N | O | R | R | I |   |   |
| C | O | S | T |   | P | O | L | I | C | E | P | O | T |
| M | Y | T | H |   | E | K | E |   | E | M | E | N | D |
| E | T | S | Y |   | N | E | S |   | D | O | Z | E | S |

**PAGE 127 CHILLY RECEPTION**

| | | | | | | | | | | | | | |
|---|---|---|---|---|---|---|---|---|---|---|---|---|---|
| A | R | O | D | | M | A | C | H | O | | P | G | S |
| L | O | G | O | | A | S | H | E | N | | I | L | E |
| B | U | R | G | E | R | T | I | M | E | | Z | E | N |
| A | X | E | | C | I | R | | | D | A | Z | E | D |
| | | | B | A | N | A | N | A | G | R | A | M | S |
| B | E | S | U | R | E | | A | L | E | P | H | | |
| E | X | U | L | T | | S | N | L | | | O | V | A |
| A | P | P | L | E | S | T | O | A | P | P | L | E | S |
| R | O | E | | | A | A | S | | L | A | I | R | S |
| | | R | O | A | S | T | | G | A | S | C | A | N |
| H | I | H | O | C | H | E | R | R | Y | O | | | |
| E | R | U | P | T | | | H | O | O | | I | A | M |
| R | A | M | | F | R | U | I | T | N | I | N | J | A |
| E | N | A | | O | N | E | N | O | | O | R | A | L |

**PAGE 128 THE HUNGER GAMES**

| | | | | | | | | | | | | | | |
|---|---|---|---|---|---|---|---|---|---|---|---|---|---|---|
| R | A | G | | | C | E | L | S | | S | L | A | P | S |
| A | L | L | | O | H | G | E | E | | W | A | N | D | A |
| C | P | A | | M | A | G | I | C | W | A | N | T | A | D |
| K | I | N | C | A | I | D | | | A | R | C | | | |
| U | N | C | A | N | N | Y | T | A | X | M | E | N | | |
| P | E | E | D | | | E | R | G | | | T | O | M | E |
| | | | E | R | A | | A | E | R | O | | O | A | K |
| B | A | R | T | A | B | W | I | R | E | F | E | N | C | E |
| B | M | I | | P | O | O | P | | X | F | L | | | |
| S | P | O | T | | | O | S | A | | | I | D | E | A |
| | | T | A | M | A | L | E | B | O | N | D | I | N | G |
| | | | B | E | D | | | I | N | C | E | N | S | E |
| B | U | B | B | L | E | J | E | T | T | A | | G | U | I |
| A | S | Y | E | T | | A | L | O | H | A | | L | E | S |
| N | E | E | D | S | | W | I | F | E | | | E | D | T |

**PAGE 129 GIVING THANKS**

| | | | | | | | | | | | | | | |
|---|---|---|---|---|---|---|---|---|---|---|---|---|---|---|
| F | L | A | M | B | E | E | D | | R | A | I | D | E | R |
| A | I | R | P | L | A | N | E | | I | N | S | A | N | E |
| C | O | N | S | I | S | T | S | | S | T | A | N | D | S |
| I | N | E | | P | Y | R | I | T | E | S | | S | O | C |
| L | E | S | T | | D | A | R | E | | | P | E | R | U |
| E | L | S | E | | O | P | E | R | A | H | O | U | S | E |
| | | | A | C | E | S | | P | R | A | I | S | E | R |
| L | I | T | M | U | S | | | | N | I | N | E | R | S |
| I | N | H | E | R | I | T | | G | I | L | T | | | |
| T | H | E | R | E | T | H | E | R | E | | A | R | E | S |
| T | E | A | S | | | E | G | O | S | | T | I | N | T |
| L | A | T | | B | O | E | R | W | A | R | | A | D | E |
| E | V | E | N | U | P | | E | N | R | O | L | L | E | E |
| M | E | R | E | S | T | | S | U | M | T | O | T | A | L |
| O | N | S | E | T | S | | S | P | Y | S | T | O | R | Y |

**PAGE 134 6 DOWN**

| | | | | | | | | | | | | | | | | | | | |
|---|---|---|---|---|---|---|---|---|---|---|---|---|---|---|---|---|---|---|---|
| ▶ | P | E | A | K | S | | S | L | U | G | G | O | | S | C | O | O | T | S |
| M | I | S | S | E | E | | C | A | R | E | E | R | | C | A | R | N | A | L |
| A | N | T | H | E | M | | A | N | G | E | L | A | | O | N | S | A | L | E |
| U | S | A | | P | I | E | R | C | E | S | | T | A | T | E | | P | O | D |
| D | U | T | Y | | S | A | V | E | D | | D | O | T | | S | L | A | N | G |
| S | P | E | A | R | | R | E | L | | C | A | R | E | W | | E | R | S | E |
| | | | N | O | S | | S | O | R | E | L | Y | | E | P | A | | | |
| | G | I | G | O | T | S | | T | I | L | T | | F | L | O | R | I | S | T |
| H | O | D | | M | O | L | E | | F | L | O | O | R | L | E | N | G | T | H |
| O | T | I | S | | P | A | T | H | F | I | N | D | E | R | | T | A | R | O |
| B | I | O | L | O | G | I | C | A | L | S | | D | O | E | S | | V | A | R |
| O | T | T | A | W | A | N | | V | I | T | O | | N | A | P | P | E | D | |
| | | | P | E | P | | P | E | N | S | U | P | | D | O | A | | | |
| S | L | I | P | | S | T | A | N | G | | T | L | C | | T | R | A | I | L |
| T | O | N | Y | S | | A | S | S | | S | P | U | R | S | | E | C | R | U |
| A | C | T | | K | E | N | T | | S | P | A | R | I | N | G | | T | O | T |
| F | A | R | R | A | R | | E | R | O | I | C | A | | A | L | P | I | N | E |
| F | L | O | U | T | S | | L | A | U | R | E | L | | P | E | E | V | E | S |
| S | E | S | T | E | T | | S | T | R | E | S | S | | S | E | W | E | D | ▶ |

**PAGE 135 AMAZEMENT 2**

**PAGE 136   SEMI-FINAL**

```
S O N G F E S T . C A R A T S
T H E A L A M O . A V A L O N
R E S T O R E R . P O M A D E
A N T E . L A S S E N . C I A
P R O . M Y R I A D . D A N K
S Y R I A . S O X . B O R N E
. . N R A . N O H I T T E R
P U F F I N S . N A P I E R S
A T L A N T I C . L E M . . .
S A Y N O . R O T . D E R B Y
T H A T . T E P E E S . H U E
R A W . B A N T A M . P I S A
A G A T E S . I M P L A N T S
M E Y E R S . C U T I T O U T
I N S A N E . S P Y V S S P Y
```

**PAGE 137   CAPITAL INFUSION**

```
A G A R . A N G S T . A S K A
R O L O . C A R T A . S P A T
M U S C A T E E R S . P O U T
S P O O L . C E E S . R A I .
. . C A I R O P R A C T I C .
. T W O I S H . . U H S . . .
D O R . L I N A . D I C E D
P R A G U E N O S T I C A T E
I N P U T . O L I O . R S A .
. S R I . . D R E S S Y . .
B A K U L A U R E A T E . .
A L I . E N T O . . T E M P E
B I R D . J U B A L A T I O N
K A T E . O R O N O . H A R I
A S S N . U N T I L . E S T D
```

**PAGE 138   ORANGE ALERT**

```
C A S K S . S E A S . S T U N
A B E A T . T A R A . A H S O
F U Z Z Y N A V E L . M E A T
. . O R A . E G A D . M I S
V A M O O S E . O R E G A N O
E L I . N C I S . Y A R N .
R I S E . A D I P . F I D E L
D E S I . R E N E E . P A R A
I N F E R . R E A L . E R A S
. L I A R . S L I M . I S E
I G O O F E D . S C A N N E R
S E R . T E E S . I N E .
L E I S . F I R S T B L O O D
A N D I . E T T E . A L E R O
M A A S . R Y A N . G Y R O S
```

**PAGE 139   ON EASY STREET**

```
. G O D . . S E I N E . Q U O
. D O R I C . B E R G E N . U N D
. K A N G A R O O C O U R T . O U I
M I Z E . R I S K . S A V E T I M E
H E R E . M I S S . D I N E R O .
A N S . D U E T . P R O A . T A C K S
R O T . A S S Y R I A N . M A S H I E
T W I T C H . L A C Y . W A I T A N D
. E E K . J A C K . F I N N . R E G
O V A L . J U N E . J I N X . F I R E
L I L . L U N E . L U R E . G E T
A L L W O R K . P O M S . L A W Y E R
F L E E C Y . C L A P T R A P . D A Y
S A Y A H . A E O N . P E W S . R U N
. V I A B L Y . C L A N . H I D E
P A R E N T A L . J O A D . S E V E
A X E . V I C I O U S C I R C L E
I L L . A M U S E D . E N D U P
D E Y . R E S T S . . G A M
```

**PAGE 140 MOVING DAY**

```
HTTP  ABEL  ASPIE  CLOYS
AIWA  METERMAIDS   HORSE
HEIRTOTHEHORNET    ESSEX
ABLER   ICONIC   APSTORY
HAIRYTECHS    ERTES
ART AWN    CORKERCHICK
   ICHABOD   OSOLEMIO
GLUEONLIZARDS     TURNTO
ABRAM   JOT   IMO  BROIL
TAGTEAM    HOOTOWL
  REARRANGEDFURNITURE
     AHEADOF    SEURATS
DEFOG  IDS    ALE  BASTA
ALINES   PERIODICBLEAT
FILETABS   MERCYME
TOOLSPIGEON    ALF  TSU
   COSTA    DEBCLOTHES
MRSGORE   RAVINE   REECE
REALM  CATSINTHECALDER
ENDOF  TRAINTRACK  LODI
DERBY  SIGNS   EROS  SWED
```

**PAGE 142 PLANE GEOMETRY**

```
DECIBEL   [Jet]    APROPOS
ELIDING   MISOS  DIALOUT
MENAGES   AMORE  JAKARTA
OVERS   OPENAIR     INTER
DEREK [Jet] ER  ASL  OB [Jet] SDART
ENA   YESMAN   BSMITH  BES
  AMU  SAAB    EELY   SLA
  MASC  INCONTROL  JEER
   SHH   TRYIT   COR
[Jet] STREAM  VW [Jet] TA  BUBBLE [Jet]
SOA   AHOY   ESO  BETH  ORS
AIRSPACES    VIDEOGAME
MESAS  KAOS  DEBT  LOFAT
  THETHUNDERBIRDS
PERSONA  NEXUS  MAESTRO
OLE  TMI  DELTA  ERR  RIA
PEAT  ELI      TSE  SUNK
DACHAS   OFFWEGO   FREEST
INTOTHEWILDBLUEYONDER
VOTRE   SALISBURY  INURE
AROOM   CNET   SESE  LAPSE
```

**PAGE 144 POST-DOCTORAL WORK**

```
MARC   FRAY   ARGON
ONOR   LIDO   TERRE
PAPADOCDUVALIER
STEVE  ORBE   INSO
  ALEC   INRE
CHIT  CHEGUEVARA
LAD   LOEW   SHEKEL
ARISE  TIE   ADEPT
STOWED  NLRB  LAO
PETERROGET    RAYS
  EYES   VETO
ABET  AGUA  DUTCH
MARIAMONTESSORI
IRISH  ODOR  ETAL
DACHA  DORE  DEBT
```

**PAGE 145 YOU CAN SAY THAT AGAIN!**

```
ETNA   HATE   DAMON
GREG   IRAN   OLOGY
GIRLSGIRLSGIRLS
SMOOCH   AINT   NEE
  WALK   SOIT
ALP  TACIT  RHODA
DORS   NAG  SEINES
DRINKDRINKDRINK
LEMONS  VII  DOSE
ENSUE   PENNS  NED
  TETE   AGES
EHS   PATS  REHASH
DELTADELTADELTA
GLUED  ROOF  IVAN
YPRES  SPOT  KAYS
```

## PAGE 151

```
M T S . A B O M B S . R I L E
Y O W . D R H O O K . A N O N
H E E . D O W N W A R D D O G
U N E S . K O O L . H I E S .
M A T T H E W . . W E I N E R
P I L E O N . M Y N A . T S K
S L Y E R . A R A B . A S T O
. . . P A U L F R A N K . . .
S T D S . P E O N . E I D E R
O E R . F O X X . P U M I C E
B E A T O N . . T H E B R A T
. N C A R . H A H A . O T R O
S A U S A G E F E S T . I T O
O G L E . O R A T E S . E E L
Y E A R . P A R A D E . R S S
```

## PAGE 152

```
D A B S . C S A . S H E D O N
I M O K . U A W . P A N I N I
D I X I E B U S . I N H A L E
I D Y L L I C . O C E A N I C
. L I C E N S E S L A V E
L E E S . D O A . O S E S
S C R E W S . S K I P .
D O N T H A T E A C O W M A N
. . A L I G . Y E O L D E
O F F A . L A A . R A Z Z
D U L L B O D Y S C A N .
O N E L O V E . C O N D O M S
U N S U R E . T E X T O N Y M
L E H R E R . N N E . W E T S
S L Y E S T . T D S . N A H S
```

## PAGE 153

```
T A C . C H E . C H A S T E
A D A . O O X . C L A I R O L
M I R . S P E C I A L M I C K
P O L E M I C V A U L T .
A S I D O . S O D . O C H S
. T I S N T . S E W . H E E
M O B . O A T . I C E A X
I S L A M I C F I S H E R
J A W E D . B U G . E S T
A T A . E R E . N A I V E
M A Y I . A R C . O R F E O
. M I C E C O M M E R C E .
B A T H M I C R O B E . I O U
A T H I R S T . Z A G . E L F
S E X T E T . E S A . S I S
```

## PAGE 154

```
P I M P . S A J A K . C P A S
O H I O . C H A K A . R A N T
E A R S L O O K I N A T Y O U
. I A N . O N E S . P I S
D E A T H C O B . W E A N S
E T C . R E V . F R A I L T Y
U C L A . E R R O R S .
S H U C K T R E A T M E N T S
. M A I L I N . N E H I
S H E E R L Y . C D E . W A D
M E N S A . F O R C U T I E
O T T . T A S E . E O S .
K E R N E L K N O W L E D G E
I R A N . M I C R O . U R I S
N O P E . S T E R N . P U N S
```

**Grid 1**

```
I C E D   R I B S   H A V E N
M A X I   O M A R   A G A V E
P L E D (B)(R)A(I)N W A(V)(E)(S)
U M M   B O I   O K R A
(R)(E)P O R T C A R(D)(S)   V O A
E X T R A   H U H   G O B I
      B T U   G E T A R O O M
S P L I T S Q U A D G A M E S
P L A T Y P U S   S E C
F O N Z   I T S   N I E C E
S T D (M)(E)D S T U D E N(T)(S)
    L E A R   A N A   T S P
(T)(W)O V I R G(I)(N)S   L I C E
S A R I N   A D Z E   S C A R
A D D L E   T S A R   D E N S
```

**PAGE 155  CLUBHOUSE DIVISION**

**Grid 2**

```
S T U C C O   R A W R   P A D
P U S H O N   E U R O   E L O
A C H I L L E S T E E N D O N
S K I   D A L T O N   O A H U
    S L I T S   D F L A T
O B T U S E A N G L E E
H O O C H   O M A R E P P S
M I R   P O B O Y   I N A
S L Y S T O N E   F I T I N
    H I P S T E E R B A N D
F W O R D   C L I M B
U R G E   S C A R F S   R E B
G O L D E N S L U M B E E R S
A T E   P I N E   A E R A T E
L E D   S T Y X   N E E D E D
```

**PAGE 156  DOUBLY FUN**

**Grid 3**

```
A C T O N   N I T R O   I R A
B L U T O   O C E A N   N A S
B U T T B E C K O N S   T V S
A B S   A B L E   C H I A
    I A M B U S H L E G E N D
    R A S E   O U T I N G
A R S E   G O A T   U M A
R U P A U L B Y T U E S D A Y
T M I   R O A M   K E D S
    R E T E L L   N O G O
G A L P A L I N A B A L L
R I B S   E B A Y   I O U
U S E   U N I X O N B O A T S
M I R   S H R U B   A U N T S
P N G   B L E S S   R I G O R
```

**PAGE 157  LET THE RIGHT ONE IN**

**Grid 4**

```
E B B E D   S A P P H O   C O O
A R O M A   A N A L O G   A U K
M A S O N I C Y O U T H   M R S
E C O T O U R   A P P S
S E M I   D E N T A L M A D A M
    C M S   O W I E   L A V A
A L C O A   S T O L E N   V I I
M A A N D P A O P E R A T I O N
P I N   D R O V E S   M A D R E
U D O N   O N E A   S U P
P A P E R P E R S O N   W I I S
    S E G A   R I H A N N A
T I N   P I T C H A P A T E N T
O D E   I C E O U T   S E P I A
M E R   D U N D E E   A R T S Y
```

**PAGE 158  NOTHING MAJOR**

**PAGE 159   SWITCHING SIDES**

```
B L U R B . G M C . F U G L Y
A U R A L . U F O . A N A I S
I N S T A G R A M . B E Z E L
L E A R H O U S E W I V E S .
. . A S O . . . H O E . . .
A C D C . F A T S O . N A G S
L U R E O F T H U M B . M O W
B R A S I . R U R . E V I T A
E L K . L A I R F R E I G H T
E Y E D . B A S S O . C A S H
. . U S B . . . C O T . . .
. M O L A R A U T H O R I T Y
L I N U X . H O M E M O V I E
E L I T E . A M A . P L A N T
O A T H S . B O N . H A N O I
```

**PAGE 160   TRIPLE FEATURES**

```
J E W E L . L O B E S . A T C
I R E N E . E F I L E . T H A
F R I D A Y G O D F A T H E R
. . . O O Z E . . I R A E
I N A F E W . T R I L O G Y
M O N A L I S A . P L E B E S
P R O B L E M C H I L D . . .
. . . U N U . . .
. . H O S T E L M A T R I X
A M O U N T . D U C K H U N T
B A D B O Y S . F A C E T S
R U D I . P E A L . . .
A L I E N M U M M Y B L A D E
D E T . F O R M E . L O W I Q
E D Y . C O N A N . T O W N S
```

**PAGE 161   VIDEO CIRCUITS**

```
T D B A N K . C A R E S S E D
O N E P E R . A D E L A I D E
(M)(A)(N) T R A . S U P E R (P)(A)(C)
A L I . F U J I . S N A P .
T A C T . T I N T . A B Y S S
O B E Y S . F O U R . I C E T
. . P U F F . S E E . U M A
(K)(Y) J E L L Y . K I N G (P)(I)(N)
E M A . K O P . E D I E .
N C I S . Z O M G . D A N S K
S A L V E . P I E R . R O M E
. B E T H . L E E D . N I N
(D)(E) A D H E A D . M U S (C)(L)(Y)
I L I K E I K E . A R E O L A
G S T A R R A W . P A C M A N
```

**PAGE 162   ONE PLUS ONE**

```
J A N D J . C A D E T . M A P
A B O R C . O P R A H . A L A
P E T E A N D P E T E . N P R
. . . D R O O L . O P T I C
N A B . D O N E A N D D O N E
A T R I S K . B I O F U E L
E M I T . P I O T R . . .
. S E V E N A N D S E V E N
. . N O R S E . O R S O
O V E R D U E . T V W I F E
H O M E A N D H O M E . E W R
S L E D S . E P E E S . . .
N U T . H A L F A N D H A L F
A M I . E D I T H . U I N T A
P E C . S O N Y S . B A N D B
```

**PAGE 163 SORTING LETTERS**

**PAGE 164 FLICKS OFF**

# Notes

1. "Why Geography Matters … But Is So Little Learned," spring 2003. Accessed May 2013, http://www.fpri.org/orbis/4702/mcdougall.geography-matters.html

2. "Puzzle Makers Exchange Cross Words," *New York Times*, August 10, 1988. Accessed May 2013. http://www.nytimes.com/1988/08/10/arts/puzzle-makers-exchange-cross-words.html?pagewanted=2

3. "Renewed Acquaintance," *New Yorker* November 26, 1979, 38.

4. "Start Spreading the Oleo," October 25, 2011. Accessed May 2013, http://www.benbassandbeyond.com/2011/10/start-spreading-oleo.html

5. Thanks to David Steinberg and Martin Herbach for uncovering this clue at the Pre-Shortzian Puzzle Project.

6. Joyce Voelker, "Glamour in the Boudoir Very Important to You," *Miami Daily News.* March 22, 1948. Accessed May 2013, http://news.google.com/newspapers?nid=2206&dat=19480322&id=A1MtAAAAIBAJ&sjid=t9YFAAAAIBAJ&pg=5859,3382542

7. "Interview with Mel Rosen," accessed May 2013, http://www.preshortzianpuzzleproject.com/p/pre-shortzian-constructor-interviews.html

8. "Rex Parker Does the New York Times Crossword Puzzle," accessed May 2013, http://rexwordpuzzle.blogspot.com/2008/01/saturday-jan-19-2008-david-j-kahn.html

9. Rosen, Mel. *The Puzzlemaker's Handbook.* New York: Random House, 1995.